how to WIRE your model railroad

By Linn H. Westcott

Contents

KALMBACH BOOKS

FIRST EDITION, 1950. Second printing, 1951. SECOND EDITION, 1953. Second printing, 1956. THIRD EDITION, 1959. Second printing, 1961. Third printing, 1966. Fourth printing, 1968. Fifth printing, 1969. Sixth printing, 1971. Seventh printing, 1973. Eighth printing, 1975. Ninth printing, 1976. Tenth printing, 1979. Eleventh printing, 1981. Twelfth printing, 1984.

1. Realistic Control

WHAT is it that makes model railroading such a captivating hobby? Why has our hobby grown faster than others in recent years?

Well, there is the irresistible lure of the railroad and the intrigue of things in miniature, but other hobbies have comparable advantages. I think the feature that makes model railroading the most distinctive hobby is that it has the greatest diversity. You can be an all-around fellow or you can specialize. And, what's more, there are many different things you can specialize in with your model railroad. Mechanics, design, art, collecting, display, handicraft, carpentry — all are phases of our hobby that you can take or leave, as you prefer.

There is another whole group of appeals; you might call them the active side of model railroading. Unlike many other hobbies, in model railroading you are only partly finished when you put the last touches of paint on a model. Here the fun is just beginning. Your new car, locomotive, or bridge is another integral part of the working railroad you build in your own home. It is no longer just a mechanical model. It doesn't have to gather dust on the mantel. Now it is a pawn or a king in the gamelike operation you can play with your pike. The active side of model railroading is the secret of the hobby's big success. First you build a *model* then you become a *railroader*.

But you are already sold on model railroading; why am I wasting your time with a sales talk on our hobby? Because I want to make this point clear: Model construction and railroading are two separate aspects of the hobby. Each is an end in itself, yet each augments the other. Between these two interlocked phases of model railroading is *control*. Control is the whole subject of making trains move, and move realistically. The man who masters control has the key to really successful model railroading.

Fortunately, control wiring is the easiest part of model railroad building. You use simple tools, there are no close measurements, and the work usually goes quickly. Your whole wiring job may be done in much less time than it takes to get ready for it.

Most model railroad beginners are not as familiar with the ways of electricity as they are with those of the hammer and nail, and that is why control looks complicated at first. When you actually do the work, all the mystery will quickly disappear and soon you may even be giving the other fellow some help.

If you build a good control system, you will have plenty of power ready to run your locomotive. When you pull the throttle, the engine will respond with slow but powerful motion. It will pull its load easily up grades and around tight curves. You should be able to run the train at scale speeds of 20, 40, or 80 miles per hour. With a good control system you can put an end to the jerky starts and stops of toy railroading. A real train takes many minutes to reach full speed and a model should take at least several seconds.

In this book I shall show you how to build a control system for your railroad that will give you convenient and responsive control. I hope to include everything you need to know to get at least one train running smoothly, with a minimum of effort, time and expense on your part.

When you are ready to run two or more trains, you will need more control equipment. This is so that each train can run at its own speed and in its own direction. The control equipment you add includes not only more power to run the second train, but also electric switches so you can keep the control of one train separated from the other even though the two trains may use the same track, one after another. I'll talk quite a lot about control for several trains.

Operation

You can run your railroad in many different ways. Some fellows like to set the throttle and watch a sleek streamliner or a 30-car freight run around and around many times.

Some fellows prefer to be towermen. For them an interlocking plant at a junction is the most fun. As several trains run about the railroad on as many routes, the towerman sets the "levers" at his junction and waits for the cars to weave through.

Almost everyone likes to be an engineer. Controls built like those in a real locomotive work well here and the engineer keeps his eye on his train no matter where it goes. He brakes for the curves and builds up speed on the straightaway.

These are only a few of the jobs that a model railroad offers, and they all center about a good control system. In this book you'll get off to a good start on control. The methods you will use are just about the easiest of any yet developed, but they will also be a sound foundation if you should care to add refinements later on.

Traffic direction

One idea, borrowed from the real railroads, will be so helpful that I want to introduce it right away. This is the concept of "traffic direction." If you can read a map, you are probably accustomed to thinking of things in terms of four directions: north, east, south, and west. But the operating department of a railroad ignores true direction almost entirely and everything is converted into two directions as measured along the actual route of the track.

Over in England, for instance, the directions are called "up" and "down," depending on whether a train or track runs to or from London. In our country, most railroads use "eastbound" and "westbound," but some lines use "northbound" and "southbound."

New York Central belongs to the group that uses the east-west nomenclature, and this line has a fine example to show what eastbound really means. The main line runs generally east from Chicago to Buffalo and Albany, but there it makes an abrupt right turn and continues south by west to New York City. On this last leg of the journey the trains sometimes turn entirely west, but they are still called "eastbound." See Fig. 1-1. All trains going toward New York are eastbound trains regardless of the twists in the track.

On your own railroad you can assign one terminal as "east." All track leading toward this terminal is then eastbound.

At first you might think this is impractical, because so many model rail-

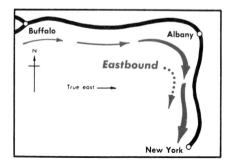

1-1 Eastbound is not necessarily true east.

roads are built in an oval or some other kind of continuous pattern. But here you have a convention you can use: just consider the generally counterclockwise direction as eastbound. Fig. 1-2 shows this.

This practice will help later on when you plan a schedule for running trains, but it is going to be very important for your wiring, too, because now you have a simple way to name the two rails of the track. If you call one rail S for south and the other N for north, you'll always be able to distinguish one from the other and not get the wires mixed up as easily. Fig. 1-2 also shows this.

Notice that the N rail is always on the inside of the oval. In effect you have placed the north pole in the center of your railroad system.

A word to the wise

As a rooter for model railroading, you can do something to help others who are just getting started. If the average fellow picks up this book he's likely to say to himself:

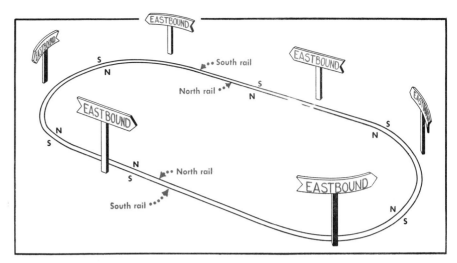

1-2 Counterclockwise is eastbound on an oval track.

"Holy smoke! If I have to learn all the things in this book just to wire my railroad, I'm going to push my trains around by hand."

Here's what you can tell your friend:

"Take it easy, brother. There are many types of model railroaders and each one wants to do some things in his own way. That wiring book has to give information to each of those fellows, and so there is much more material there than you will ever use."

I'll try to do my part by letting you and your friend know when you come to places you can skip over.

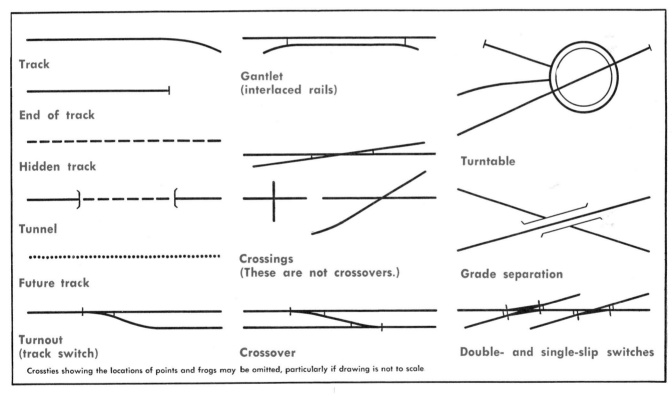

Track

End of track

Hidden track

Tunnel

Future track

Turnout
(track switch)

Gantlet
(interlaced rails)

Crossings
(These are not crossovers.)

Crossover

Turntable

Grade separation

Double- and single-slip switches

Crossties showing the locations of points and frogs may be omitted, particularly if drawing is not to scale.

1-3 Use these symbols whenever you draw track plans for wiring purposes.

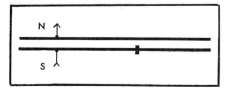

1-4 Arrowheads and tails are convenient symbols to show feeder wire connections to S and N rails on your wiring sketches. Heavy crossbar represents a gap.

1-5 The same symbols can be used with one-line track plans. Here crossbar shows an insulated rail joiner or gap in only one rail. Insulated gaps are used to prevent electricity from passing beyond a given point in the rail. You can get plastic joiners, or cut the rail.

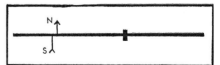

1-6 This is the same as Fig. 1-5 except that the crossbar indicates a need for insulated gaps in both rails this time. Often the place where you put gaps and feeders isn't very critical, as you'll see in Chapter 10.

2. What You Need

WHEN you are getting ready to wire your model railroad, it's a good idea to draw a plan of your track right away. You can draw two lines for a track — that is, one for each rail — but that's a lot of work. It is much easier to draw only one line to represent both rails, and this will be good enough for wiring planning.

Use the symbols on page 3 and be sure you get all the turnouts (track switches) in the right relationship to each other. Except for this, your drawing can be very crude. Of course, a large drawing will be easier to use than one on a letterhead size sheet.

You won't add any wiring to your plan for a while, but it is still a good idea to keep this drawing nearby. Since I'm going to say some things in this book that will apply to someone else's railroad instead of yours, it will be best to keep your own track plan handy. This will make it easier for you to sort out the data you need.

Perhaps you want to build a small test track first and a bigger railroad later on. This is very sound planning on your part, because every model railroader does a better job each time he starts a new railroad. The wiring for a simple test oval or yard is as easy as pie, and you won't have to read even half of this book to do it.

Before leaving track planning, let me assure you that no matter how you design your track, you *can* wire it. There's no need to change a track plan to make the wiring easier. Your track plan should be arranged for good train operation, practical switching moves, and interesting railroading.

First equipment

As a beginner, the control equipment you need for your first railroad is shown in Fig. 2-1. Power is provided by a one-train size power pack. A toy transformer cannot be used as it delivers alternating current, A.C., instead of direct current, D.C. Alternating current won't run our motors.

The pack has a built-in speed controller or throttle and also a reversing switch. You also need two wires long enough to reach from the "controlled D.C." terminals of the power pack to a terminal track section. Of course you will have a lot more track than is shown, but often it won't require any more wiring as long as you run only one train.

However, if your track plan has a return loop in it (Chapter 6) or if you happen to use solid frog track switches (Chapter 8), you will need some special wiring even when running only one train.

You may want special wiring for remote-control switches, lamps, and other accessories. While adequate instructions usually come with these, you'll find some special help given in following chapters.

How many trains will you run?

The place where wiring help will be most needed is when you are ready to run two or more trains at the same time. On a real railroad, each train is controlled independently; that's what we want too. However, to do this we must have some way of separating the control of one train from the next even though both trains may use the same track at different times. Thus it takes more than twice the equipment to run two trains than it does to run one. You need separate speed and reversing control for each train, usually using two separate power packs. Then you need some kind of control panel to separate the control of each pack so it reaches the right train. That's the main concern of Chapters 10 and 12, but much of our planning in other chapters is a preparation for multi-train control. The rest of this chapter will give you some electrical background. You don't need this so much to build your control system as you do later on if you have to hunt for trouble or mistakes in wiring. So I'll leave it up to you whether you take your electrical lessons now or later.

The control circuit

The diagram in Fig. 2-2 shows how electricity is harnessed to run a locomotive on your system.

Notice the cast of the scene:
1. Power source.
2. Controller unit.
3. Feeder wires.
4. Track rails.
5. Locomotive.

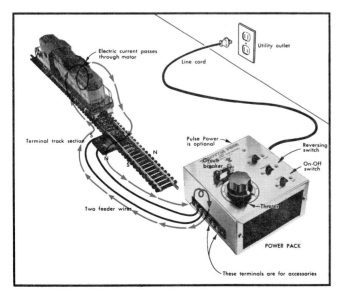

2-1 Control for one train.

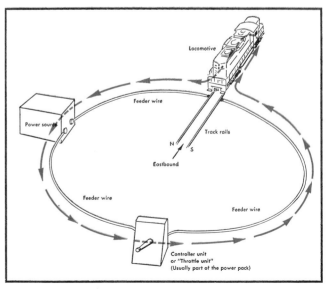

2-2 Electricity flows only in loop paths.

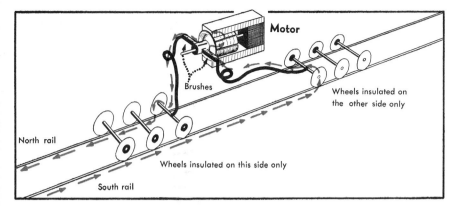

2-3 Electricity passes from one rail, through the motor, and back by the other rail.

Notice something else that is very important. All of these components are connected in a sort of necklace of events around which the electric current can circulate. The electric power is pumped around this daisy-chain by the power source. A feeder wire guides it to the controller unit which is a sort of valve that regulates the flow. Another feeder continues the path to the track. Electricity can flow through metals but not through air, and that is why it stays in the feeder wire. The rail of the track is also metal, so the electricity can move along the rail as far as necessary to reach the locomotive.

At the locomotive, the electric current leaves the rail and passes up through a wheel or special collector shoe to a short wire and finally reaches the motor, Fig. 2-3. Here it develops the power to pull a train.

But this is only half of our story. Electricity has to pass *through* a motor, not just to it. And if it must flow through, you'll need another path to return the current home again. This return path is the other rail of the track and then another feeder which

reaches the other terminal connection on the power source, Fig. 2-2.

Now we have the underlying principle of electric power machines. You must have a complete "circuit" of metal wires, rails, or other conductors so the electric current can flow around and around passing through each component in turn. So let's remember this:

Electricity can flow only if there is an unbroken path from the power source, through the other elements of the circuit, and back to the source by another route.

Locomotive wiring

You might wonder why the electricity flowed along the rail past the first wheels and on to the second in Fig. 2-3. This is because there is a small bushing of plastic near the hub or the rim of all the wheels on the near side of the near truck. This "insulation" prevents electricity from flowing up to the locomotive because there is no all-metal path here. The electricity can flow into the second truck because these wheels are not insulated.

In a similar way the other truck returns electricity to the other rail.

The connecting wires usually connect to the truck frames, but often one truck frame and one motor brush are in contact with the main frame of the engine, which replaces one wire. Then we say the motor has "one brush grounded." This is illustrated in Chapter 5.

Series and parallel

All the components, including the wires and rails, of our daisy-chain were connected end to end in a series, so this is called a "series" circuit. All circuits have at least two elements in series, but sometimes a part of a circuit can be "parallel" to another part. Suppose you have another locomotive and you put it on the track as shown in Fig. 2-4.

Now electricity has two routes at the right side of the circuit. It has a choice of passing through either locomotive. Well, electricity is very democratic and it will always divide itself, part of it going each way, whenever there are two paths. Thus each locomotive will receive part of the power and the two are said to be in "parallel." This may be more clear if you study the schematic diagram of Fig. 2-5.*

Electric current

As you know, all materials are supposed to be made of ultra-small particles called atoms, and each atom has much smaller particles called electrons that dance around it. When you make something warm, all you are really doing is making the electrons dance faster.

In metals, the electrons may not always dance around the same atom. Instead they migrate from one host to another in haphazard fashion. If you can make the dancers migrate a little more in one direction than any other, as they bounce and whirl, you have an electric current, Figs. 2-6, 2-7, and 2-8.

Now it is easy to see why you must

---

*Schematics are a type of shorthand that is much easier to follow than a pictorial diagram when you want to show what is happening in an electric circuit. On the other hand, because they are made of unfamiliar shapes and do not look like the actual parts, schematics are not as good to show how to build and wire a control system.

2-4 Electricity can divide and flow "in parallel" via two simultaneous paths.

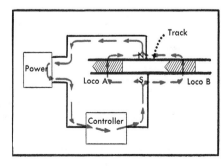

2-5 Same diagram in "schematic" form.

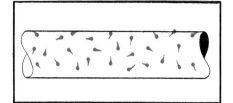

2-6

2-7

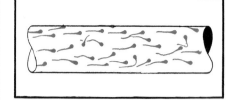

2-8

These diagrams represent a wire and the dots with tails represent the paths of electrons. Ordinarily the electrons dance about in a hap-

hazard fashion, 2-6, and when the wire is hot they do it more rapidly, 2-7. If you can make the electrons move more in one direction than

in any other, 2-8, you have an electric current. The current will also produce more heat in the form of disturbed electron moves.

have a complete circuit for electricity to move around. If electrons cannot move all the way around, they will pile up somewhere; the parade stops and no useful work can be done. Fig. 2-9 is an example of this.

In many control systems, the voltage pressure is always left full on, 12 v., but other devices like switches and rheostats are used to control the ampere current by obstructing the loop path.

You may have heard that electricity travels at the speed of light, but this isn't strictly true. The dancing electrons actually migrate rather slowly through a wire. The thing that moves fast is the push of one electron upon another.

This works like a row of dominoes touched at one end: each domino falls over and touches the next. In a second or so the wave of pressure may be several feet away, yet each domino has moved only an inch.

When you push an electron it moves slowly, too, but the wave of pressure is nearly instantaneous. That's why the motor in a locomotive starts to work the moment you pull the throttle.

When only a few more electrons move in one direction than in the other, as all of them dance, you have a weak electric current. If a great many electrons move onward, the current is heavy. Current is measured in units called "amperes" or just "amps" and usually abbreviated "a." Most HO gauge locomotive motors will pull

their loads with about half an ampere of electric current flowing through their coils, but some big O gauge motors use 4 a. or more.

In many ways an electric current behaves like water passing through a pipe. If the pipe is level and filled with water, the water still won't flow unless you have a pump or something else to push it. In the same way, although a wire is already filled with electrons, you need some kind of electrical pressure to make the electrons move in one direction.

Again, suppose you have some pressure but water doesn't flow fast enough to suit you. To make more current flow you have to pump the water with greater force. This same thing happens to electricity moving through a wire. If the power source can push it with greater pressure, more current will flow. This push in electric currents is measured in "volts." Actually the 12 v. pressure used in model railroad circuits is a relatively low voltage and that's why we don't get serious electric shocks when running trains.

The 110 v. pressure of the wall socket is much more dangerous and on occasion has caused death. Not because the pressure is great, but because a high pressure forces so much more electric current through the wire, or a motor, or your arm, or anything else that becomes part of a circuit.

Higher pressures are rare in model work, but thousands of volts of pres-

sure are used to force electric current through some radio, television, and power transmission apparatus.

Electric force can be present without a current just as you can push against a stone wall without moving it. Electric pressure, volts, can push down a wire, but only when you close a switch to make a continuous loop back to the power source will any amperes flow.

Likewise the amperes are always potentially there but not effective if there is no pressure to push them.

Resistance and heat

When you try to force electricity through any circuit, you have to overcome friction just as real as though you were pushing a heavy carton over a concrete floor. This friction in a wire or other electrical device is called "resistance" and resistance is measured in units called "ohms." Copper wire has low resistance, minimum friction, so we use it for most of our connections. Some other materials have very high resistance and it takes more volts of pressure to push a current through them. Here's what happens in a wire that produces the resistance to electric current.

You may remember when we first talked about electrons I said they danced around at all times. If they dance fast you have heat. If you push a box over a concrete floor you are going to agitate some of the electrons on the bottom of the box and some on the floor. These move around faster so you have heat. If you slide down a rope too fast, this agitation produces so much electron activity that you are burned.

Well, then, if electricity means you are merely pushing dancing electrons along a wire, you're going to agitate them this way too. The harder you push, the more current there will be and the hotter the wire will become. This agitation is in the wire, but it is going to bounce against nearby electrons in the insulation and air surrounding the wire. All energy thus lost in heat is never going to help run your locomotives. It is energy wasted where you don't need it.

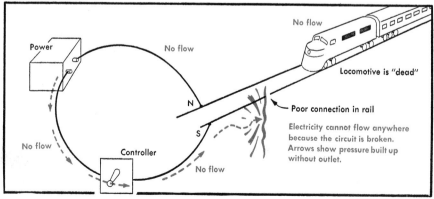

2-9 Electricity can't flow unless there is a complete loop circuit. This circuit is "open."

When a wire is small, the current has to pass through a restricted path and there is much agitation. In this "high resistance" the wire temperature goes way up and much energy is lost.

Likewise, a long wire has more resistance than a short one and wastes more power.

If the wire is a big one, the current has lots of elbow room and there is slight agitation—less energy is wasted. That's why we want to use large wire between the power pack and the track, so more energy reaches the engine; we want wire with "low resistance."

The kind of material in a wire or any other kind of "conductor" makes a difference, just as do the size and length. Silver and copper are smooth paths for electricity and thus have low resistance, produce little heat.

Iron and lead have a higher resistance, and the electrical friction produces much more heat. At the right is a list of commonly used materials to show the amount of resistance in each.

Notice that all conductors listed except carbon are metals. Electricity will also pass through many other materials if they are damp. Pure water will not pass electricity very well, but add some salt or an acid or many other chemicals and you have a fairly good conductor.

You might compare copper wire to a water pipe with a smooth inside wall. Water flows through the pipe easily and electricity does the same through copper.

Iron wire isn't as good a conductor; you could compare it to a rusty pipe stuffed with a lot of steel wool. Water has to be pushed pretty hard to get much through. The same holds true for the iron wire. If you want much electricity to flow through, you have to push harder — apply more volts of pressure.

As a matter of fact, the amount of current you can get through a metal conductor is directly proportional to how hard you push it. If you have a copper wire that resists current with 1 ohm of electrical friction, it would take 1 v. of pressure to force 1 a. of current through. Increase the pressure to 2 v. and 2 a. will flow.

These effects are neatly summed up in a mathematical formula called "Ohm's law." You may occasionally have use for the rule, but there is little need to try to memorize it or even understand it. Here's how it looks:

Let
   I represent current in amperes
   R represent resistance in ohms
   E represent pressure in volts
Then
$$E = IR$$
Which means that if you want to push a current through a circuit or

Relative resistance

Silver	1.6	Phosphor bronze	7.8
Copper	1.7	Nickel	7.8
Gold	2.4	Platinum	10.0
Aluminum	2.8	Iron, steel	10.0 and up
Magnesium	4.6	Solder	16.0
Tungsten	5.6	Lead	22.0
Zinc	5.8	Nickel silver	33.0
Brass	7.0	Nichrome	100.0
		Carbon	900.0 and up

The values represent the resistance in ohms of a wire 100 ft. long and 0.025" (approximately size 22) in diameter at 68° F. Resistance rises slightly in most metals when temperature increases; it drops in carbon.

part of a circuit, you multiply the desired current, in amperes, by the resistance, in ohms, and the product is the required pressure in volts.

You can use this formula in three ways, depending on which of the three terms, I, R, or E, is the unknown. Here are the other two forms:
$$R = E/I$$
$$I = E/R$$
This means you divide either current or resistance into pressure to find resistance or current.

Insulating materials

Most plastics, wood, fiber, paper, cloth, porcelain, waxes, and cements are very poor conductors when dry. Their resistance is a matter of millions of ohms, and so little electricity passes through them that we call them "insulators." In model railroad work you can choose your insulating material for its mechanical advantages and not worry about how much power is wasted in heat. The amount is negligible.

Big calculations

You can use Ohm's law in many useful ways, although at first you may not even want to try.

Look back at Fig. 2-2. Each part of that loop circuit has an ohm value, perhaps something like these:

Power pack	3 ohms
Feed wires in all	½ ohm
Controller unit	0 to 40 ohms
Rails	½ ohm
Locomotives, motor stalled	6 ohms

The resistance of the controller varies with the speed adjustment with zero at top speed. The effective resistance of the motor decreases when it is moving, especially with light loads.

Now, when several elements are in a loop circuit, like Fig. 2-2, you can add up all the ohms to get the whole circuit's value; in this case it would be 10 ohms with the motor stalled but the throttle at full-speed position. The average "12 v. power pack" actually pushes with about 16 v., so Ohm's law

would indicate that under these particular circumstances 1.2 a. would flow. A test with actual meters would come close to this figure.

Each device around the loop will get only part of the total 16 v., but all the voltages will total 16 v. The amount each device gets is proportional to its ohms value. So if a loco has one third of the resistance of an entire loop, it will also use one third of the voltage.

The current flowing around the loop is the same through all the devices. That is sometimes a helpful thing to know. For instance, if you can figure the current at one place, you know it's the same at a place where you can't figure it.

In Fig. 2-4, the parallel branch circuits can also be figured by a little detective work. Since the two locos are in parallel, they both get the same voltage. But the current through them will divide in inverse proportion to their resistances. For instance, if one loco has a 3-ohm motor and the other a 6-ohm, the 3-ohm will draw twice as much current. Think about it and you'll see that this would be ⅔ of the total current too.

These figures are with motors stalled. In Chapter 4, you'll see that when motors are going they change the voltage of the whole circuit.

Plus and minus

Direct current terminals, on a power pack or battery, are said to be positive (+) and negative (−) or just "plus and minus." Usually we say electricity flows from plus to minus. Actually this was a bad guess made before folks knew what electric current was, for later it was found the electrons actually moved the other way. However, I'll follow convention and talk about current going from plus to minus.

As you'll see later, the reversing switch in the power pack actually changes the plus and minus train-running terminals around. Reversing the current flow by any means is called changing "polarity."

3. How to Select Your Power Pack

YOU cannot use a toy train transformer to run scale model railroads because transformers produce the wrong kind of electricity. The output of a transformer is "alternating current," usually just called A.C. In a wire carrying A.C., the electrons flow in one direction for a while and then they stop and move the other way for a while. This alternating goes on so fast that the electrons swing forward and back many times every second.

If the current swings forward and back 60 times every second, it is called "60-cycle A.C." This is the "frequency" of the A.C. in most parts of our country, but not everywhere.

A toy transformer may produce around 12 v., but it is still unsuitable because the current alternates and the motor in a scale locomotive will just sit and cook if you try to use it. The motors need D.C. (direct current).

However, you can buy a device called a "rectifier" which will change the A.C. into D.C. when attached to the toy transformer. The rectifier acts as a sort of traffic regulator and sends all the electrons around the circuit in one direction even though they come out of the transformer going alternately both ways, as in Fig. 3-1.

A transformer and a rectifier are exactly what you get when you buy a power pack, but you also get the convenience of having the whole works in one box and some added features as well.

When you buy a power pack, be sure it is rated for use in your community. This is usually an input of 115 v. 60 cycles, but might vary from 110 v. to 125 v. Other voltages of less than 50 cycles require a special pack.

On the West Coast, many cities have 50-cycle A.C., but the difference between it and 60-cycle is so small that model railroaders can ignore the variance. In Upper New York, 25-cycle A.C. is used and special transformers and power packs must be used there.

When you go to a hobby shop to buy a power pack, you may be faced with an amazing array — little packs, big packs, packs with throttles and packs without them. There's a good sales argument for each kind, too, so before you buy, here are some questions to ask yourself:

1. Do I have to be economical in buying a power pack or can I afford to spend a little more to get better operation?

2. Do I want to buy my power supply a little at a time rather than pay out a big sum at the very beginning?

Financing is only one consideration. Here are other points equally important about how you plan to build and operate your railroad:

3. Will I always have a small railroad?

4. Or will it start small but grow until I can run three or four trains?

5. Do I want the controls arranged so that friends or perhaps others in the family can also run trains?

6. Will I let the trains run more or less by themselves while I do other things around the pike?

7. Or do I prefer to stress smooth starting and stopping — with emphasis on the engineer?

I'm sure the answers will help you in making power pack decisions, so let's get started. First, let's figure roughly how much power your railroad will eventually use by making a guess and a simple addition. Estimate how many locomotives you will eventually acquire. If you're in TT, HO or S gauge, make a list and allow 1 a. apiece for one-motor engines and 2 a. for two motors, etc. O gaugers must allow 4 a. for the largest motors and 2 a. for the rest.

This kind of figuring has a limit because model railroaders often acquire more engines than they can run at one time. If your track will handle only three trains at a time, strike off all but the three biggest engines from your list and then total it. Here's an example:

Two-motored diesel ....2 a.		
4-6-2 ....1 a.		
2-8-2 ....1 a.		
Diesel switcher ....1 a.	Strike out
0-4-0 ....1 a.	Strike out
Total: 6 less 2 is ....4 a.	Maximum

This will be conservative because many engines do not draw as much as 1 a. apiece. Add to your total the power needed for any other equipment, such as lamps and crossing gates, that you'll be running from the same pack. Lamps may be the biggest item. They look innocent enough but they use a lot of electricity. If you don't know the actual current rating for your bulbs, figure them at $\frac{1}{6}$ ampere for normal 12 v. or 18 v. bulbs or $\frac{1}{12}$" ampere if they're the smaller grain-of-wheat size. (Lamp bulbs are discussed in Chapter 13.)

3 - 1 Rectifiers are made by several firms for attaching to a toy transformer to convert it into a power pack for running scale trains. The inside of any ordinary pack also contains a transformer and rectifier similarly connected. Lower diagrams indicate path of electric current in the rectifier at two moments 1/120 of a second apart. When A.C. happens to flow one way, rectifier switches it straight through. When A.C. reverses, rectifier automatically crosses the paths so output is still going in same direction and is D.C.

Your grand total may be something like 2 a., 6 a., or as much or more than 15 a., but this doesn't necessarily mean that you should go out and buy a pack that size. You may want to split the power among several packs. Here are the advantages of using one big pack, followed by a list of the advantages of having several small packs instead. Keep in mind your answers to the questions in the first part of this chapter as you read.

Single power supply

The one-big-pack idea is called "single power supply," and it is the most obvious and oldest way to power trains. Its biggest advantage is one of cost. You get more ampere-handling capacity for the dollar in a big pack. You aren't paying for any duplication of parts in the pack.

When you use a single pack to run two or several trains, quality is very important. Maybe you've noticed how water pressure drops in the shower when someone turns a faucet on somewhere else in the house. The same can happen with model railroad power.

When you use one power supply to power two trains, a slow train may stall completely when you start a second train. To minimize this, you must buy a quality power pack, perhaps one that is rated well above actual requirements.

Regulation of a pack

A typical power pack has about 16 v. output, but as load is increased this gradually drops to 12 v. The percentage of loss is called "regulation" and 25 per cent is common. If you want less regulation, use a pack only to part of its rated output. For instance, using only 2 a. from a 4 a. pack may give you about 13 per cent regulation instead of 25 per cent. Some of the better packs are conservatively rated this way in the first place.

Typical wiring

In Fig. 3-2, I have greatly simplified the wiring of a railroad to show how double-pole switches must be used in control panels when a single pack powers two trains or more. (Actually other connections made at YY and XX are likely and they account for the need of doubled wiring in this instance. It's all explained later on.) I've also shown how separate "controller units" or side "throttle units" can be added to power more trains when you get them. You can enlarge a one-throttle pack in this same way if it has reserve capacity in amperes.

The other way to wire your power is called "multiple power supply" and it completely eliminates trouble from poor regulation.

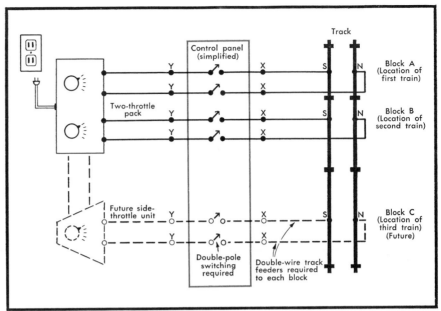

3-2 SINGLE POWER SUPPLY.

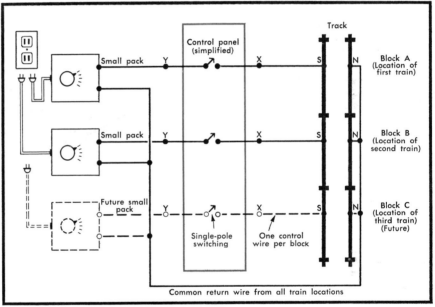

3-3 MULTIPLE POWER SUPPLY.

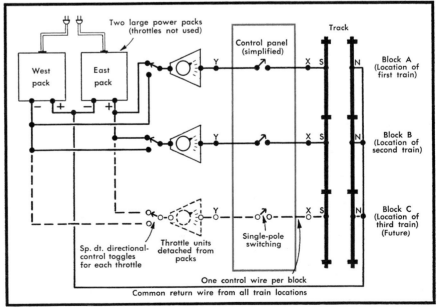

3-4 TWIN POWER SUPPLY.

9

TRANSFORMER

Connect A.C. accessories here.
A.C.

Path of positive electricity shown in color.

Primary coil Secondary coil

Connect D.C. accessories here.
D.C.

RECTIFIER

Magnetic core

Connect feeders to track here.
N S RN RS

DIRECTION CONTROLLER

PILOT LAMP

ON-OFF SWITCH

CIRCUIT BREAKER

Break here to insert meter

See back view below

AUXILIARY DIRECTION CONTROLLER
You may want to add this to handle loops, a wye, or the power to a turntable.

AMMETER

RHEOSTAT

VOLTMETER

N

Faster

Slower

THROTTLE

S

3-5 The interior of a typical full-wave power pack is wired something like this, although some of the accessories, or even the throttle and direction control toggles, may be omitted. Circuit breaker is sometimes installed between the transformer and rectifier to protect the latter more effectively.

Multiple power supply

Here you start with one pack, but instead of getting a pack big enough to handle all future trains and to insure good regulation, you do the opposite. You buy a small, perhaps cheap, pack that will handle one train or perhaps a double-header. When your railroad is ready for a second train, you get a second small pack. If you plan a four-train railroad, you eventually get four packs. In the long run you'll pay more for this kind of power supply, so what are the advantages? Here's what users of multiple power supply point out:

1. Low first cost.

That's because you start with a small pack. The quality of the pack can be lower too, a possible further saving in cost.

2. Installment plan buying.

You pay for your power plant a little at a time as you add more packs to run more trains.

3. Nothing becomes obsolete.

Since your power plant grows with your railroad, it's never too big or too small. The units will be equally suitable for any other size of railroad — if you move to a new home or change the size of your pike.

4. Best possible engine performance.

Since each train will operate from a different power pack, there will be no slowing down, stalling, or shooting ahead of one train when others are started and stopped. Also, there is no need to have good regulation in the pack. This is why you can use a lower quality pack, yet still have perfect locomotive performance.

5. Packs can be suited to their jobs.

This is more important on a big railroad with many trains. You can have one or two of your power packs larger than the others to handle four-motored diesels, double-headed freights and the like.

6. Wiring can be simpler.

This is a most important point especially for medium and large railroads. When you build enough controls so you can handle three or more trains and do some yard switching at the same time, anything that can keep the wiring simple is worth a little more money.

Diagram 3-3 shows the difference in wiring with multiple power supply. Now control panel switches need only one moving pole per block of track. Also, only one wire need run from the control panel to each block, and one additional "common rail return" wire to the N side of all blocks. Sometimes the insulated gaps in the N rail may also be omitted.

The common return is the secret of wiring simplicity with multiple power supply. It isn't possible with single power supply. The reason is this: You can join two separate electric circuits at any one common point without having one affect the other, but if you join them at two separate points you may have trouble. Since connections are usually joined inside the multithrottle pack of Fig. 3-2, you can't join wires anywhere outside the pack and each train must have independent wiring. With multiple supply no wires are joined in the packs, so it is safe to use the common return.

Which system to choose

You may not understand all the differences between single and multiple power supply at once, so here is my personal opinion about which is best for whom. Single power supply is for the man who wants to keep the total cost down, and also for the man who is not so much interested in the operation side of the hobby as he is in just getting a test or display track going where he can run his rolling stock.

Multiple power supply is for the man who will appreciate the simpler wiring. It is also for the man who isn't sure how large his railroad will grow. Multiple power supply also offers better opportunity to run trains in a realistic way with smoother starts and stops. If in doubt, use multiple power supply.

If you already have a large power pack but would like to get the advantages of the simpler wiring, there's another power system called "twin power supply" which you can use.

Twin power supply

Twin power supply is a sort of compromise system with some of the advantages of both single and multiple power supply. It is a way in which a man who has already purchased a big power pack can still have the advantages of common rail return wiring. It is also practical for use with storage batteries or motor generators where ordinary power is not available.

With twin power supply you have the advantage of a fairly low total cost (although the initial investment is high). You have the disadvantage of running more than one train from the

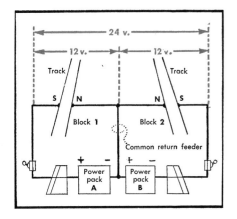

3-6 Even though two electrical circuits are often linked through the common rail return feeder system, the fact that this common network is connected to every N rail prevents 24 v. from ever reaching the motor and lamps in the trains. In rare instances 24 v. can make trouble if you run a train across gaps into a block that has not been properly aligned for the train's direction of travel — but that isn't good operating so shouldn't be a cause for complaint about the wiring.

same pack and therefore more of a tendency for one train to shoot ahead when another stops. This effect is negligible with storage batteries. Most important of all, you have the same advantages of simple wiring in your control panel as with multiple power supply.

Two large power packs are used with twin power supply and neither need have any speed or direction control devices for they are useless on the packs, Fig. 3-4.

All trains running in the eastbound direction at any moment will be powered from the first pack while the second pack is in reserve for all trains that happen to go west. Thus the load varies with each pack and each must be big enough to handle most of the trains in case they go the same direction at once.

Throttle or controller units are fed from the packs through a direction selecting switch that can tap power from either pack.

Since both twin power supply and multiple power supply railroads are wired for common rail power return, you can use both power supply schemes on the same railroad. If you outgrow the original twin supply, additional cabs can be powered by multiple supply.

No short circuit through common rail

Notice that the plus side of one pack is always connected directly to the minus side of the other with twin power supply and frequently with multiple power supply, Fig. 3-6. This common connection is also tied in with the N feeders of all blocks. This plus-

to-minus doesn't constitute a short circuit because plus and minus terms are relative and refer only to an individual power source. If you connect a voltmeter across the packs it measures 24 v., but this much never reaches the trains, as only one pack or the other is connected between the S and N rails of a particular block at any particular time.

Power pack throttles

For most purposes you'll want power packs with built-in speed controllers or throttles (two names for the same thing). One type is a slider that moves across the transformer windings inside the pack when you move a lever or knob outside. This is a built-in "variable transformer" type. The other is a separate device called a "rheostat" that's wired into the pack. Since it is an extra part, it isn't found in low-price packs as often as the slider.

In either case, you want a control that will stand up mechanically and your dealer can tell you which types come back least often for mechanical or electrical repairs. If the slider type is well made, it has the advantage that trains will not vary as much in speed when loaded with more cars or when going up and down hills. This is called good "speed regulation."

External throttle units

I've already mentioned the possibility of adding side controller or throttle units to a power pack so one pack can run more trains. We did this with the single power supply scheme, Fig. 3-2, for the third train. You could use the same side controller units with a one-throttle pack or with a pack that has no throttle at all. This scheme is used in some Marnold, Lionel, Model Rectifier, and other units.

External throttle units like these can also be used to salvage a power pack with defective built-in controls. Just turn the pack's defective throttle all the way on and use the side throttle.

Of course, whenever you run two trains from the same pack with side throttles or built-in throttles, or both, you have single power supply because of the internal connections.

Still another form of external throttle unit is the variable transformer explained on the next page.

What's inside a pack?

The picture diagram in Fig. 3-5 shows the parts you might find in a very complete power pack. Most packs don't have all of these parts. The two parts you'll find in every pack are the transformer, upper left, and the rectifier next to it. These convert A.C.

(alternating current) electricity from the high voltage of your house mains into low-voltage A.C. current and then into D.C. (direct current) which is necessary for the permanent magnet motors in your trains. All the rest of the parts are conveniences, except perhaps for the circuit breaker. This is insurance. The circuit breaker is supposed to open the connection before any damage is done to the power pack due to a derailed train or other causes of a short circuit.

When the manufacturer designs a power pack — or any other electrical equipment for that matter — he is particularly concerned with how he is going to get the heat away from the various parts and into the air. This is why a 10 a. pack must be made of heavier parts than a 5 a. pack. It's going to produce more heat, so needs more surface area on the parts to keep it cool.

Pulse power

The pack shown has a full-wave rectifier. This means that the current is switched so that each half of the A.C. wave forms a D.C. pulse that is furnished to your train. Sometimes a pack is provided with a switch marked "pulse power." This switch is located right in the white wire just above the words "circuit breaker" in Fig. 3-5. When opened, only one half as many D.C. pulses reach the train and there is a space of 1/120 of a second between these pulses when no power reaches the train. This pause tends to vibrate the armature in the locomotive motor ever so slightly; nevertheless this mechanical vibration loosens tight bearings and friction so stiff locomotives can start smoothly. With pulse power you can run a locomotive so slowly that it may take a minute for a wheel to make one turn. This is mostly a stunt, but pulse power is handy in coupling cars accurately, in switching smoothly, and in running an engine by slow motion to see what

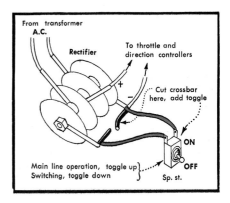

3-7 You can use ordinary power packs to run trains at slow and medium speeds by cutting a connection and adding a toggle.

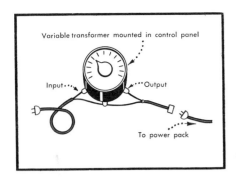

3-8 Variable transformers are sold with or without a case. If you fit your own cords and plugs, as above, you can save a few pennies, but be sure to insulate the unit in a ventilated can so that no one can touch the high voltage windings or terminals on the units. You can mount a variable transformer in your control panel for maximum convenience.

causes a derailment at some trouble spot.

Pulse power can be added to almost any power pack. In most, it's done by adding a sp. st. toggle connected as in Fig. 3-7. If you want a smooth change from pulse to regular power, use a 100-watt 300-ohm rheostat in place of the toggle.

Motors always develop heat when pulling a load and the heat is nearly double when you use pulse instead of regular power. Ordinarily this won't matter, but if you load your engines to near capacity it should be considered.

If you limit the motor current to about ⅔ the rated current, you should be safe. This means pulling fewer cars. For short periods a motor can take more current until it is warmed up.

Variable transformers

Another method of greatly improving operation can be used separately or in addition to pulse power. This is using a variable transformer instead of a rheostat to adjust the voltage.

You can get excellent operation with any pack by leaving the rheostat full on (or using a pack without a rheostat) and adding a variable transformer to adjust the high voltage before it gets to the pack, Fig. 3-8.

The smallest variable transformers made, such as Superior's model 10, will handle all the power you can draw from your pack. Speed control will be smooth and gradual. If it isn't, the trouble is in the locomotive or track.

The v.t. may be rated at only 1.25 a. but this is still adequate to handle a pack up to 10 a. size because the input to a pack is much less in amperes than the output.

You can't use a v.t. pack combination to power accessories because all of its voltages are varied. Also, for two trains you need two v.t.'s, two packs, and something extra for accessories.

Comparison with rheostat

As you know, it takes a few volts just to get a train started. But all volts that reach the train above this develop speed. So if you deduct the "starting voltage" from track voltage you get a "speed voltage." Train speed will be in proportion to the speed voltage if wheels don't slip.

On the level, starting voltage might be 3 v. for a particular train. But starting voltage changes in proportion to the motor load, so going uphill it isn't surprising to find the starting voltage might rise to 4 v. This takes away 1 v. from whatever the speed voltage was and slows the train accordingly.

This is all that affects speed when you operate a train at any particular setting with a v.t. pack. But with a rheostat matters are more serious.

Instead of having an adjustable voltage, the rheostat pack always furnishes about 16 v. Then the rheostat is used to waste some of the volts in a manner described in the next chapter. The trouble is that the rheostat waste isn't constant. It also varies with load and just the wrong way. This lowers the track voltage seriously when the train climbs and after you deduct the starting voltage you may have nothing left for speed. The train stalls, or else you have to keep readjusting the throttle handle.

Actually we don't mind adjusting the handle. But the same instability that requires it on hills can make for rough operation beyond our control when operating through turnouts where the loads change often and suddenly.

Accessories

Power packs come with a lot of handy features, such as an on-off switch, pilot light and terminals arranged in a place where you can make your connections conveniently. There are also features which are necessary to train operation and if they are not included in your pack, you are going to have to provide for them. These include the throttle, usually a rheostat, and a toggle for reversing the train.

Voltmeters and ammeters are very useful and when bought with the power pack they may cost less than when bought separately. Sometimes you'll find that a power pack comes with a fuse instead of a circuit breaker. By all means replace this fuse with one of the little circuit breakers sold in hobby shops. It will slip right into the fuse clip. A fuse is good for only one power failure but the circuit breaker is used over and over again.

Very few throttle-type packs seem to be designed for real convenience to the user. Some have no provision for mounting to the side edge of a railroad table. Some have connecting terminals in an awkward place; at one side is most convenient. The control levers on some packs don't move very far between slow and fast speeds so it's difficult to regulate speed. Generally levers that pull to and from you are the best, while small twister knobs are less convenient as speed controllers.

One maker has plug-in controller units so that you can add any number of rheostats just by plugging them into a large power unit. Another manufacturer has substituted a special kind of rectifier for the usual selenium rectifier in order to get better regulation. This same pack uses a potentiometer instead of a rheostat for speed control, giving good regulation and particularly good control of trains at low speeds.

Packs using transistors in place of ordinary rectifiers can automatically regulate voltage or even speed and also provide gradual speed changes, a sort of "fly-wheel" effect produced electrically. Throttles can also be made with these features using transistors.

Maintenance of power packs

Here's about all you have to do to keep a power pack in good condition:

1. Keep it in a drafty location, or at least where air can circulate freely around the pack to keep it cool.

2. See that the fuse or circuit breaker is rated for no more or little more than the maximum amperes the pack is supposed to deliver.

3. Use the pack at least once a month. This keeps it from deteriorating chemically.

4. Clean all the dust from the parts about once a year. Sometimes you can blow the dust out through the ventilating openings. If there are no ventilating holes, the pack won't need inside cleaning.

Technical requirements

Finally, I'd like to point out that the most important things in buying a pack are:

1. The pack should be able to deliver its full rated load of amperes for six hours without overheating.

2. The voltage across the terminals of the pack, while delivering its full rate of current, should not be lower than 12 v. It doesn't matter if it's somewhat higher.

3. If the pack is to operate several trains at the same time, the regulation should be good. The simplest test for this is to run two trains slowly and see how much one train's stops and starts affect the speed of the other. But this regulation is not important if you use multiple power supply.

4. Motors and Speed Control

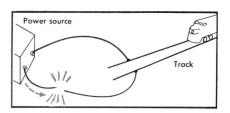

4-1 A broken circuit stops the train.

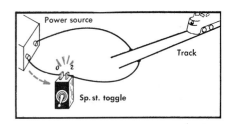

4-2 An on-off toggle is a more convenient way to stop a train, but all it really does is break the circuit.

THE throttle in your power pack, whether it be a rheostat, variable transformer, or transistor device, controls the speed of your train by regulating the voltage available to the motor. With the variable transformer, the voltage is truly varied right in the power pack. With a rheostat, on the other hand, the pack always produces about 16 v. and the rheostat merely wastes some of the voltage so it doesn't reach the train. Let's see how this works.

Suppose we deliberately break a wire in the feeder system, as shown in Fig. 4-1. Now one of the paths is interrupted and current cannot pass *through* the motor even though the other path is intact. The train stops dead in its tracks and won't go until you restore the connection and make the circuit complete.

When we want to open a circuit and close it at will, a break in the wire isn't convenient, so we use an electric switch such as the simple toggle shown in Fig. 4-2.

This kind of toggle is called a "single-pole single-throw" or sometimes just an "on-off" switch. The abbreviation *sp. st.* is used in catalogs and that's what we shall use in this book too.

Since the word *switch* can be confused with track switch, I'm going to use the word *toggle* most of the time. But you can always substitute any kind of sp. st. switch or contacts whenever I refer to an sp. st. toggle. The only thing to watch for is that the contacts of the switch or toggle are rated to handle at least as many amperes as will pass through your circuit. This is usually the case.

The sp. st. toggle is fine for cutting power in a circuit — and that's what we'll use it for later on. It isn't good enough for controlling a locomotive because it stops the engine too suddenly. What we need is something with a more gradual action and the device most often used for this is a "rheostat." See Fig. 4-3.

A rheostat produces electrical friction that wastes power. The more power it wastes, the less voltage is left to run the train. Thus, as you turn the handle on a rheostat, your train moves more slowly until it finally stops.

A rheostat consists of a small coil of resistance wire wound around a heat-resisting form such as porcelain. One edge of the coil is polished clean, and a metal or carbon wiper slides over it from one end to the other.

Most rheostats are designed so the wiper doesn't touch any metal at the "off" end. This cuts all flow of current and the train will not run.

Some rheostats are made without any off position, but the small current flowing through the train when stopped is usually not enough to cause motor overheating. However, an "off" switch can be added (Fig. 4-4) or the reversing switch may have an off position.

When you turn on the rheostat gradually, the wiper contact rides over the coils so that less and less resistance wire is left in the circuit. Thus the rheostat wastes less and less voltage and the motor gets more. When the wiper reaches the extreme "on" end of the rheostat, no voltage is wasted here and the motor gets full voltage from the power pack.

Rheostat ratings

Rheostats are rated two ways — in ohms, for their maximum resistance, and in watts or amperes, for the amount of power they can waste safely.

You should pick the ohms value to match the smallest motor you are going to run, but the watts rating should be large enough to handle the largest load.

For most small- and medium-size motors, a rating of about 40 ohms is

4-3 Most rheostats look like this from the back side. Electricity enters at the terminal lug 0 and passes to the central moving wiper. This slides over the coil of resistance wire. Current leaves via lug 2. A shaft protrudes from the other side and you can fasten a knob or a controller handle to the ¼" shaft. The wide black place at the lower right is where the wiper can rest when trains are not running. As you turn the controller on, the wiper first reaches a section of small wire. Later heavy wire is cut in. This "tapered" feature makes a rheostat better able to carry heavy currents when trains are running at nearly full speed. This particular rheostat has three sizes of wire as you can see in the photo. The numbers 0 and 2 are used in this book merely to help get connections straight if you must make a substitution.

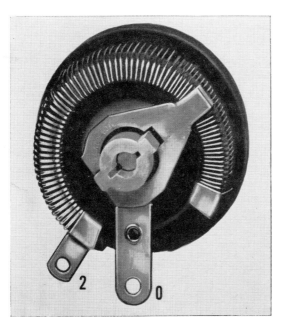

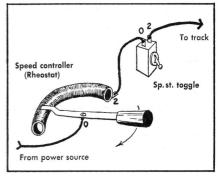

4-4 Toggle added for "off" position.

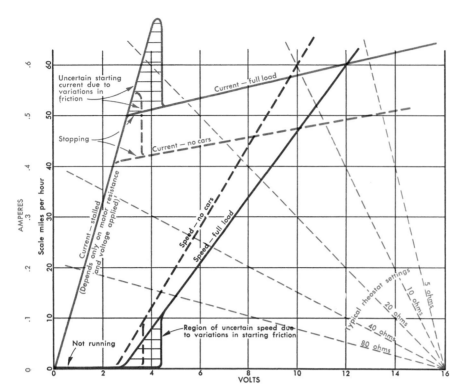

4-5 Voltage, speed, and current of a typical model locomotive.

just right. Less than this will not stop some engines when running light.

In O gauge, 20 ohms is more often used because small motors are rarely run in this gauge. Very large O gauge motors can be controlled more easily with a rheostat of only 12 ohms.

For single-motor trains, a 50-w. rheostat is adequate. If you want to run double-headers or two-motored engines frequently, or two trains from the same rheostat, you will be better off with a 100-w. or even larger rheostat. This idea is better than trying to fasten two rheostats to the same shaft.

Some manufacturers now rate rheostats by their ampere capacity instead of the older watt method. This is safer because you know exactly how much load you can control. Add up the total load in amperes just as you would for power packs, page 8. Of course, you add up the total of the load that will be controlled by this one rheostat only. Then the ampere rating of the rheostat must be at least as great.

How speed control works

When a motor runs it develops two things. First, pulling force — enough to handle the cars you put behind the locomotive. Second, it develops speed. The relation between speed and load and the electricity going into the motor is a thing you may not understand at first reading, but I'll try to make the action clear.

In Chapter 15, we'll learn how you can connect an ammeter into your control panel to see how much current your train uses. We'll also use a volt-

meter to see how much electric pressure reaches the train. Let's imagine we already have these and we are about to start a train.

Well before the moment when the train starts to move, the ammeter and voltmeter needles move upward as we pull the throttle. They show that both the pressure (voltage) and current (amperage) to the motor is increasing even though the motor doesn't yet move. Actually it is the volts that make the amperes increase, as Ohm's law showed us.

If you coupled a miniature scale between the engine and first car at the same time, you would see it registering more and more pull. So we have the first law of locomotive motor mechanics:

Pulling force is proportionate to the amperes of electric current.

So far it's also proportionate to the voltage, but let's pull the throttle back until the wheels start to turn. From this point on, the pulling power doesn't increase very much because it's already sufficient to move the train and there's nothing extra it can pull save a little increased friction at high speeds. Since the amperes are proportionate to pull, they reach a ceiling too, at the moment the train starts, and they don't increase much more unless something changes the load.

But if current doesn't increase much after the train starts, what does happen when we pull the throttle back still more? Well, above the voltage needed to move the current, all extra

voltage merely develops speed. Speed increases in exact proportion to this excess voltage. Here's the rule:

The voltage below the stalling* threshold point serves to develop current to pull the load.

Above this point the excess voltage develops speed.

If you run a train with, say, 6 v., and if some 4 v. of this is used to develop the load current, the other 2 v. develops speed. If this is the case, then 8 v. will run the same train twice as fast as 6 v., 10 v. three times as fast, and so on. Extra voltage won't burn out the motor, but too much speed might make the motor fly apart or at least wear out more quickly.

Now let's change the load. If we add more cars, it will take more current to get the train started. Thus the threshold voltage will be higher, say 5 v. Now the train still will be stalling if we give it 5 v., while at 7 v. it will run about as fast as it did before at 6 v.

Curves add slightly to the load, but grades will add or subtract depending on whether they are up or down. In general, the load is doubled on a grade of about 2½ per cent. So, then, is the motor current and the heat.

When you use a rheostat, the power pack always develops 12 v. or a bit more. We use the rheostat to waste some of this voltage, but this is where the rheostat is a bad actor. The voltage it wastes is proportionate to the current going through. Thus the rheostat wastes more voltage with a heavy train than with a light one.

There is no place on a rheostat where you could mark it "half speed" or "slow crawl" because the load is different for each train, so the voltage wasted will also be different.

The worst trouble with rheostats is in up- and downhill running, as mentioned on page 12.

Motor characteristics

These facts are shown graphically in the chart of motor performance of a particular Varney Berkshire, Fig. 4-5. Other locos will develop the same shape of curves, but with different slopes and values. Voltage increases to the right as you pull the throttle. The black line shows that the engine doesn't start until about 3 v. Also, up to this point the colored line shows current increases along a straight line "current stalled."

After the loco starts, speed increases along a virtually straight line and current increases only with the extra friction of higher speeds.

*I changed the wording to stalling instead of starting in this rule because it is more accurate. Due to a property of friction, the load is greater than normal until a train actually starts. The stalling point current properly represents the rolling load of a train.

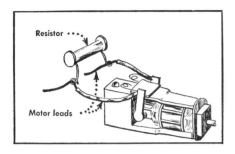

4-6 A fixed resistor across the two wires leading to the motor will help if the engine will not come to a smooth stop. Solder the two pigtail leads of the resistor to the motor leads. If one motor lead is grounded you may also connect one end of the resistor to the frame. The resistor may be tucked into almost any small space inside the loco or tender.

Technically minded readers may find the dotted lines radiating from the 16-v. corner interesting. These represent rheostat settings in ohm values and where they cross the current curves they indicate the actual voltage the motor will receive with and without load. (They have no relation to the speed curves so you have to figure the speed by finding the voltage first.)

Jerky stopping of small locos

Small locomotives may sometimes move even at the lowest setting of a rheostat. This is because they draw too small a current for the rheostat to lower the voltage below the stopping point. Installing a headlight almost always cures this, because the headlight draws just enough more current to lower the voltage properly. Another solution is to connect a fixed resistor of 25 ohms and 10-w. rating across the wires that lead from the power pack and rheostat to the track. If the loco has the space, you can put the resistor in the engine as in Fig. 4-6.

Power

If you multiply the amperes a motor uses by the volts across its terminals, you get the amount of power it consumes in watts. Here's the formula with P representing power:

$$P = IE$$

Some of the power to a motor is wasted as heat, but if the motor is not stalled the rest of the power is useful mechanical power. You can figure out all three if you know the stalling threshold voltage and the current needed to pull a particular load.

Let's say a motor has a load that makes it draw ½ a. and we find the threshold stalling voltage is 4 v. If we run the motor, the amount of heat wasted will be 2 w. If we increase the running voltage to, say, 6 v., the total watts will be 3 w., of which 2 w. still will be wasted as heat. But the extra 1 w. will be mostly useful power to pull the train.

Preventing burnouts

Practically all damage from electricity is due only to the heat developed by the current. Each watt of electricity raises the temperature of any electrical device a certain amount every second. At the same time, the air and other materials around the device start to carry the heat away. Eventually the temperature reaches a maximum point when the heat carried away equals the heat generated by the electric power.

You can control the temperature of anything electrical in two ways: you can limit the current or watts of electricity, and thus the rate of heating, or you can increase the rate of cooling by using a metal heat-dissipating fin, a big mounting plate, a blast of air, or an oil bath, etc.

Most devices are designed to work with only free air to carry the heat away. A "1-w." resistor, for instance, is usually made about 1" long and ³⁄₁₆" in diameter, because if it is this big the air can keep it cool enough to avoid destruction. That's all the watt or ampere rating means, that the temperature will be safe.

Knowing this you can often make a good guess as to how much electricity you can put into a device. You can think about how hot it could safely get without melting any metal or plastic parts or charring insulation. Then compare its size with some other device you do know the watt rating of. If it has more surface, it will be proportionately cooler for the same watt rating, for instance.

Of course, mechanical construction makes a difference too. Blowing a blast of air at a lamp bulb won't prevent it from burning out on twice its normal rating, because the air can't reach the filament to take the heat away as fast as it's generated. The temperature goes up so high that the filament vaporizes in less than a second. Poof, one useless lamp.

If you're in doubt about safe currents, with a motor for instance, it isn't likely to be damaged if it never gets so hot it will sizzle moist fingers touching the armature. Usually the temperature can go quite a bit higher than sizzling; some fellows put a droplet of oil in the windings, expecting to see a vapor wisp as a warning of high heat.

Selenium rectifiers should run somewhat cooler than the sizzle point.

Now, since it is temperature that does the damage, you can see that a short spurt of motor operation at more than the rated current (as when running a train up a short steep hill)

won't do any harm. Just watch that you don't overload a part so long that the temperature gets too high. This takes longer with big metal parts than with small things.

If you measure the watts going into a motor, or any device, you'll find about 1 w. per square inch of cooling surface is usually about the limit, as this raises the temperature 180°F to 200°F *above* the surroundings.

There is a good way to protect motors in locomotives. You adjust the weight of the engine so it slips its wheels when the motor current reaches its maximum safe rating. Then if you apply more voltage the wheels just slip faster without the motor current rising any more. Of course, if current rises due to mechanical defects inside the loco, such as a binding side rod or chipped gear, the motor can be overloaded without pulling a thing.

If you should burn out a coil, don't be too dismayed. All coils can be either rewound or replaced for a reasonable cost. There's nothing that can go wrong with your model railroad that cannot be repaired.

Heat from rheostats

The rheostat may be rated in watts, but that means for the whole coil. If you're using only half the coil at a particular moment, that part of the rheostat can develop only half the watts and still have a safe temperature. That's why a rating in amperes means more with a rheostat than a watt rating.

Watts and ohms cooperate

Before I go on, let me point out how useful the watt relation and Ohm's law are when you want to find out "what cooks" in your electrical equipment.

Ohm's law was stated three ways:

$$E = IR \quad I = E/R \quad \text{and} \quad R = E/I$$

Similarly you can learn about power in three ways:

$$P = IE \quad I = P/E \quad \text{and} \quad E = P/I$$

And you can go a step beyond this and relate power to resistance:

$$P = I^2R \quad P = E^2/R$$

This shows that power increases as the square* of the voltage or current in any particular device.

With these relations you can figure out not only how your motor is behaving, but also how the rheostat and track feeders affect the circuit.

In our example of the motor using only ½ a. at 6 v., you can also find out what is happening in the rheostat. First, we know the current in the rheostat is also ½ a., because the same current passes through both the motor

---

*The "square" of a number is the number multiplied by itself. Thus, the square of 5 is 5 times 5 or 25. A small ² raised above a number indicates that you should "square" it to work out the problem — 5² = 25.

and rheostat. All elements in a series circuit receive the same current.

Then we know that if the power produces 16 v. at no load (which is typical for so-called 12-v. packs), there must be another 10 v. wasted somewhere in the circuit. Most of this is wasted in the rheostat, so let's assume all of it is. Then by Ohm's law we find that the rheostat must be adjusted at a point putting 10 v. divided by ½ a., or 20 ohms, into the circuit, since ½ goes into 10 twenty times. This is halfway around a 40-ohm rheostat.

By using Watt's law we can also figure that the rheostat will be wasting ½ times 10, or 5 watts of power.

The whole rheostat is rated at 50 w. (usually) and we're using half the coil, 25 w., so our 5 w. isn't going to heat it up very much.

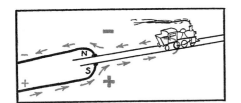

4-7 When the S rail is positive trains will be eastbound.

4-8 When the S rail is negative trains will be westbound. This is true regardless of which way the cowcatcher points.

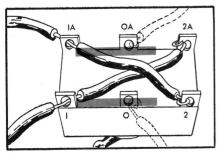

4-9 Whenever a double-pole double-throw toggle is used for reversing polarity, crossed wires are added to it as shown here. This is a rear view. When the toggle handle points to the left, terminals 0 and 1 are connected together as are terminals 0A and 1A; color shows this internal connection. Throwing the handle the other way connects 0 to 2 and 0A to 2A instead. You can substitute other kinds of dp. dt. switches. Label the terminals to the moving poles 0 and 0A in this same way. Then number the fixed contacts in the order of their use.

Direction control

IN our diagrams so far I have shown the electricity going around the control circuit in a counterclockwise direction. Suppose we made the electric current flow the other way around.

With ordinary motors this wouldn't make any difference. But motors for scale model locomotives are usually designed so that they will reverse and turn the other way when you "reverse" the polarity of the electric current, Figs. 4-7 and 4-8.

Notice how I managed to get the electricity to flow the other way around in Fig. 4-8 by interchanging the wires before they reach the track. Reversing an engine this way is just as awkward as it was to start and stop it by breaking a feeder wire, so again we resort to a toggle switch.

You can use ready-made reversing switches, such as the Atlas Twin, which actually contain two reversing switches. See Fig. 6-5. Or you can make up your own reversing switch starting with a dp. dt. (double-pole double-throw) toggle switch. Fig. 4-9 shows the back of such a switch and how short wires are added across diagonally opposite corners to make it into a reversing switch. The colored bars represent the internal connection in the switch when the handle is to the left. When the handle is moved to the right, the internal connections are also.

There is an easy way to add the crossed wires to the back of the dp. dt. toggle. Remove 1½" of the insulation from two of the connecting wires. Slip one of the connecting wires through the terminal lug at one corner of the dp. dt. toggle, and then wrap a short piece of friction tape around the wire where it was stripped. The last ½" or so should be left bare and pushed through the opposite lug. Now solder both corner lugs and then add the other crossed wire in the same way. With some kinds of insulation you can save a small tube and slip it over the wire instead of taping it.

Again, as before, you can substitute any kind of dp. dt. switch for the toggle as long as it will carry the current. A 3 a. rating will do for all but railroads running large locomotives or several locomotives from the same toggle. Then you need 5 a. or more in the rating of the toggle.

You can buy dp. dt. toggles that have an off position in the center of the handle's throw. These make it unnecessary to add a separate toggle for quick emergency stops.

Now, if you connect the reversing switch between the power pack and the track, as in Fig. 4-10, and then throw the lever, as in Fig. 4-11, you reverse the flow of electricity through the motor and this reverses the train.

If you have the train running, say, east, as in Fig. 4-7, and pick the locomotive up and turn it around on the track, it will still go east when you put it down again, even if it's going cowcatcher east at first and backing east last. This is hard for many to believe until they try it. But the reason is that you are reversing the wheels to opposite rails when you turn the engine around, which sends current through the motor in the opposite direction. You've reversed both the engine and its electric current, so it still goes eastward.

Strictly speaking, a single reversing

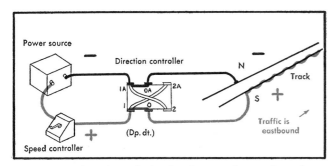

4-10 For eastbound travel, the direction-controller toggle sends positive energy to the S rail of the track. The short conductor from 0A to 1A is the contact inside the toggle. 0 to 1 is the same.

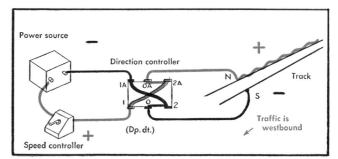

4-11 To reverse polarity, the toggle can direct electricity through the crossed wires. Now trains run west and the contacts inside the toggle have moved to the right. The toggle is shown from the rear.

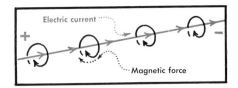

4-12 The color shows the path of electrons along a wire. The dark arrows show the magnetic force produced around the current.

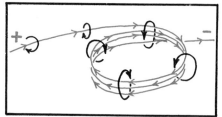

4-13 If several wires carrying electrons are brought close together, the magnetic effect around each wire complements the force around the others. The force is strongest through the center of the coil but exists everywhere.

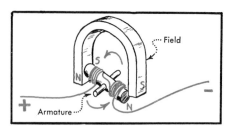

4-14 If you pivot an electromagnet between the poles of another "field" magnet and force current through the coil, the electromagnet will try to complete a magnetic circuit by bridging the poles of the field magnet.

switch is more of a "direction controller" than a "reversing switch." In practice it's better to provide more reversing switches and use a different switch to set up direction than the one already in the power pack.

Three reversing switches

For convenience, I recommend three reversing switches, Fig. 4-15. Here is how you use them:

1. Use the switch on the power pack for forward and reverse moves, as when switching in a yard or picking up cars at a spur. This is the engineer's reverse lever.

2. Sooner or later you add another reversing switch, probably on a control panel, and you use this to determine whether east or west is forward. You don't touch this switch unless your train reaches the end of a run and is ready to come back.

3. A third reversing switch is used in this same way to determine which way is forward in a return loop.

In chapters on return loops and on building control panels, we'll see how these three reversing switches are put to use.

How the motor works

I told you about amperes being a flow of electrons and how the push that makes them move is a pressure or voltage, and I told you how the flow of electric current always produces heat. But I didn't mention one other important thing about electricity up to now. That is the magnetic effect of electron flow. It so happens that when an electric current moves along a wire, it produces a magnetic force around the wire as shown in Fig. 4-12.

The force around the single wire isn't very strong unless you increase the current to a value that might melt the wire. But if you put many wires side by side as in a coil, the magnetic forces around each wire in the coil will add to the others and produce a very strong magnetic field, Fig. 4-13.

Put a piece of soft iron through the coil and you have an electromagnet that can lift nails or scrap metal, all depending on the size of the coil, the iron field, and the current flowing through.

This electromagnet is just like a permanent magnet as long as electricity flows through the coil, but it has the advantage of losing its magnetism when you cut the current.*

*Permanent magnets are made by using hard steel or special alloys in place of soft iron. They retain magnetism after removal from the coil.

The magnet will pull or repel any other magnet, electric or permanent, all depending on the relative polarity of the two. Poles are labeled N for north and S for south.

In an electric motor, several magnets are arranged to interact by attracting and repelling each other.

Suppose you mount an electromagnet upon a shaft so that it can turn, and surround it with a horseshoe-shaped permanent magnet, Fig. 4-14. The moving part is called the "armature" and the big magnet is called the "field"—short for field magnet.

If you force an electric current through the coil, the armature becomes a magnet and it will try to move to a position across the poles of the horseshoe. The N poles try to approach the S poles and the poles of like polarity try to move away from

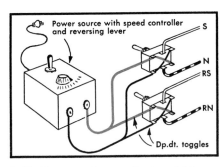

4-15 Two reversing toggles in addition to the one in the pack make for the most convenient control of direction.

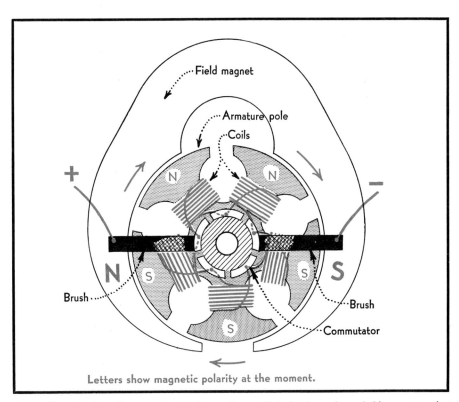

Letters show magnetic polarity at the moment.

4-16 If you look at the motor in your locomotive you'll find it has a large field magnet and a three, five, seven, or nine "pole" armature magnet. The coils of the armature are joined in a daisy chain and each junction is connected to a segment of the armature. This motor is shown as viewed from the commutator end. There are five commutator segments in this motor because it happens to have five poles.

Motor Current Ratings

If you operate a motor at not more than the current values listed, you should have no overheating. In most ratings a 20 per cent safety factor is included to allow for variations in individual motors and ammeters. Voltage has little to do with motor heating.

MAKE AND MODEL	SAFE CURRENT AMPERES
All-Nation, older motors, obsolete	1.0
Pittman DC-92, DC-94	1.5
Pittman DC-95	2.0
American Flyer (S scale)	
Small motor	0.85
Large motor	1.5
Diesel motors, each	1.2
Add for smoke unit	0.4
Athearn, small motor	0.6*
Large motor	0.8*
Bowser, all models	0.7
Central Locomotive Works,	
Pittman DC-95A	2.0
Fleischmann	0.3
Gilbert (HO scale) all motors	0.85
Add for smoke unit	0.3
Herkimer, uses Athearn motor	0.6*
Hobbytown, Pittman DC-70	0.7
H. P. Products, Romford Midget	0.5
Kemtron, Thomas Flyer	0.5
(Lindsay motors have L numbers; some models use Pittman motors.)	
L-170, L-180 (discontinued)	0.8
L-190	0.7
L-570, L-580, L-582	0.5
L-740	0.8
KL-766	0.5
L-1010, L-1030 (discontinued)	0.5
L-1045 (discontinued)	0.8
00-666	0.8
PM-10	0.5
TT-105	0.5
X-130, Romford Midget	0.5
X-300, Romford Phantom	0.5
X-301, Micro	0.5
Kendrick & Davis, 117-1	2.0
117-2	2.8
117-3	4.0
117-4	5.0
Kidder, Japanese imports	0.8*
Lindsay (now Kemtron; see L numbers)	
Lionel, HO, 1959-1960 models	0.7
O gauge and O-27 gauge	2.5
Lobaugh, 6100	1.75
6200	2.75
6300	4.0
Mantua, 3352 (small)	0.6
33565 (General tender motor)	0.6
33572, 33573, PM-1	0.6
Diesel power truck	0.6
33574, 33575 (Pittman DC-70)	0.7
Miller (S scale power truck),	
per armature	1.0
After starting, current should be lower.	
Model Die Casting, Pittman DC-60	0.7
DC-62A	0.6
Formerly used Lindsay motor	0.5
Model Engineering Works	
Pittman DC-60	0.6
Formerly used Lindsay motor	0.5
Model Pike, DC-60	0.7
Nord, M1	1.35
Pacific Fast Mail, Tenshodo, MV-1	0.75
MH-2, MH-3	1.0
United, DC-195	0.5
DC-295	0.95
Pittman DC-70	0.7
DC-62A	0.6
DC-71B	0.8
Penn Line (uses Pittman motors)	
Pennsylvania Scale Models,	
ES-160 diesel	0.5*
Traction motor	0.5*
Pittman (rubber-band replacement motor)	
DC-62A	0.6
DC-60, DC-62, DC-65	0.6
DC-70	0.7
DC-703	0.6
DC-702 (Early RDC cars)	0.5
DC-71A, DC-71B	0.8
DC-80 (obsolete)	0.85
DC-81, DC-85	1.0
DC-91	1.3
DC-92, DC-94 (obsolete)	1.5
DC-93, DC-95 (obsolete)	2.0
DC-94A (discontinued)	1.5
DC-95A	2.0
DC-100	3.0
DC-204A, O gauge trolley truck	0.7
AC-92, AC-94 (obsolete)	1.2
AC-93 (obsolete)	1.8
AC-95 (obsolete)	1.8
Revell, diesel loco motor	0.6
Switcher motor	0.6
Add for smoke unit	0.3
Rivarossi	0.5*
Romford, Phantom, etc. (see H. P. Products or Kemtron)	
Roundhouse (see Model Die Casting)	
Sims, Pittman DC-71B	0.8
Japanese motor	0.6*
Suydam, HO, S-143	1.0
Tenshodo (see Pacific Fast Mail)	
Thomas (uses Pittman Motors)	
Tyco (same as Mantua)	
United (see Pacific Fast Mail)	
Varney, all smaller locos are	
Pittman DC-60	0.6
F-3 diesel, Pittman DC-70	0.7
Berkshire, heavy Consolidation,	
Pittman DC-71B	0.8
Formerly supplied own motors	0.75
Wagner, Pittman DC-60	0.6
Pittman DC-71B	0.8
Pittman DC-94	1.5
Walthers, HO power truck,	
Pittman DC-60	0.6
O scale truck uses K&D motor	
Wilson	0.5

* Estimated; no verification received.

each other, so both pulling and pushing forces are at work at each end; there are four forces in all.

This particular device will flip-flop only a half turn and then is magnetically locked in position. But in a motor, a switching device called a "commutator" is added to reverse the connections to the coils each time the armature reaches the crosswise position. Two contacts called "brushes" ride over this commutator. If you look at an actual motor and then study Fig. 4-16, you'll be able to figure out how your motor works.

The current from the brushes reaches the coils in the armature through contact plates called the commutator. As the motor shaft turns, the brushes and commutator act like a direction-controller toggle and reverse the polarity of the poles twice in every revolution. This keeps the lower poles trying to move to the left and the upper poles to the right as long as electricity flows in the same direction. To reverse the motor, you reverse the electricity, and thus the magnetic polarity of each armature pole. This makes them seek the opposite pole and turn the other way.

Some motors have an electromagnet for the field instead of the permanent magnet. You cannot make these motors turn the other way by merely reversing the electric current because the polarity of the field is reversed at the same time as the armature. That's why we used a rectifier to keep the polarity of the field the same in Fig. 5-7.

Choosing a motor

When you build your own locomotive, you have a big choice of motors to select from. An ideal motor would have a very strong magnet; this makes for cooler operation, more pull, and slower speed. Some off-make motors may look just like known brands, yet have magnet alloys that cannot be magnetized as strongly.

Big motors are not needed for pull, only for speed. You can pull any load with the smallest motor if you have a high-enough gear ratio. But if you need pull and speed too, the motor must be bigger with less gearing. If you use the smallest motors in freight locomotives, with sufficient gear ratios, you can actually pull longer trains because the small motor leaves space for more weight in the locomotives.

More poles in a motor are better because the armatures turn more smoothly. Skewed armature slots also help. If the motor will have a worm gear, the thrust bearings in the motor will be of utmost importance because they will bear more than the entire pull of the train.

Sparking brushes

An uneven commutator or bad brushes or too heavy a load causes brush sparking. In severe cases, the loco gets a pitted commutator and eventually stalls. Sparking can be reduced if you can adjust the brush springs for best speed at a given voltage. If the commutator needs smoothing, use delicate methods such as a strip of crocus cloth over the end of a small stick while the motor runs. High speeds will aggravate sparking trouble, but ordinarily do little harm to a motor.

5. Locomotive and Car Wiring

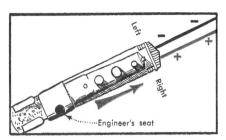

5 - 1 For forward operation the right-hand (engineer's side) rail should have positive polarity. This is true regardless of whether the rail happens to be the S or N rail. If you lift this engine and turn it the other way, the engineer's side of the cab will then be over a negative rail. This will make the locomotive back up. But since it is turned around, backing up would still be in the direction of the colored arrow. The only way you can run the engine toward the left of this picture is to change track polarity.

THE first essential in locomotive wiring is that the locomotive should move forward when the rail on the right side is connected to the positive power terminal. See Fig. 5-1. You can check track polarity with a meter across the rails, but usually a comparison with other locomotives will weed out any connected backwards.

Sometimes you can correct a wrong-way loco mechanically. For instance, you can reverse the twist of rubber-band drives. Sometimes you can turn a truck around so it picks up from the opposite rail, or turn all the wheels in a truck end for end.

More often, the best way to reverse a locomotive is to interchange the two wires connecting to the motor brushes. Usually one of these is a strap, lug, tab, or spring that connects this brush to the motor or loco frame. This ground connection has to be opened by bending up the lug (or sometimes even by cutting it). For an example, see Fig. 5-2. Next, you transfer the "hot" power wire to this motor brush, taking it off the second brush. Finally, you devise a new all-metal ground connection for the second brush.

Failing other methods, the engine can be reversed by turning the magnet in the motor end for end. This isn't recommended because removing either the armature or magnet from many motors weakens them instantly.

Wheel insulation

If all-metal wheels and axles were used in a model, an electrical path would create a short circuit from rail to rail. This can happen accidentally

and shows up first as a slowing or jerking of the locomotive; later, as the wheels get cleaner, the train stalls completely and the wheels may be pitted from sparking.

To prevent this kind of short circuit, some plastic has to be used somewhere between the wheels. Sometimes the wheels themselves are plastic, but plastic wheels are a problem for model railroad car lighting and signaling, and also won't do for a power pickup on locos. Sometimes metal wheels are mounted on plastic axles. More often they are mounted on metal axles, with a plastic bushing at one or both ends to separate the wheels electrically. Sometimes a coat of baked enamel is deposited right on the axle for insulation. Large wheels are more often made in two parts with the rim separated from the body with a thin ring of plastic or fiber.

Sometimes both wheels are insulated from the metal axle, but more often only one wheel is insulated. With the other wheel "grounded," the axle can then be conveniently used as an electrical power connection.

These half-grounded wheel axles can cause a lot of mysterious trouble if one axle in a truck should get turned the wrong end about. This has happened to me even with brand new trucks as they came from the factory. Power goes in one wheel to its axle and from there to the metal frame and the other axle. From there it goes out to the opposite rail. This can take a while to show up if the wheels have a coating on them. The same kind of short frequently occurs with metal-frame cars and particularly tenders

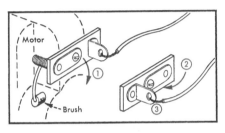

5 - 2 This shows how one brush in a Kemtron-Lindsay motor is grounded and how to "unground" it by removing the center screw and bending up, 1. Now bend the other brush terminal down and replace the screw, 2. Finally, connect the "hot" wire to the other brush, 3.

when a whole truck gets accidentally turned half way around.

If you cannot see the insulation, the test in Fig. 5-3 will show which wheels are grounded to their axles and also find if the insulation has been punctured on the other end of the axle.

Power pickup

When power is needed for the motor or lamps in cars or engines, some wheels are arranged to pick up from one rail and the other wheels from the other rail. Both Athearn Hi-F and Sims locomotives have a clever way to pick up from all wheels on both rails,

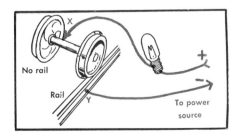

5 - 3 This test shows which end of an axle has the insulated wheel. It can also be used to find defective insulation. Wire X can touch either the axle or the truck frame. If the bulb lights, the wheel touching the rail is not insulated. The lamp bulb should have a voltage as high as the power source used.

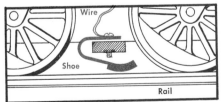

5 - 4 When a locomotive has no trucks or tender to pick up current from the left-hand rail, you can install a spring shoe to ride on the rail. The shoe is made thick where it will wear most. See also Fig. 5-5. Connect the shoe to the hot brush of the motor. Sometimes shoes are provided at front and rear ends.

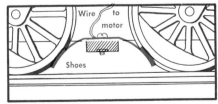

5 - 5 This arrangement is even better because it does not tend to lift the engine off its drivers and thus lose some pulling power. The shading represents insulating material to which the spring shoe is bolted. You can use any other arrangement that will insulate the shoes from the frame of the engine.

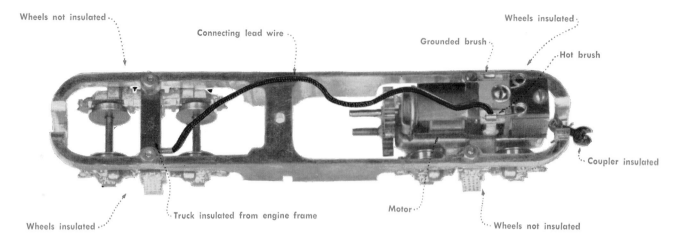

Wheels not insulated

Connecting lead wire

Grounded brush

Wheels insulated

Hot brush

Coupler insulated

Wheels insulated

Truck insulated from engine frame

Motor

Wheels not insulated

5-6 Typical motive power uses the two trucks as collectors. The forward truck picks up at the right and the other wheels are insulated. One or both trucks must be insulated from the main frame Front and rear couplers should always be insulated from the frame to prevent short circuits when you run double-header trains. In steam locomotives the link between engine and tender should also be insulated

but more often the arrangement is like this:

The front wheels and axles are turned so they connect to the right-hand rail and the axles and front truck are grounded to the loco main frame. See Fig. 5-6.

The rear truck is insulated from the frame and its axle-grounded wheels are turned so they pick up from the left rail. The "hot" wire to the motor goes to the rear truck frame.

This is just the usual method, and doesn't rule out many other good schemes that are used. With steam-type locos the whole engine is treated as the front truck and the whole tender picks up from the left rail. This requires a fiber drawbar and enough separation so the tender doesn't short circuit against the loco when they go around tight curves; see Fig. 5-10.

When pickup is faulty or there aren't any grounded wheels available for power connection on one side of the engine, wiper-type contacts are provided so they either rub on the rails or upon the sides, rims or axles of otherwise insulated wheels. Both schemes are shown in Figs. 5-4 and 5-5.

Faulty pickup

Poor pickup connections result in jerky operation or complete stalling whether caused by a short circuit or broken circuit. Be sure all insulation is in good condition to avoid shorts. Check to see that metal frames of insulated trucks don't touch the main frame on curves or rough track, causing short circuits. Also, see that the terminal connections of wires at trucks and motors are not shorting on the inside of the body or some part of the frame. Often locos won't run with the body in place because of interference between the shell and the motor brushes. A poor ground connection at the pivot of a grounded truck frame is also a common trouble spot.

On diesel-type locos, where two wheels are insulated on each side, faulty pickup can occur if the trucks don't have enough freedom to nod and tilt. A washer placed between the truck pivot and main frame helps here.

Without the washer, it's possible for the pickup wheels to lift entirely off the rails on twisted track, and there you stand, powerless.

Flexible connections

The wire between a motor and swivel truck or tender may get stiff in time and then should be replaced. A good type of wire sold in many hobby shops is what is called in the radio trade "indoor antenna wire." It is size 25, stranded with a grayish, limp plastic covering. This size is big enough for all HO locomotive wiring and comes in handy for other short-distance connections about the layout.

I fasten a No. 4-0 female dress snap to the tender end of the motor wire on my steam locos, taking care that the solder doesn't foul the spring in the snap. Then I file the head of an 00-90 screw round like a ball so the snap will attach to it. (The diameter will just pass through a No. 51 drill hole.) This screw is mounted at some convenient place at the front of the tender. Then I can easily detach the wire from the tender. The same scheme is handy for connecting a string of lighted cars.

Headlights and car lights

You'll find an important discussion about lamp bulbs in Chapter 13, and

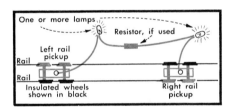

5-7 One or several lamps in a series can be wired like this with two-truck equipment. All lamps in a string should have the same ampere rating, but voltages can differ. Total lamp voltages should exceed 16 to 20 volts to avoid burnouts or else dropping resistors are recommended.

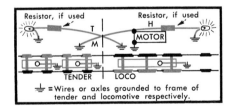

5-8 When one motor brush is grounded to frame, one headlight wire may also be grounded, simplifying wiring. This also shows how tender light can be grounded to both tender and locomotive frames. If you don't want the two wires between loco and tender, then insulate one tender truck from body, turn it half way around, and connect lamp wire T to it instead.

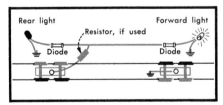

5-9 Each headlight burns when engine goes in its direction but darkens going the other way when you install rectifiers in the wire going to each lamp. Any small one-cell rectifier will do if it can handle up to 20 v. and as much current as one bulb. Usually a low-cost diode will do, such as type 1N90 or 1N91 A diode rated at 100 ma. is the same as 1/10 a.; this is the minimum to use with a grain-of-wheat type bulb. If lamp goes on when it should go out, reconnect the diode end for end.

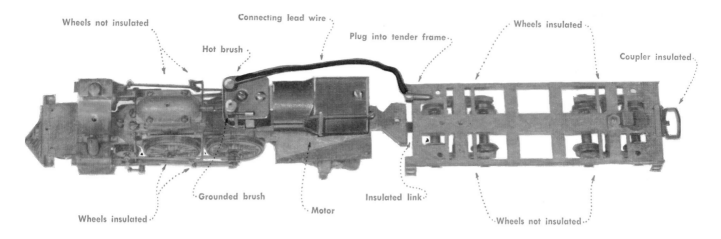

Wheels not insulated · · · · Connecting lead wire · · · · Wheels insulated · · · ·
· · · Hot brush · · · Plug into tender frame · · · · Coupler insulated · · ·
· · · Grounded brush · · Insulated link · Wheels not insulated · · · · ·
· · Wheels insulated · · · · · Motor

5 - 10 We wire steam-type locomotives to collect electricity from the right-hand wheels of the engine and to return it through the left wheels of the tender. All other wheels are insulated. Current from the track passes through the engine frame to the grounded brush of the motor. Return current flows through a wire to a connection on the tender frame. Which brush is hot and which grounded depends on motor construction.

you'll see that sometimes it's wise to include a voltage-dropping resistor or more than one bulb in the lighting system for a particular car or loco. But whether the string has several bulbs and a resistor or only one bulb, the power connections for the string are the same. In Fig. 5-7, one power connection is made to each truck of a car or diesel loco. Each truck has wheels insulated at one end only with the grounded wheels placed along the right rail in one truck while the other truck is turned so its grounded wheels are on the left. If there is a metal frame, one or both trucks must be insulated from it.

You can put the lamp bulbs anywhere you wish, headlight, behind marker lights, in the cab, firebox, etc. Just be sure the wires don't short against metal body and frame parts by using good insulated wire or sleeves. If you use grain-of-wheat bulbs with pigtail wires, a drop of cement at the base of the bulb will

help prevent the wires from breaking off from the continuous vibration.

On locomotives you can use the same wiring scheme or you can connect each end of the lamp string to one of the motor brushes, whichever is more convenient. Since one brush is often grounded, you can then ground one end of the lamp string anywhere for convenience. Fig. 5-8 shows a grounded headlight and also shows how to light a tender headlight on a steam-type locomotive. You have the choice of connecting this light to the locomotive frame or to an insulated tender truck.

Locomotives in switching service keep both the headlights on, but road locomotives usually have only the front headlight burning. Fig. 5-7 shows how to connect a small rectifier so the headlights switch on and off, depending on the polarity of running current.

If you want the train lights to shine when the train stops, electronic lighting is available. This consists of a special power supply and means to separate the lighting and running power in each car. For further information, write Leyghton-Paige and any other manufacturers. Also, see *Model Railroader* for April 1950, and

April 1955, and *Model Trains* for January 1957. A reprint booklet of these articles is planned for 1960 publication.

Universal motors

Not all motors used in scale model railroading are of the permanent magnet type. The universal motor has a coil to produce its magnetic field, and if you want reversing you must have the current pass through this coil in the same direction at all times. Small rectifiers especially for this purpose are sold through hobby shops, and they are connected as in Fig. 5-7.

Insulating trucks and couplers

Except for cases of power pickup, trucks and also couplers should usually be insulated from the frame of any car or locomotive to reduce the chance of short circuiting. Often trucks can be mounted on wood or with plastic bushings that fit in the metal frame. Fig. 5-12 shows a scheme for homemade insulation of trucks under metal cars. As for couplers, metal ones seem preferable to plastic mechanically, whether you use one style or another, and the clever PFM Six-Way plastic coupler pocket is a good solution to the insulation problem in most cases; the only disadvantage is that you may sometimes have to remove a bit of metal to make way for it. Sometimes the whole pilot of a locomotive or the end sill of a car can be insulated from the main frame more easily than just the coupler pocket. Kadee fittings for their K-6, K-7, and K-8 couplers are insulated and sometimes it may help to buy this coupler and graft the type of coupler you use onto the shank to solve an insulation problem.

Parting advice: Don't forget left and right are backwards when you work on cars and locos bottom side up. Our drawings in this chapter show them from above.

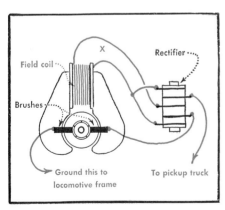

Field coil · · ·
X
Rectifier · · · · ·
Brushes ·
Ground this to locomotive frame
To pickup truck

5 - 11 By adding a small rectifier, any A.C.-D.C. or "universal" motor can be made to reverse just like "permag" motors. Notice that the field coil is connected to the middle and outside terminals of the rectifier. If you find the motor runs the locomotive in the wrong direction, interchange wires at X.

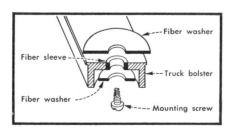

Fiber washer
Fiber sleeve
Truck bolster
Fiber washer
Mounting screw

5 - 12 Two fiber washers, such as are sold by Kadee and others for truck shimming, can be used together with a small piece of model airplane fuel tubing, hard plastic sleeve, or drilled-out fiber rod to make an insulated mounting for metal trucks under metal cars.

6. Loops and Other Turning Tracks

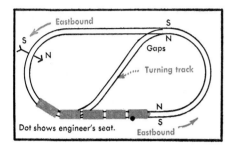

6-1 Train goes eastbound before crossing.

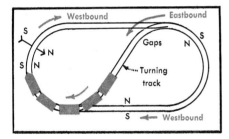

6-2 Whenever a train uses the turning track, it is automatically turned from eastbound to westbound even though it doesn't back up. This happens no matter which end of the turning track the train leaves from. The same occurs on all return loops, wyes and turntables.

LOOK at the oval railroad in Fig. 6-1 and imagine a train eastbound, or moving counterclockwise, around the line. After a few trips, throw one of the turnouts to guide the train across the diagonal track in the center. When the train crosses this diagonal, it will regain the oval on the other side but now it will be westbound, Fig. 6-2.

Notice how the train, without ever backing up, has turned to go in the other direction. Thus, the diagonal track can be called a "turning track."

A turning track exists whenever you are able to get a train turned end-for-end, whether it's done by a return cutoff, as we've seen, or by a loop, wye, or even a turntable. If we use the convention of calling clockwise westbound, then we can say we have a turning track wherever we can change a train from heading eastbound to westbound, or vice versa.

Turning tracks are easy to find if your track plan is an oval. Some kinds of turning track are more subtle and I'll show you how to find all of them in the next chapter. The reason you must find them is that you need special wiring to prevent trains from stalling.

Wherever there is a turning track, an isolated electrical "turning section" is needed. This may coincide with the actual turning track or it may merely overlap into it a little. So get this: Turning *track* is a mechanical situation of operation and turning *section* is an electrical circuit to accommodate it. Here's why we need the section:

When the train first ran around the oval in Fig. 6-1, the grounded wheels and grounded motor connection were on the engineer's side of the locomotive, connected to the S rail of the oval; see the black dot. But after leaving the turning track in Fig. 6-2, the engineer's side with the grounded wheels rides on the N rail side of the track.

In Chapter 5 we saw that the right-hand side of a locomotive must be connected to positive polarity for the engine to go forward. Since this positive side changes from being over the S rail to being over the N rail, it is obvious that the main line (oval in this case) must have its electrical polarity reversed if the train is to continue forward.

This requires a mainline direction-control reversing switch (preferably in addition to the one already furnished on the power pack). But we want the locomotive to go smoothly forward all the time, so when the mainline direction is reversed, this action must have no effect on the locomotive itself. This makes for the other requirement:

There must be a place that is isolated from the effect of the mainline direction controller where the train can run continuously forward during the moment when the mainline direction controller reverses the mainline polarity. See Fig. 6-3.

This is accomplished by providing a separate electrical circuit in the track, a "block" or "section" where the train can run independently of the mainline direction controller. This

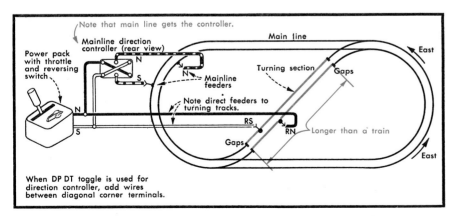

6-3 MINIMUM LOOP WIRING. By providing one extra direction controller, mainline polarity can be changed smoothly from eastbound to westbound while train is within the colored turning section. If turning section is long enough, this can be done easily without stopping the train and without jerking. The reversing switch on the power pack is still needed for back-up moves on either main line or return track.

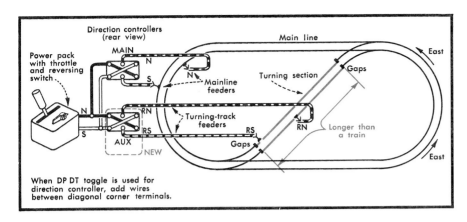

6 - 4 PREFERRED LOOP WIRING. By providing two direction-control levers or toggles next to the reversing switch on the power pack, train operation is much more convenient. Some complicated track plans may require a third controller for additional loops, wyes or turntable.

6 - 5 The Atlas Twin contains two direction-control levers built into one printed-circuit unit. Each has off and reverse.

block is also called a "return block" or a "turning section" and its feed wires are labeled RS and RN, or in some other way to warn you of special wiring. You'll find the letter R appears on many published track plans to show where a turning section should be provided.

Gaps and insulated rail joiners

The black bars at the ends of the turning section represent plastic rail joiners or open gaps in all rails. They are necessary because there is bound to be a polarity mismatch between the turning section and the mainline rails first at one end and then the other.

These gaps should be far enough apart so you can get the whole train into the turning section. If not, metal wheels will have to cross mismatched gaps and heavy short-circuit currents will interfere with train running and also pit the metal wheels of cars.

You can remove metal rail joiners and replace them with plastic joiners, but if track is already laid it's easier to saw gaps right through each rail. Do this by hand with a razor saw or with a motor tool equipped with a large diameter and very thin abrasive cutting wheel. After cleaning metal chips from the cut, squirt a little Ambroid cement into the gap so it cannot close when the rail expands in hot weather.

Usually the gaps should be close to the frog end of the nearby switches, because this allows you to get the maximum train length between the ends of the turning track. The gaps can be staggered or opposite, as you find convenient. See Chapter 17 for detail considerations in gap location.

Auxiliary direction controller

The scheme in Fig. 6-4 is a big improvement in operating convenience. Now an auxiliary direction controller AUX is provided in addition to the MAIN controller. In all you now have

three reversing switches, and here's how they can be used conveniently:

REVERSER. The lever on the power pack. This is used like the reverse lever in a locomotive cab to make the engine go forward and back. It is used in switching operations almost exclusively. Proper operation is to stop the train before reversing it.

MAIN DIRECTION LEVER. This is the added reversing switch that controls only mainline polarity. It is used like a dispatcher's lever to determine whether eastbound or westbound shall be forward on the mainline districts of the railroad. In proper operation this lever is moved only when a train is in the loop (not on the track influenced). The idea is to get this direction properly set up before the train reaches mainline track.

AUXILIARY DIRECTION CONTROLLER. This is the added reversing switch that controls the principle direction of travel only through a loop, wye, turntable, or return cutoff. It could be marked LOOP or TURN instead of AUX if you prefer. Its use is exactly the same as the main controller except that you move the lever at a different time; you move it to set up the traffic direction in the loop before the train gets there.

You can label the power pack reverser "Forward" and "Reverse," the main controller "East" and "West," and the AUX controller "Normal" and "Reverse" if you wish, to help keep the preferred uses in mind. In cab control you'll have two or more sets of these three controls.

I've explained these levers somewhat laboriously because this arrangement will be new to many model railroaders. Those who use it find it far more convenient than older schemes for wiring loops and wyes.

How to operate the turning track

When your train approaches a turning section, glance at the toggle

marked AUX to see that it is lined up properly. The AUX lever should be turned one way if you will enter the turning section by the usual end, but flipped to "Reverse" if this time you plan to enter the turning section by the back door.

After the train is completely within the turning section, you flip the mainline controller lever. This reverses mainline polarity so your train can continue back in the other direction.

That's all you do each time your train reaches a turning section. The train never stalls or jerks. If you wish to stop and do some switching, then you use the reverser on the power pack regardless of the direction-controller arrangement.

Electrical equipment for loops

The direction-control levers can be any kind of electrical reversing switch. In Fig. 6-5 the identical circuit is shown using Atlas "Twin" knobs as MAIN and AUX controllers. If you prefer to build your own control panel, you can use any kind of switch that has at least two poles and two positions. Then you wire it as a reversing switch as shown on page 16. Several types are discussed in Chapter 14.

Some fellows wonder why relays aren't used more often to automatically reverse mainline polarity for a turned train. This is because it's simple only if you run a single train; see Fig. 8-18. If two trains use the same main line, the circuit has to be able to reverse individual parts of the main line differently for each train, and to do this with relays results in more complication than we can discuss in this book.

Other track patterns

So far we've only shown the return-cutoff type of turning track, but the wiring is really the same for all the others. The differences come only in

Continued on page 26

Reference Data for Turning Sections of All Kinds

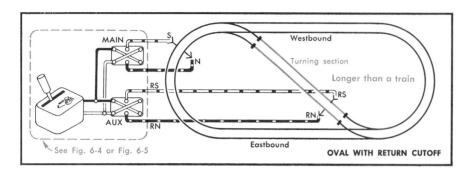

OVAL WITH RETURN CUTOFF

6 - 6 RETURN CUTOFF, METHOD A. Compare this drawing, which repeats the method used in previous examples, with the scheme in Fig. 6-7 below. In this first method the isolated turning section is entirely within the diagonal return cutoff

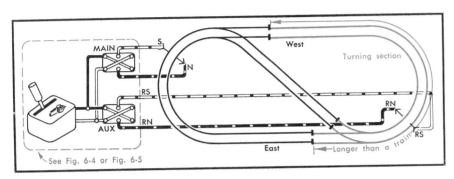

6 - 7 RETURN CUTOFF, METHOD B. Here most of the isolated turning track has been extended past one track switch and around the oval. The advantage is that this can accommodate longer trains. It is essential that at least some part of the diagonal track (the real turning place) still be included in the electrically isolated turning section. In this example, very little of the diagonal is part of the turning section, but more could be added by merely shifting the gaps up the diagonal any distance you wish. Note six gaps are needed

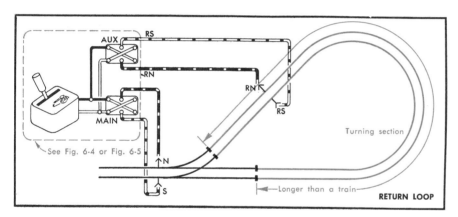

RETURN LOOP

> Turning sections shown in color in all diagrams.

6 - 8 RETURN LOOP Here's the standard wiring for a return loop. If the loop is large, it is permissible to make the turning section shorter as long as it will still hold your longest train. The track switch cannot be part of this isolated section

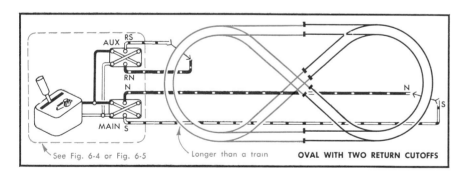

OVAL WITH TWO RETURN CUTOFFS

6 - 9 FIGURE-EIGHT OVAL. You might think you'd need two turning sections for this plan but if you gap it as shown you need only one. Also, this allows you to operate in either oval or figure-eight pattern continuously without having to flip direction-control handles on each lap of the trip Be sure each section is as long as your trains As with all plans, it's really arbitrary which section is called AUX and which MAIN for the wiring is really the same for each, and each must be long enough to hold a returning train

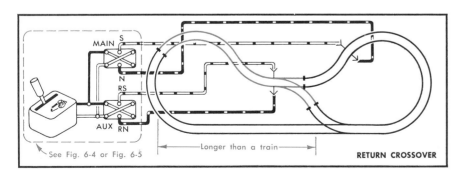

RETURN CROSSOVER

6 10 RETURN CROSSOVER, DOG-BONE PLAN This is exactly the same as Fig. 6-7 except for track distortion If you prefer, the entire left part of the layout could be included in the turning section by merely shifting the gaps nearer to the track switch in the foreground One switch should be in each section. That's because the actual returning occurs when a train crosses the crossover

24

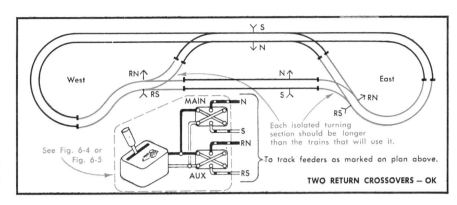

TWO RETURN CROSSOVERS — OK

Each isolated turning section should be longer than the trains that will use it.

To track feeders as marked on plan above.

6-11 TWO CROSSOVERS ON DOG-BONE
Sometimes the obvious way to provide two isolated turning sections is also most convenient on a dog-bone plan.

6-12 TWO CROSSOVERS WITH SHARED SECTION. If the crossovers are about a train-length apart, this arrangement will be preferable to that in Fig. 6-11 because only one turning section serves both crossovers. The only difference in actual operation is the timing of when you flip the direction-control levers. Note two ways where section must be longer than a train.

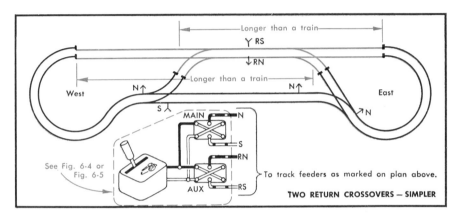

TWO RETURN CROSSOVERS — SIMPLER

To track feeders as marked on plan above.

Dog-bone Layouts
Three methods:

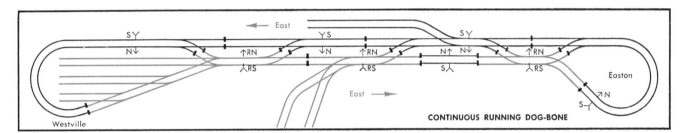

CONTINUOUS RUNNING DOG-BONE

6-13 METHOD A. This favors around-the-oval running, as the only time you must operate direction controllers is when switching through the crossovers. Then the whole train must be within one of the turning sections before regaining main track on other side

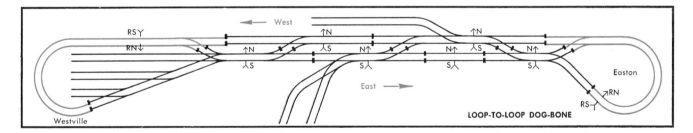

LOOP-TO-LOOP DOG-BONE

6-14 METHOD B. This favors switching as now controllers must be flipped when trains use end loops, but not when using crossovers.

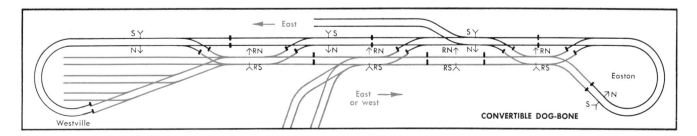

CONVERTIBLE DOG-BONE

6-15 METHOD C. By providing return sections all along one main, you can operate either for switching convenience or for oval running by merely setting controllers one way or the other. This is often more complicated, but gives maximum operating advantages.

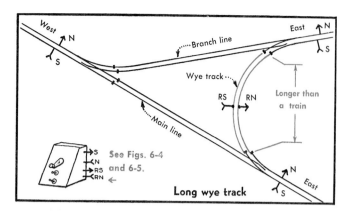

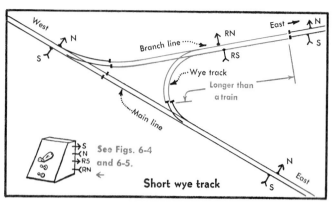

6 - 16 WYE, METHOD A. If side of wye is long enough to hold entire train, this method of wiring is convenient at junctions.

6 - 17 WYE, METHOD B. More often one of the turnouts is included in turning section. Section may be short if for turning locos only.

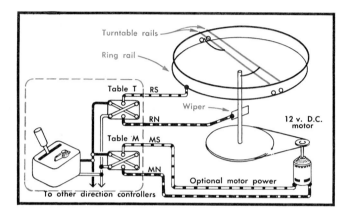

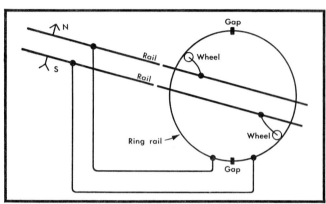

6 - 18 TURNTABLE. Usually power to the rails on a turntable is fed by the center pivot and the ring rail. This requires connection either to the regular AUX direction controller or to a separate direction controller as shown here. In either case, an off position is required so engine on table can stand while table turns. Note how motor can be added; all you need is another direction controller. Regular power pack throttle controls turntable motor as though it were another train.

6 - 19 RING-RAIL GAPPING. By putting gaps in ring rail, insulating support wheels from other metal parts, you can make the turntable operate as its own direction controller. Then no matter which way you turn the table, its track polarity will match that of the approach track. Each support wheel is connected to one rail, and polarity depends on whether this wheel is on near or far side of divided ring rail. Locate gaps so turntable is between track positions when wheels straddle them.

how you decide to locate the boundary gaps to make the isolated section. In all cases, the power pack and direction levers are wired the same way whether you use toggles, the Atlas Twin, or some other switch. Each ends up with four feeders which I've marked S, N and RS and RN. The differences in the following examples then come only in where these feeders are connected to the track and where you cut the gaps. Each diagram covers one of the typical arrangements you might have on your own railroad.

Dog-bone layouts

The dog-bone type of plan can be operated as an oval or as a point-to-point line with loops at each end. The first method requires wiring as in Fig. 6-13; otherwise you'll have to flip toggles every time a train reaches an end loop.

But Fig. 6-14 requires less toggle flipping when switching through crossovers, so it is preferred for point-to-point and switching type operations. The more ideal scheme in Fig.

6-15 is like 6-13, except that all the blocks along one main track are made into turning sections. With this arrangement you can leave toggles one way for convenient continuous running or another way for convenient switching.

How many direction controllers?

You can run most railroads with two direction controllers. One handles all mainline sections, the other all turning sections. In a few rare instances a third controller is required.

However, this minimum is not a must. For convenience you can divide the main line and turning sections up into many subsections, each with its own AUX direction controller.

For instance, if it seems foolish to have the AUX controller that determines the left-end loop of Fig. 6-14 also determine polarity in the right-hand loop, just add another reversing toggle (or Atlas Twin or the like) so each loop has its own direction controller. Each added AUX controller takes its power directly from the

power pack in the same way as the one you already have installed.

Changing section boundaries

I've given general examples about changing section boundaries, and you'll learn a lot by comparing the diagrams. However, in the next chapter the material on finding return tracks will also be helpful in planning section boundaries or readjusting them for operating convenience. Also see Chapter 10.

RS and RN feeder order

It doesn't really matter which rail of a turning section is marked RS and which RN, but I like to put the RS on the right side of trains going in the more frequently used direction if practical to do this. What is more important is that if you operate adjacent blocks of a turning section *from the same* AUX controller, then both blocks should have the RS on the same side of the track. This is so a train running from one of these blocks into the other will continue on the same polarity.

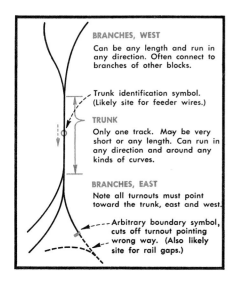

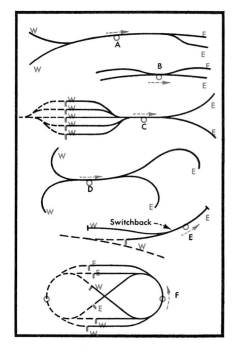

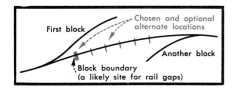

7-1 BASIC BLOCK ANATOMY. All track plans can be divided into basic blocks similar to this and those in Fig. 7-2 as an aid in planning for simplest wiring.

7-2 Each basic block has a trunk marked with O in color, and two ends which usually divide into branches. Which group of ends is called "East" is a matter of choice, but affects wiring.

7-3 The basic block boundary comes between track switches that point away from each other. The actual boundary can be anywhere between the turnouts, but is usually best near one of them.

7. Basic Blocks and How to Find Turning Tracks

HERE is a brand new way to search your track plan to find not only if you have some turning tracks hidden away somewhere, but also to find the most likely locations for all track feeders, block boundaries and rail gaps. We'll use it first to find turning tracks, but save your plan-sketch because you can refer to it later when you add wiring to handle two trains, special switches, etc.

You know that a house plan is made up of basic units called rooms. Well, you can divide all track plans into basic blocks. By this I'm not yet talking about blocks with wires and gaps; they come later. I'm talking about operating units of track that are connected together to make up the whole plan. All of your track can be divided into units like those in Fig. 7-1 and 7-2.

Notice that the basic block always has a single track at its trunk, and this may branch into limbs and roots at each end. Most basic blocks have branches at both ends, but the switchback at E in Fig. 7-2 has a dead end and a branched end because the trunk ends at a bumper. Notice also that the trunk and branches can be long, short, straight, curved or coiled, and that they may cross other track.

If you divide your track plan into basic blocks, it will then be easy to locate all turning tracks, to plan control blocks for running several trains, and to locate special wiring to prevent short circuits, etc. So here's how to mark your plan.

Dividing the plan

First, draw a sketch of your track, omitting any turnouts that merely lead off to a bumper, as at an industrial spur. In Fig. 7-4 I've done this for plan No. 67 from the book *101 Track Plans*. This sketch need not be to scale, but the remaining track switches should be arranged in their correct order.

Now study these track switches. Some point toward each other, so mark an O over the track at these locations. These places are the trunks of basic blocks.

Next, find places where track switches point away from each other, and draw a boundary bar across the track between them. These are the limits between two basic blocks. All the remaining stretches of track should also be checked, but if they start at the frog of one switch and end at the point of another you need no marks, as wiring is not usually required.

In making boundaries you might wonder whether to put the mark near one of the turnouts or the other; see Fig. 7-3. You can put the boundary anywhere along here and usually the final exact location decision is made later on, depending on which adjoining basic block needs more length. However, the boundary is usually near one turnout or the other, rather than near the middle.

Generally speaking now, the places where you marked an O are safe places to connect feeder wires to your plan. The places where you marked a boundary are likely to need rail gaps in both rails later on when you're ready to build a control panel and run two trains. Right now they're still just marks on paper.

Finding turning tracks

Note: New model railroaders should skip to the next paragraph unless wiring things come easy. Others should now add in any other block boundaries needed for multitrain operations (Chapter 10). Mark the trunk, etc., for all blocks whether basic or created. Then treat all blocks alike in the following steps.

Now, to find turning tracks the first thing to do is to mark which way is "eastbound" beside each O mark, using an arrow as shown in Fig. 7-4. Actually, you have the option to make the arrow point the way you prefer, but wiring is simplest if you can arrange all or most of the arrows along any much-traveled (and especially along round-and-round routes) so that they point the same way along the line. This is the case along the route 2, 3, 4, 5, and around to 2 again in the example. That's the only continuous route on the plan where this can be done because other con-

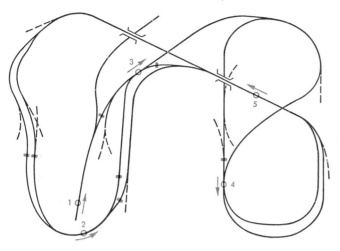

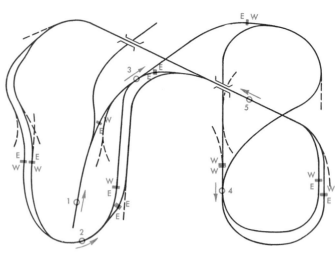

7 4 Your basic block sketch may look something like this when you have marked it ready for planning the wiring Save the sketch for future planning

7 5 These marks are added when you wish to find turning tracks Every place where two east or two west branches come together is a turning track.

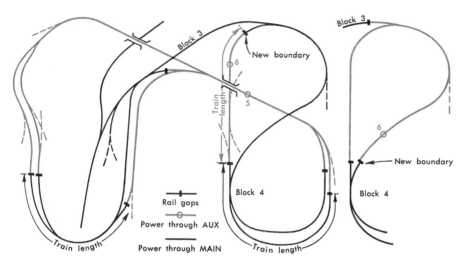

Rail gaps

Power through AUX

Power through MAIN

7 6 Block 5 was chosen as one turning section because it adjoined two of the turning places shown in Fig. 7-5. Block 6 was created between two turnouts for another turning section

7 7 Above, right If the length of Block 6 in Fig. 7-6 is too short to hold a train, it can be increased. This was done here by robbing track from Block 4 so the entire loop becomes a turning track. You can create block boundaries anywhere you wish for purposes like this. This section needs six rail gaps instead of the four of Fig 7-6 because it now touches Block 3

tinuous routes here are loop-to-loop routes where the main line is traversed in alternate directions.

Blocks may have several branches at each end. First go to all the block boundaries at the east ends of all blocks Mark a little E just short of each boundary. Remember these are the branches only in the direction of each arrow. Then put a little W just short of all the boundaries going the other way. See Fig. 7-2.

This step is the place where you can most easily go wrong, either by omitting some letters or by putting E's at both ends of the same block, so check carefully here

Notice in the example at the bottom of Fig. 7-2 how the E and W branches of the same block actually cross each other Here it's particularly important to label E and W correctly.

Finally, check all the boundaries Normally there will be an E at one side and a W at the other side of each boundary. This is normal, just as it's normal for the east side of one house to face the west side of the next.

But wherever there are two E or two W indications, make the boundary bar extra heavy This is a turning track because any train crossing this boundary changes from eastbound to westbound or vice versa. You have now found all turning tracks automatically

Location of gaps

As we learned in Chapter 6, we have to create an isolated turning section beside every turning track. This must be long enough to hold an entire train and it must have gaps in both rails at all boundaries. You have choices in just where you create this section,

but it must at least include some part of the track where you marked the heavy boundary bar.

Take a look back at Fig. 7-3 again, and assume that this boundary happens to be a turning track boundary Where do you create the turning section?

The simplest wiring occurs if there is enough distance between the two switches to hold an entire train. Then you put gaps in both rails near each switch and the track between is your new turning section. An example of this is in Fig. 6-6.

Often your trains are too long for this treatment. Then you can include one of the turnouts (never both) and some track beyond as a part of the turning section. To do this, make the entire block on one side or the other of the boundary into a turning section. Install gaps in both rails at *all* boundaries of the block chosen (not just the heavy-bar boundary). For instance, in Fig. 7-6 a total of 12 rail gaps are required for section 5 and only 4 gaps for section 6

If your railroad has several heavy boundary bars indicating turning tracks, try to find blocks that have more than one turning boundary These blocks might very well be made into turning sections because only one section will serve the several turning boundaries. This is true of section 5 in Fig. 7-5, and that's why it was chosen for the turning section.

On the other hand, section 5 is mighty long. If you're going to run several trains, you don't want turning sections much longer than the trains For this reason, it is all right to divide large basic blocks into smaller ones at any time. I'd say any block that's long enough to hold more than one train is a mighty good candidate for such division. That's one of the things explained in Chapter 10.

8. Turnouts Make a Difference

THIS used to be one of the most-needed chapters in the book, but now you could build a big railroad with hardly any reference to it. The difference is in ready-to-use plastic turnouts we now use. Electrically they are "beginner's turnouts" because they save many wiring problems for you. Where much of the material that follows used to be essential, you can now consider it more as a guide to raising your railroad to above the average in operating possibilities.

The difference comes in the way turnouts are wired. The ready-to-use turnouts send power down each branch all the time. That makes it easy to get a one-train railroad going. The kit-built, and most homemade, turnouts, on the other hand, have an automatic provision that sends power down only one branch or the other. You can have a loco standing on each branch and when you turn on the power only the loco on the favored branch will move. This is handier when you operate several locos in the same area.

Fortunately, both types of turnouts can be converted to work either way. Sometimes you'll want the advantage of fixed control's sure power everywhere. Sometimes you'll want the operating convenience of selective control's one-route-at-a-time power.

When you use fixed-control turnouts, you can connect them together in any arrangement, then merely connect power feeders at one place and power will travel up and back on all the various rails so the whole combination is powered. That's why they're so nice for beginners.

When you use selective-control turnouts, you may need some extra gaps to prevent fouling their control, or in some cases to prevent short circuits. These gaps are explained at the end of this chapter.

The other things discussed in this chapter are the details of turnout wiring, and some of the ways you can use selective-control turnouts advantageously to improve operation, particularly in dead-end tracks.

Now here are some terms with special meanings for our needs:

Ahead and **behind**. The track leading to the points of a turnout is "ahead," while "behind" is the area of the branch tracks.

Feeder rails. The rails to which the power feeder connections are made. Sometimes power reaches them through jumper wires or directly from other trackage.

Frog rails. The rails behind a turnout leading directly from the frog (the inner rail of each branch).

Stock rails. The outermost two rails along a turnout. They may be feeder rails, but not if they are frog rails to some other turnout in either direction.

Fixed-control turnout. A track switch in which each branch track is always electrically connected to the track ahead of the points.

Selective-control turnout. A track switch with some kind of provision to shift power connections from one branch to the other when the turnout is thrown.

Throw rod. The mechanical connection to throw the turnout.

Tie rod. The mechanical connection between the two points.

Metal tie bar. A tie rod or any connection that joins the points electrically. Found in most kit-type turnouts, also in Rivarossi.

Insulated points. No electrical connection from one point to the other. Found in Atlas Custom and Snap switches.

Solid frog. A metal frog or at least a connection joining the two rails that cross through the frog, as in most kit-type turnouts and Rivarossi. However, in Rivarossi, gaps behind the frog limit the area affected.

Insulated frog. A metal or plastic frog where no electrical connections pass through. Little used today.

Bridged frog or **jumpered frog.** A frog in which each rail continues through electrically without connection to the rail it crosses. Found in Atlas Custom and Snap, Fleischmann, and also shown in Fig. 8-1 at C.

Fixed-control turnouts

The well-known Atlas Custom and Snap switches and Rivarossi's turnouts are the fixed-control type. Fleischmann's Super Track switches are built so you can use them as fixed or selective control at will.

The fixed-control type of turnout is distinguished by the fact that both branch tracks are electrically connected to the track ahead of the points at all times.

In the Atlas turnout, the rails that cross at the frog actually play leap frog inside the plastic molding; see Fig. 8-1, A. Thus power flows right through to each branch track. This is one type of "bridged frog."

Other turnouts have gaps behind the frog like the Rivarossi arrangement at B. Here the frog rails get their power from straplike jumpers that reach over to the feeder rails in a sort of lateral pass arrangement.

You can make any turnout into a fixed-control turnout by insulating the frog rails with gaps in this same way and adding lateral jumpers.

Spring switches are turnouts with spring-loaded points so trains always take one branch. Atlas Custom and Snap switches are usually operated this way. The wiring should always be fixed control when making use of the spring-switch feature.

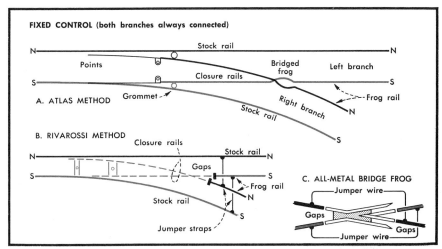

8-1 Most ready-to-use turnouts are made with fixed-control wiring.

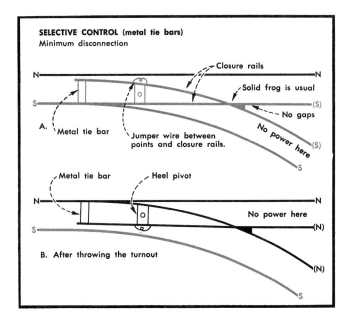

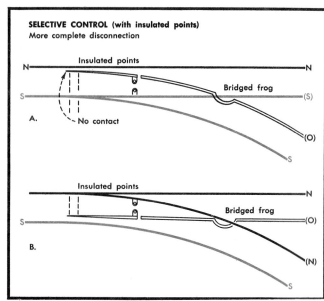

8 - 2 Kit-type turnouts, and Tru-Scale as well as Atlas regular line turnouts, are normally wired in this arrangement. The forward portion of Rivarossi, including the frog, is also wired this way, but has additional gaps and jumpers as shown in Fig. 8-1.

8 - 6 If you drill out the grommet (see Fig. 8-5), an Atlas Custom or Snap switch becomes a useful selective-control turnout with wiring like this. This can also be done with other turnouts if you install an insulated tie bar between the points and a bridged frog.

The fixed-control turnout has one important advantage. Since there are no electrical contacts, there is less chance of having dead track behind the turnout when it should be alive.

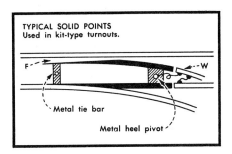

TYPICAL SOLID POINTS
Used in kit-type turnouts.

8 - 3 An advantage of solid point construction is that both points can be one metal assembly. This should be narrow enough so wheel flanges don't cause short circuits by touching at F. A flexible pigtail wire may be needed at W. Sometimes rail joiners are used instead of an actual pivot at the heel; sometimes rails merely bend as in real railroad turnouts.

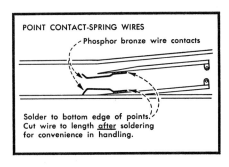

POINT CONTACT-SPRING WIRES

8 - 4 Small spring wires of brass, or preferably phosphor bronze, may be added to make better electrical contact between points and stock rails. Use hot soldering iron.

Selective-control turnouts

Up to now all the kit-built turnouts I have seen and most other turnouts not specifically mentioned are of the selective-control type. This includes Atlas's regular line and Tru-Scale.

The distinctive thing about the selective-control turnout is its ability to switch off one track or the other as the points are moved. In the kit-type turnout, this is accomplished by the actual metal-to-metal contact of the points against the stock rails of the turnout, Fig. 8-2.

At A the points are aligned for straight running. The points are made in one all-metal assembly with a metal tie bar and heel plate, Fig. 8-3. One point touches the S feeder rail. Since there are no gaps in the closure rails or frog, these and the frogs rails are then all electrically

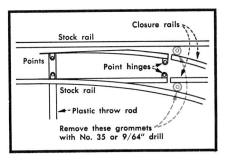

8 - 5 Grommets tucked between closure and stock rails act as electrical jumpers in Atlas turnouts. You can drill them out for selective control. Drill on mainline side only if you want spur-track feature shown in Fig. 8-15. This makes turnout fixed along main, selective for the spur branch.

connected to the S rail through the point. Thus S power reaches along one side of the straight branch and trains can plow right through. On the curved branch both rails are connected together through the point so no trains move here.

After the turnout is thrown, the other point touches the N rail. Now both frog rails are connected to the N rail and power now favors trains on the curved branch, as things should be.

It may confuse you a little that both rails of a branch may be connected to plus 12 v. at the same time, but this won't run a train any more than when both rails are connected to zero volts. Only a difference between rails runs a train. Raising two ends of a plank won't help you slide down it!

The weakness of the kit-type turnout is using the switch point itself for an electrical contact. It is easy for this to get misadjusted or dirty. The simplest remedy is to use a throw rod or switch machine that keeps the point well against the stock rail with spring tension at all times. Or you can install little feeder-wire contacts as in Fig. 8-4. Many thousands of these turnouts are giving excellent service without special attachments, however.

The Rivarossi turnout is really a selective-control turnout of the solid tie bar type, but the maker has added lateral jumpers and gaps behind the frog to make it into a fixed-control turnout. You can reverse the procedure to turn it back into a selective-control turnout.

In Fig. 8-2 the two points were tied together electrically by a metal tie

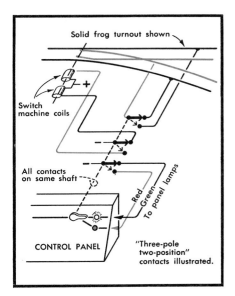

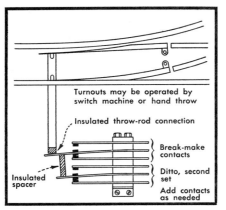

8 - 8 One of many ways to install contacts so electric circuits are changed when you move the points of a turnout. Contacts that operate with turnouts can simplify many control problems on any model railroad.

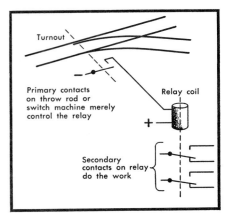

8 - 9 Often it's much simpler mechanically to install one contact at the turnout and let this control the coil of a relay. Then you can have any number of contacts attached to the relay for other purposes.

8 - 7 Any number of electric contacts can be provided on a panel lever to control many things simultaneously. Actual mechanical construction rarely looks like this, but all multiple-contact electric switches are similar electrically. Here the first moving pole switches panel lamps to show which way turnout should move. Second pole operates coils of switch machine. Often this set of contacts is specially made to flip current on only momentarily as coils must have current cut off after operating. Third pole is for selective control of rails behind turnout.

bar and metal heel pivot. If you use insulated tie bars and heel pivots you can improve the wiring a little, Fig. 8-6.

This can also be done by altering the Atlas Custom or Snap or similar turnouts which already have electrically separated switch points. In the Atlas turnouts you'll find two small metal tabs, or more recently two metal grommets, as indicated in Fig. 8-5. Drill these out with a No. 35 or a $^9\!/_{64}$" drill and you automatically have a selective-control turnout. This still

depends on good point contact but it has the advantage that the frog rail on whichever branch is dead is not connected to anything, Fig. 8-6.

If you contrive a way to insulate the points from each other on a kit or homemade turnout, you still need a bridged frog to make this scheme work. Gaps and jumpers can do this as shown at C in Fig. 8-1.

Added contacts

A more professional way to handle selective control is to use electrical contacts made for the purpose. The so-called "polarity" contacts sold with some switch machines can be used for this purpose. Also, you can buy control panel levers to handle the switch machine coils with extra contacts added for track power, indicating lamps, etc., Fig. 8-7.

An alternative is to install electrical contacts that are moved by the throw rod itself, Fig. 8-8. (They must be insulated from it.) This system is often awkward to install and maintain but

is practical otherwise. Contacts for the purpose are sometimes sold in hobby shops or they can be made from relay parts kits; see Chapter 14.

If you can afford it, a much better scheme is to install a single contact and have it operate a relay, Fig. 8-9. Relays come in all voltages and with all possible contact arrangements. While the switch machine shifts the rails, the relay responds and shifts the electric contacts at the same time. All a relay is is a one-coil switch machine for electrical contacts instead of track points.

In all these methods, what matters to us here is only that the contacts change the frog rail connections at the time the turnout is thrown. Regardless of the location of the contacts, the electric connections are the same to the rails.

Sometimes you may want to convert one type of switch to another. Figs. 8-10 and 8-11 show how to get the equivalent of Figs. 8-2 and 8-6 respectively by adding contacts that

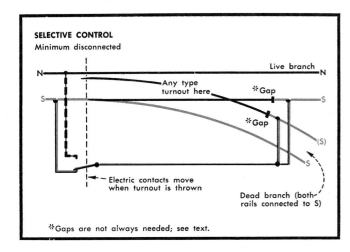

8 - 10 Any turnout can be wired as the electrical equivalent of Fig. 8-2 with one moving contact like this. This scheme is handy in stub yards, enginehouses, and other places with only one branch track live.

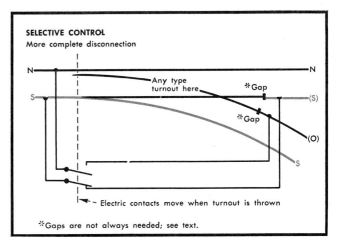

8 - 11 Two contacts plus gaps convert any turnout to the electrical equivalent of Fig. 8-6. This will do everything that Fig. 8-10 will do with less chance of wheels short circuiting over gaps.

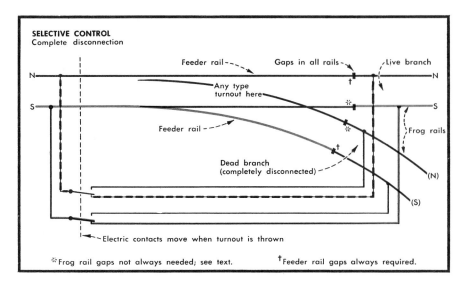

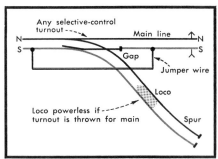

8-15 Half selective turnout controls power in spur but doesn't affect trains on the main line Feeders to main line can be to right as shown or to left, as is convenient.

8-12 This arrangement gives complete disconnection of both rails of the idle branch

operate at the same time you throw the points. You can also use these schemes to reinforce the electrical system of turnouts that are already wired as in the earlier figures; in this case the gaps back of the frog aren't needed.

In Fig. 8-12, two sets of contacts plus gaps in feeder rails are used to achieve complete disconnection of the unused branch. This is handy when you want to power the branch line from some other place at times, for instance from the opposite end of a double-ended yard. This is the best method of wiring turnouts, but is not always warranted since it's on the complicated side. Fleischmann turnouts have these contacts built in, one moving pole connected to each feeder rail. You must add the gaps and connections beyond the frog when you use this turnout for selective control.

PFM switch machines have contacts that can be used for the Fig. 8-11 scheme, while Kemtron's imported machines have enough contacts for all three schemes. However, there are many uses for switch machine contacts and no machine has enough con-tacts for the maximum uses. More about this in the chapter on switch machines.

Which type of turnout to use

Fixed-control turnout wiring is preferable where the block is cut short on each branch behind the turnout. This includes turnouts at the ends of passing tracks and double-ended yards and in short blocks with a congestion of turnouts. Fixed control is preferable for temporary track arrangements and is suitable for stub yards where only cars will be stored on the various tracks.

An exception to the above is when you feed power from behind the frog, as explained on pages 33 and 42.

Selective-control turnouts are preferable when you have a branch behind a turnout that's long enough for a locomotive or two to stand in. This includes storage yards where locomotives might stand, industrial spurs, and less congested groups of turnouts. Selective control is also useful for creating dead sections to protect against a train entering from the wrong branch.

Tricks with turnouts

IN stub-type yards, selective control is almost always preferable to other schemes because only one track at a time is operated and because the mere throwing of the track switches also switches the electric power; see Fig. 8-13. Notice how all the rails on one side of the selected track are S and all the others N. Only one track connects to both S and N feeder rails so only one track has power to run a loco. Locos on all other tracks will not move as long as the turnout connections are firm (good contact).

At an industrial spur along a main line somewhere, it is nice to have power extend all along the main but into the spur only when the turnout is thrown for the spur. This allows the switching engine to go into the branch and work on the main too. But if a mainline train wants to pass by, run the engine into the spur, throw the turnout, and the spur is then disconnected so the mainline train can go by.

This is accomplished with selective-control turnouts, but with a jumper wire around the turnout on the mainline frog rail. In this way the throwing of the turnout doesn't influence power on the main line — just the spur, Fig. 8-15. The result is a turnout that is

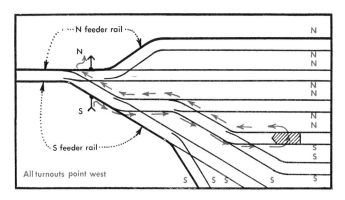

8-13 Any of these seven yard tracks can be energized depending on which turnout points touch the outermost "feeder rails."

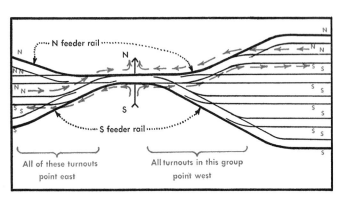

8-14 Two groups can share the same pair of feeder rails as in any basic block. All turnouts must point toward the central trunk.

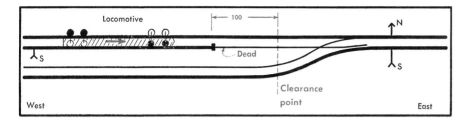

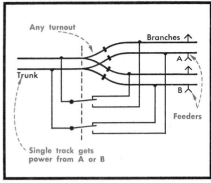

8-16 The solid circles represent the wheels that pick up current for the locomotive motor. When the pickup wheels of the leading truck cross the gap into "dead" track, the locomotive stops. The track is dead because the selective-control turnout is aligned for the other branch.

fixed control for the main, selective for the branch.

Another use that's made of the dead branch feature is to have a train stop automatically when it approaches a turnout from the rear, waiting until the turnout is thrown for it, Fig. 8-16. The locomotive comes from the left and after the right front wheels cross the gaps, the loco will stall. This is because power reaches this part of the frog rail only if the turnout is set for the straight branch. Throw the turnout and away she goes.

For this method to be successful, you must locate the gaps far enough behind the turnout so the loco will coast to a stop without fouling the other track at the clearance point, perhaps 100 scale feet.

Many operating men frown on this scheme because it makes the trains stop and start abruptly and because it's a good idea to be personally responsible for stopping trains as you run them. Others like this scheme because of its built-in protection from turnout derailments and from side swiping, in case a fellow does overlook the situation. While I would rarely use this scheme myself, I think it is a good one for the man who wants to run several trains with a shortage of manpower but a desire for some automatic protection with a minimum of gadgetry.

Power connections behind a turnout

Sometimes you'll read a rule stating that you should never connect a track feeder behind the frog of a turnout. But there are times when there's an advantage in this even though it takes a little of knowing what you're doing. We've seen an example of one use of

this where the mainline S feeder in Fig. 8-15 is in the frog rail but protected from the frog itself by a gap (usually required).

In Fig. 8-17, power feeders are connected to both rails of each branch and a turnout with complete disconnection is used (as in Fig. 8-12). This scheme is handy in double-ended yards where the lead tracks at one end may line up with a different track from the other end. More often it would be used to power short stretches of single track through narrow bridges or tunnels or at an interchange of several routes.

By merely throwing the turnout, the trunk is powered from either branch track. This saves toggles on a control panel.

You'll see a particularly fruitful use of this idea in the "interchange blocks" discussed in Chapter 10.

Another use is to reverse mainline polarity at a return loop, as in Fig. 8-18. When you throw the turnout to let the train back onto the main line, it automatically corrects the mainline polarity too. But before you grab this little gem too quickly, remember it's good only for the train in the loop. If there are other trains on the main line too, you don't want them reversing just because their cousin went around a loop. This scheme is for one-train railroads or districts on larger railroads where only a portion of the main line is influenced by the turnout.

Gaps needed behind selective turnouts

It used to be that all HO turnouts were wired like that in Fig. 8-2 with solid frog and metal tie bar. In those days we had to have elaborate track

8-17 Complete disconnection wiring allows single track to be powered from either of double tracks, depending on which train passes through turnout first. This is handy in tunnels, bridges, and at junctions where several tracks converge and spread out again.

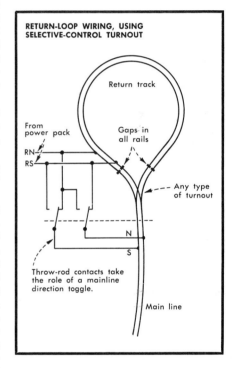

8-18 Mainline polarity approaching return loop is automatically controlled by turnout when train goes around the loop. Not recommended for more than one train. This circuit is useful in automatic display layouts where track contacts operate switch machine which throws turnout plus contacts for mainline polarity. It is unsuited for multitrain railroads because throwing the turnout will affect operation of any train already on main track.

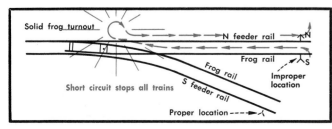

8-19 Feeding power to frog rail of solid-frog turnout causes short circuit when turnout is operated for branch.

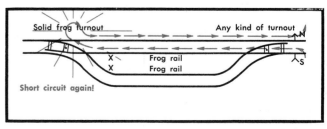

8-20 Same short can occur from power reaching frog rail through other trackage down the line. Gaps needed.

wiring rules to prevent short circuits by way of the frog rails.

We must still take precautions when selective-control turnouts are used and in a moment I'll give you two rules for it. But you'll find they can be a lot simpler than the old rules because of the basic block sketch you prepared for Chapter 7.

In Fig. 8-19, power feeders are connected so that one attaches to the frog rail of a solid-frog turnout. You can see that when the turnout is thrown, electric current from S can flow to the frog, across to the points, then to the feeder rail that's also connected to N. This creates a dead short and stalls all trains. The remedy is to move the S feeder to the S feeder rail. If you must attach a feed wire to the frog rail, then you must have a gap between this feeder and the frog.

If the turnout had had more complete disconnection, there would be no short circuit but it would still be impossible to power a train up the curved branch without an additional

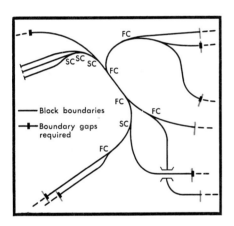

8 - 21 Illustration of a basic block with some fixed-control turnouts, FC, and some selective-control turnouts, SC. Note where gaps had to be placed at block boundaries. Of course, some block boundaries might need additional gaps because of turnouts in adjoining blocks.

feeder connection to the S feeder rail.

While you might not deliberately connect a feeder to a frog rail behind a selective-control turnout, there might be such a connection by way of other trackage as shown in Fig. 8-20. Here power passes through the points of one turnout at the right (not necessarily selective control either) and then it goes down to the selective-control turnout at the left where the same short circuit occurs. The remedy here is to put gaps in the frog rails at X, X. Later you'll see that you will want more gaps than this, but for control rather than electrical reasons.

You'll never get these kinds of short circuits if you make the basic block sketch as explained in Chapter 7 and then check the plan with these two rules:

Gap rule: If a block contains one or more selective-control type turnouts, put gaps in both rails at every block boundary in all the branches behind the selective-control turnouts.

Gap rule: If for any reason power is connected to the frog rail behind any selective-control turnout (or to rails that eventually lead to the frog rail), place a gap in the frog rail somewhere between these places.

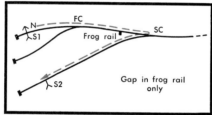

8 - 22 Illustration of single gap to separate S1 feeder wire from frog of selective-control turnout. Gap is needed even though a fixed-control turnout is between feeder and frog rail. No gap is needed in other frog rail as power comes to it normally from N via points of turnout, colored path.

How to Avoid Complication

Some folks want simple wiring that's a minimum tax on the mind. Others expect a book like this to provide ideas beyond average practice.

Much of the material that appears in Chapters 8 and 9 is for the experts and for those who want to run two or more trains at a time. Beginners can skip these chapters providing they

use only the types of turnouts and crossings made with bridged frogs and usually sold as components for sectional-track layouts. Atlas Snap and Custom (but not regular line), Rivarossi, and Fleischmann turnouts are in this class. I suggest that you come back to this material before you build a large railroad, however.

9. Crossings an
Fancy

A GOOD crossing should have as much of its rail electrically alive as possible to reduce the chance of power trucks and four-wheel locomotives stalling for lack of pickup contact. On the other hand, metal rails of a crossing should not be so long or so located that they might be grazed or crossed by wheels of cars running on the other track. Otherwise, momentary short circuits cause jerky operation, wheel pitting, and sometimes stalling.

The best way to wire a crossing is with four bridged frogs similar to the bridged frogs we discussed in the previous chapter. This is accomplished in Atlas crossings, Fig. 9-1, by a clever notching and bending scheme so the

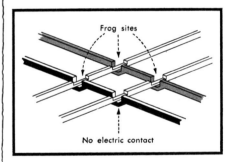

9 - 1 X-ray view of plastic crossing shows how rails actually leap in the frog. Each track is electrically continuous yet independent of the other lines.

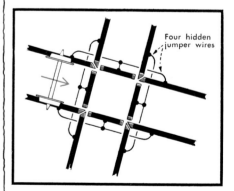

9 - 2 Even though the lines are insulated at the mitered frogs of this crossing, wheels will touch crossing rails and cause short circuits at the points shown in color. Operation is better if all parts shown in color are plastic.

rackwork

rails actually cross each other without electrical contact inside the plastic frog. When separate rail parts are assembled, jumper wires must be added to connect all the rail segments in any line; an example of this is shown in Fig. 9-2.

This construction is practical, but it has the fault that wheel treads and flanges are likely to short circuit at all the places marked in color. In order to avoid this fault, part of the frog and guard rails of a crossing can be made of wood or plastic, including at least all portions shown in color.

Another scheme is to build the entire crossing in one metal assembly (the parts are usually soldered together). Then secure all parts of the

track to the base permanently with screws, pins, or cement. Finally, saw four places around each frog, as shown in Fig. 9-3, and slip thin strips of insulating paper into each saw cut. While the frogs are metal, they won't cause short circuits since they are insulated from other rails. To saw the rails, use a 3-0 jeweller's saw, starting through a small hole drilled near the base of the rail. For extra security you can make two saw cuts at each frog one day and fill them with cement. This will hold all the parts in position until you make the remaining cuts on the following day. Needless to say, this is a workbench job and the whole completed crossing should be installed as a unit after insulation operations are done.

Experts may prefer a more mechanical rail fastening, such as the use of optical screws or small pins as in Fig. 9-4. Again, you cut the gaps after providing all the fastenings.

When the crossing angle is medium

to small, the jumper scheme of Fig. 9-5 may be an advantage. When crossings have a large angle, 60 degree to 90 degree, you can omit the powered section of rail between frogs as in Fig. 9-6, providing this is done in territory where trains will not move slowly, or providing you have no four-wheel-only pickup trucks or locos.

Cautions about gaps and feeders

The crossings through Fig. 9-6 have bridged frogs of one sort or another and can be used with no particular consideration given to feeder connections and gaps. But many of the remaining crossing diagrams in this chapter require their own track feeders. In such cases, these crossings become the natural feed points for a block of track and this block, large or small, must be insulated with gaps so there is no interference with other feeders in other blocks. For instance, in Fig. 9-7 the two routes through the crossing are electrically tied together.

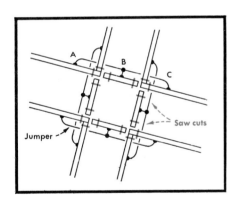

9-3 Solid frame of crossing is built in one piece, then sawed at 16 places marked in color to isolate each frog. This is electrically the same as Fig. 9-1, but easier for home construction.

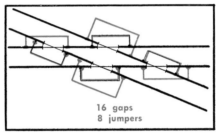

9-5 Jumper scheme for crossing from around 15° upward.

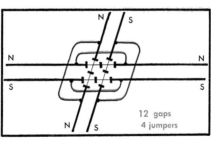

9-6 Fewer gaps can be used on 60° to 90° crossings if in fast-moving territory.

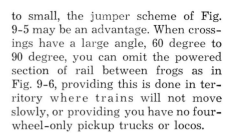

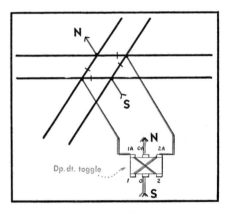

9-8 This very old scheme requires the fewest gaps of all and there are no dead spots. While it has the fault that both lines get power from the same feeders (see feeder remarks), only one line or the other can be powered at one time due to the reversing switchlike connections to the toggle or other contacts used to select the operating route. This can be used as a crude stopping-block protection since train on dead track will stop, presumably before reaching train on live track.

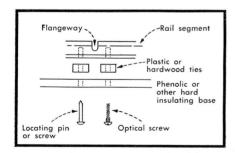

9-4 Accurate work is required with this method to drill holes running up through center of rail web. An alternate that's easier is to drill from above, turn screw in from above, file off head flush with rail, then use a nut below.

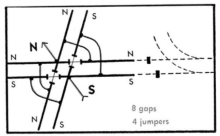

9-7 This is one of the simplest wiring schemes for homemade crossings. It has the limitation that all four approaches are powered from the feeders, no separation between lines. This limits it to one-train railroads for the most part. See feeder remarks.

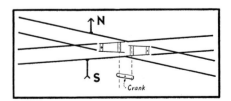

9-9 Crossings of less than 12° are usually built with moving points that work in opposition through rodding or with separate switch machines. Here solid frogs are used and all-metal point assemblies. The rodding must be insulated electrically from one or both sets of points. See feeder remarks. This type of crossing can also be built like two fixed-control turnouts face to face and with bridged frogs.

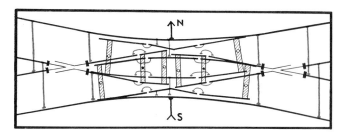

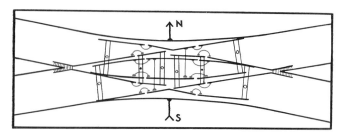

9-10 Slip switch wired for fixed control requires insulated tie rods to separate pairs of points. End frogs must be either bridged or insulated and lateral-pass jumpers are needed for rails of each branch

9-11 Selective-control wiring for slip switch requires no gaps; only favored branches get power. Metal tie rods must not short circuit against rails above them. End frogs can be solid.

For this reason, it is wise to power the crossing independently from any other routes nearby. Feeders are provided at or near the crossing as shown. Then a block boundary must be created with rail gaps as shown at the right, to separate this crossing from other routes that don't use the crossing — such as the curved track of the turnout.

In other words, crossings requiring feeders can be treated the same as the trunks of basic blocks running in four instead of the usual two directions. Those crossings requiring this special attention are indicated in the following paragraphs with the words, "See feeder remarks."

Other crossing schemes

The advantage of Figs. 9-7 to 9-9 is that fewer gaps are needed when you build these crossings. This made them popular some years ago, but bridged frogs are now the most popular. Figs. 9-8 and 9-9 have no dead frogs, so are ideal from the wheel-pickup viewpoint. Electrically, both are equivalent to two solid-frog selective-control turnouts and have the same wiring limitations as such turnouts.

The de luxe scheme in Fig. 9-12 requires a four-pole set of contacts for selecting the desired route and making the connections to the rails. However,

it has ideal electrical wiring connections and no dead spots. Each route is independent and can have its power supply fed from either end, as with bridged frogs.

When a train approaches this crossing, it will stall when the loco reaches the dead rails on the unfavored route. So if you want this feature, be sure to locate the outer eight gaps more than coasting distance from the center.

Slip switches and gantlet tracks

A slip switch requires two, four, or six pairs of moving points depending on whether it's a single slip (one curved track) or double slip, and whether frogs or moving points are used at the center. In all cases, the wiring can be either fixed control, as in Fig. 9-10, or selective control, as in Fig. 9-11.

The selective-control type of slip switch has little advantage in wiring as it is usually used as the center of a short interchange block with gaps in all four approach tracks. However, fewer gaps, solid frogs and all-metal point construction may make this slip easier to build with home methods.

While slip switches usually have moving points at the center, frogs are used on trolley lines and occasionally on heavy railroads too. The frogs must be of the bridged type if the selective-control scheme is used.

When rails of two routes are interlaced for some distance, the track is

called a "gantlet." The turnout in Fig. 9-13 might be used in tight quarters where the railroad company didn't want to maintain switch points in a pavement or on a bridge where there was no room for a man to stand. But electrically you can use any of the turnout wiring schemes of Chapter 8, as we've merely stretched a normal turnout.

The gantlet of Fig. 9-14 is used where double track must squeeze through a small tunnel, narrow bridge, or between buildings in an alley.

The most convenient way to wire a gantlet is to use bridged frogs. If you'd like the same kind of route-selecting train-stopping protection we used on crossings, you can do it with a toggle or other contacts. Use a dp. dt. toggle wired as shown and located on the control panel. Relay contacts of the types A and B could also do the job; see Chapter 14 about contacts and about relays.

Three-way turnouts

Often two or more turnouts are overlapped into each other's territory when space is crowded; the most common example of this is the three-way turnout. Wiring is the same as for

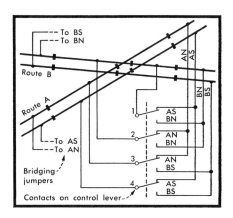

9-12 De luxe crossing wiring has none of electrical faults of other schemes. Throwing hand lever changes wiring connections to favor one road or the other. Power is picked up from proper approach track at right.

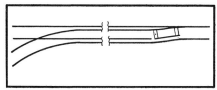

9-13 Gantlet turnout

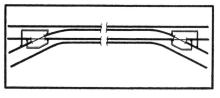

9-14 Gantlet double track

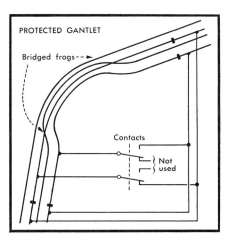

9-15 Route selection contacts added so only one route of gantlet can be used at a time. Note it is not necessary to gap and switch opposite rail of either track as breaking only one rail is sufficient to stop power from flowing through motor in loco.

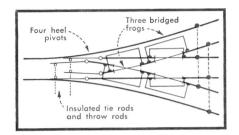

9-16 Three-way turnouts with individually hinged points can be wired either for selective control (of power to one branch at a time) or for fixed control by adding the dotted feeders (all branches tied to power). Three bridged frogs are required; see Chapter 8.

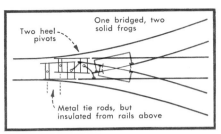

9-17 When metal tie rods join points, two solid frogs and one bridged frog are used in a three-way turnout. Tie rods must not touch rails of other track above them or unwanted feedbacks occur.

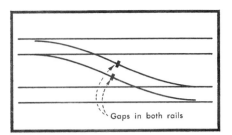

9-18 Gaps are almost always required in both rails of any track connecting between other tracks, whether in a crossover or longer arrangement. These are required to prevent short circuits when selective-control turnouts are used. They're also needed to separate control of train on one outer track from another train on the other outer track. Beginners can forget about these gaps until they are ready to run two trains — providing Snap, Custom, Rivarossi, or Fleischmann turnouts are the only kind used.

ordinary turnouts in principle and you can have fixed or selective control. Fig. 9-16 shows a three-way turnout constructed with individual hinge points. This becomes fixed control only if you add the colored dashed jumpers at the rear (right on drawing). Note that any type of bridged frog wiring can be used. Fig. 9-17 shows a three-way turnout constructed along the lines of the solid-frog, metal tie-bar principle, but one bridge frog is still needed. This is always selective control.

Double or scissors crossovers

The diagram of Fig. 9-19 shows one of several simple ways to wire the scissors-type crossover, and the caption explains the importance of having double gaps in all four through routes (both rails each). The only exceptions to needing all these gaps are rare cases where one gap can be omitted on a common power-return rail, or sometimes in one-locomotive territory as on the ramp to a car float.

Commercially made double crossovers usually have inadequate wiring and new gaps must be cut in them at X and Y if you want to eliminate intertrain control interference. When

you make a scissors using sectional track, be sure to use eight plastic rail joiners, one in each rail of each branch of two of the turnouts. Homemade double crossovers can be made with either fixed or selective turnouts, but there is no real advantage to the latter.

Other combination trackage

Most complicated trackwork is really only a group of ordinary turnouts with a crossing or two thrown in. Thus there is no special wiring problem. You just want to use gaps skillfully for these same reasons as are described in detail in their proper places in this book:

Some gaps will be needed to separate the control of a train at one place from another train on another track or waiting on a branch of the same track. See Chapter 10.

Some gaps will be needed if you use selective-control turnouts. See Chapter 8.

And you may need gaps if the boundary of a turning section happens to be in that region. See Chapters 6 and 7.

An example of combination trackage that is seen once in a while on a large layout or more often on an interurban line is the double junction, Fig. 9-20. In this example, individually hinged points and bridged frogs are used in the turnout. The crossing is also shown with bridged frogs. This is what would occur if you made the arrangement with sectional track components.

The same arrangement using solid-frog turnouts might look like Fig. 9-21. In each case the wiring is not really

special at all. It's just ordinary wiring for a crossing and for two turnouts. Each would be wired the same whether or not the others were nearby. By adding many ordinary turnouts and crossings you automatically arrive at correct wiring for any combination of trackage.

Reading published track plans

Most working track-plan drawings include symbols to show where to use gaps and where to attach feeder wires. Books of plans put out by track makers usually assume you will use the maker's own type of turnouts and crossings. But with the information in this book in Chapters 8 and 9, you can use any make of turnout or crossing in any plan with a minimum of wiring changes.

More advanced track plans, such as those in the book *101 Track Plans*, can be built with either fixed or selective-control turnouts of any make (providing they fit the space). However, in any plan it is generally better to re-wire turnouts for selective control in stub-type yards and on industrial spurs, as already discussed in Chapter 8.

The crossings in modern plans are assumed to be of the bridged frog type, like those sold commercially, rather than older types. Fig. 9-7 represents an older type found in published plans some years ago.

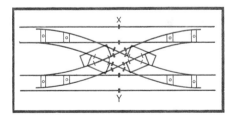

9-19 While the wiring of a double or "scissors" crossover can vary quite a bit — depending on where gaps are located, what kind of turnout wiring is used, and type of frog used at the center — one thing is required: that all four corners should be completely isolated from each other. This means there must be gaps or other isolation somewhere along each of the eight rails that runs left to right. In this example, insulated frogs serve as such gaps for four rails. The other two center frogs are preferably bridged to eliminate dead spots that might stall locos. Also see text.

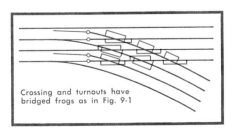

Crossing and turnouts have bridged frogs as in Fig. 9-1

9-20 Double junction with hidden bridge wiring under frogs indicated in color.

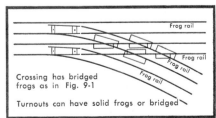

Crossing has bridged frogs as in Fig. 9-1

Turnouts can have solid frogs or bridged

9-21 Double junction using solid frogs and point assemblies in the turnouts.

10. Block Wiring

WHEN your railroad is ready to operate more than one train, you'll want to add a control panel with toggles and other contro'lers so you can run one train fast and another slow, even when they follow each other along the same track. This is accomplished by dividing the track into "control blocks." No matter how you build the control panel the block dividing is done the same way, so let's get that done first.

A control block is a place where you can stop or slow one train without affecting any of the other trains (in other blocks). It's a sort of electrical island and your railroad will consist of a half dozen or perhaps many more of these islands, each with a separate electric control wire running to your control panel.

Each control block will be separated in one or both rails from all other blocks with insulated rail joiners or gaps (page 23). This is so the electricity sent down the block feeder wires to run a train won't get into other blocks and run other trains too.

In planning control blocks, you can mark block boundaries with a bar drawn across the track diagram just as we did to create basic blocks in Chapter 7, only this time we're likely to have more boundaries.

You can have any number of blocks you wish, of any length, and you can put the boundaries anywhere you wish too. This is important to remember.

However, the more blocks you create, the more toggles and other equipment you will need on the control panel. This not only increases expense, but also requires more manual operations for a given train move. Generally you'll want to follow some suggestions in placing block boundaries. The basic rule is to:

Provide enough blocks so that each train is always in a different block from all other trains.

Fortunately, this is an ideal that is easy to realize. The result is that you will create at least twice as many blocks as there will be trains operated simultaneously. You need twice as many because you need a block for each train plus an empty block that it can run into without fouling the other train as it moves along.

More likely there will be three to five times as many blocks as trains on a large railroad. This is because the more blocks per train you have, the more train moves can be made without getting two trains into the same block.

You can plan blocks by two methods. The "quick easy method" is like solving a simple puzzle. You get the job done but you don't learn much about railroading from it. The "operating man's method" is to study where trains will go first, then be sure there's at least one block boundary between trains at all times.

Quick easy method

Start with the basic block sketch you made in Chapter 7. As before, you needn't show industrial spurs that run to a dead end (unless they are so long you'll either be operating in them or holding a train there while another goes by).

Study each basic block, especially large ones. If you find any block has a branch so long you can hold a train in it, separate the branch into a new block, Fig. 10-1. Keep this up until no basic block is left with a train-long branch. (An exception is when the branch ends in a bumper and a selective-control turnout controls the branch.)

This process may have more than

doubled the number of blocks, which is fine. The number isn't important.

Now look for any blocks, original or just created, that are still so long you can get two trains into them at the same time. Divide them into two parts. Excessively long blocks might be divided into three or four parts so most of the blocks are about the same size, a little longer than a train. Fig. 10-2 shows examples of this lengthwise subdivision.

Now you can skip the rest of this chapter. However, it won't hurt to read the operating man's method as a check on your work. You'll also become more familiar with detailed block planning.

Operating man's method

Draw a plan of your track and drag limp pieces of string (to represent engines and trains) around the lines — you'll learn a lot of things about operation planning.

This string-on-paper idea is more fun to do if you get another model railroader to help. With four hands you can handle the "trains" more easily and it will be like playing a game.

While you study your future operations, consider all these possible train movements:

1. Train arrives in yard, road engine is sent to the enginehouse, caboose to the crummy track.
2. Switcher sorts cars and arranges them into new trains.
3. Road engine couples on for another run, and leaves for the main line.

Be sure these operations are ones you can really do. For instance, if your arrival track hasn't a switch at the far end, your locomotive will be trapped beyond the train. See Fig. 10-3. Also, plan the same operations two ways, entering the yard caboose first as well as engine first.

Next, plan your mainline train movements. What you can do will depend on the kind of railroad you have and how large it is:

4. Consider the effect of other trains running past the yard while you try to make the switching moves already listed.
5. How about trains going in both directions on the main at the

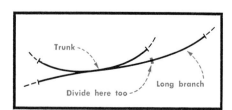

10 - 1   Lop off long branch routes.

10 - 2   Subdivide blocks that are too long.

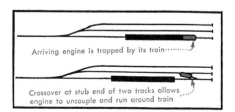

10 - 3   Every yard needs a runaround track.

same time? Will they make "meets" in passing sidings and along stretches of double track?

6. How about a fast train overtaking a slow one?

7. Will you operate a local freight that will do a lot of switching along the main line?

8. Are there any crossings, junctions, or other bottlenecks where trains will have to wait their turns to pass over the same piece of track?

9. Are there to be any places where helper engines will be cut off?

When you get the actual operational possibilities of your railroad in mind, you're ready to plan your "blocks."

Let's go through all those train operations again, but this time let's pencil some block boundaries across the tracks. We need enough such boundaries so that at least one boundary separates each train from every other train at *all* times.

For example, consider a train waiting on the side track for another to pass, like this:

I've drawn the two block boundaries in color so the train will not be in the same block with another train, no matter which direction the other comes from.

After the No. 2 train has passed, the first train wants to get out on the main again so we need a third boundary, like this:

This insures that the two trains, now both on the main line, are separated by at least one boundary. These three boundaries are a minimum requirement at any passing siding. But even this is not ideal. If train No. 2 should happen to arrive first, you'd need another boundary at the right to keep the train separated from the approaching No. 1. So four boundaries are best:

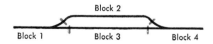

You can analyze every part of your track in this way, and you'll end up with from half a dozen up to 20 or more such boundaries, depending on your track plan.

When you're through, the lengths of

BLOCK DEFINITIONS

BLOCK. A part of the track set aside from other trackage for operating or electrical reasons. Electrical blocks have insulated rail joiners or gaps in one or both rails at each block boundary so the electrical control of one block has no effect on the next.

BASIC BLOCK. This is the kind of block that results if you divide your railroad at every place where turnouts point away from each other; see Chapter 7. It is a short cut in planning any kind of block.

CONTROL BLOCK. An electrical block isolated from other blocks to aid in controlling more than one train independently; see Chapters 10 and 12.

SIGNAL BLOCK. An electrical block isolated from other trackage in order to control signals or other devices when trains are within its boundaries. A "track circuit." See page 44.

INTERCHANGE BLOCK. A control block which is tied into adjacent control blocks through contacts operated when the turnouts are thrown. See pages 34 and 42.

STOPPING BLOCK. A block, usually short, where power is temporarily disconnected so a locomotive will stall when it reaches the place.

BLOCK TERRITORY. This may mean all the track within a particular block, but in signaling it means that part of the railroad that has been divided into signaling blocks.

SECTION. This often means the same thing as a block. In this book it means a part of the track under the influence of a particular throttle or reversing switch, and may be one or a group of blocks. Thus you find a *return section* at a loop and a *mainline section* where there is no loop, each having its own direction controller.

track extending between one boundary and the next are your "blocks," or more properly "control blocks."

This process would be tedious if you had to figure everything out, but you don't. Here are some simple rules that apply to common track patterns, and they'll account for most of your blocks, if not all of them.

1. Try to keep the blocks longer than your trains, Fig. 10-4.
2. If there is room, blocks should be considerably longer than your trains in any territory where the trains will move fast, Fig. 10-5.
3. But where traffic is heavy, you

may want to allow only about half a train length per block. This makes shorter blocks that permit trains to follow one another more closely, Fig. 10-6.

4. Along any given route, whether oval or point-to-point, allow enough blocks so that there can be an empty block per train in addition to those blocks the trains actually occupy, Fig. 10-7.
5. If a switcher must sometimes use

Short blocks help keep heavy traffic moving.

10 - 6   Half-size blocks expedite dense traffic.

Most blocks should be longer than your trains. Leave a little room at each end.

10 - 4   Train-length blocks save wiring.

Where trains move fast and rarely stop, blocks can be longer if space permits.

10 - 5   Longer blocks for speed territory.

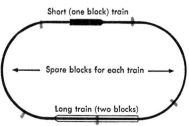

Allow for an average of one empty block per train in addition to the blocks actually occupied.

10 - 7   Spare blocks keep traffic moving.

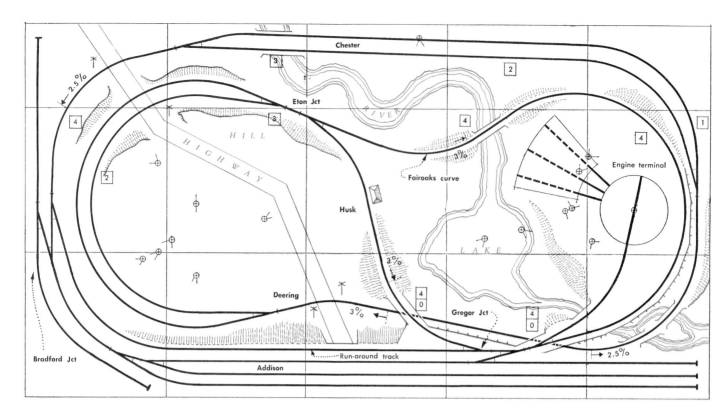

10-8 This is the track plan used in many of the wiring examples through the following chapters of this book. It is a good operating plan for such a compact space since it provides for round-and-round as well as terminal-to-loop operation. Of course, a number of industrial spurs should be added to facilitate roadside switching, but such spurs do not affect block wiring. There are three passing sidings in the twice-around oval, a good operating combination because trains running in opposite directions need not always meet at the same sidings.

part of the main line near a siding or at the end of a yard, consider a short block in the main line near the yard. This allows the switcher to use that part of the main line but it still permits any of the mainline trains to approach closer to the yard before waiting for switching maneuvers to be completed. Without such a short block the mainline train might have to wait at quite some distance from the yard. See block B6-2 near the yard on Fig. 10-10.

6. Places where trains will pass over the same point in quick succession, though over different routes, such as at crossings and junctions, should be isolated into small "interchange" blocks. This is so one train can get into the zone as soon as another has cleared it; see block B6-1, Fig. 10-10.

7. Be sure to put a block boundary in the middle of any crossover between double track whenever trains might move on both tracks at the same time.

8. Consider the use of short blocks at the bottom and top of grades so that the control of the helper and the regular road engine can be separated when the helper is coupling on or uncoupling from the train. In this case the block boundary should be located approximately under the coupler of the helper engine.

9. Yard tracks with a ladder turnout at each end should be treated with two boundaries, the same as we did with the passing siding. Single-end yard tracks can remain part of the approach track block. See Fig. 10-9 and also page 32.

10. If in doubt, having too many blocks will do little harm, but will add to the cost of the toggles on your control panel.

A practical example, block numbering

The railroad in Fig. 10-8 takes only a modest space considering its track pattern, and it's a good one on which to practice block planning. It also shows the boundaries I'd recommend for most model railroad operations.

I've assigned each block a number, too. This helps keep your wiring untangled. On a small railroad you can number blocks any way you want. On a bigger railroad, it pays to be more systematic.

The planners of real railroads number their signal blocks according to the distance from some arbitrary zero point, perhaps the largest terminal on the line. They often assign even numbers to any predominantly eastbound tracks and odd numbers to westbound tracks. Thus on a particular railroad a block 24 miles from base and on track 1 might be numbered 241. A block on the next track opposite (or the eastbound main if it's a double track) would be 242.

Another railroad company might

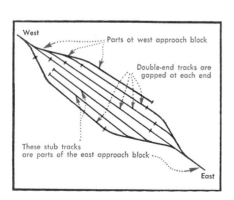

10-9 Only double-ended tracks in yards need be blocks. If single-ended tracks will store waiting locomotives, use a selective-control turnout to cut power.

use the same idea in a different way, having a number like this: 24-1; or still another railroad might use 024.1 or even inverted as 1024.

These prototype block numbering systems are often confusing when you try to use them on a small track plan. You get too many similar numbers such as 21, 22, 12, etc. But if you use the letters A, B, C, D, etc., for parallel tracks, and a number for the distance from the starting point, the confusion is reduced. That's how I numbered the blocks on the Fig. 10-8 plan.

B is for blocks along the main track.

A is for blocks on the alternate track.

C, D, E, etc., are for additional tracks if there are any.

Interchange and other blocks too short to hold a train are given a sub-block number. Sub-blocks B6-1 and B6-2 share the 6 of block B6.

Engine terminal blocks can be given the number 0 so they don't interfere with the distance numbers.

Naming stations in alphabetical order is helpful to your guests while learning to operate your railroad.

Let's see how trains would use some of these blocks. Notice how block B1 includes all of three yard tracks and a switchback spur as well. Why isn't some of this divided into separate blocks?

Well, I figure that even though you do one kind of switching in the yard and a different kind of switching in the zig-zag spur, you can't do both at the same time. At least it's very unlikely. So, since two trains will not operate at the same time in all this territory, you need only one block.

Block A1 must be separate from block B1 because mainline trains may want to run by on A1 while the yard is used for switching moves. These two blocks can also be used as a main line and passing track and also as a run-around track to move engines to the other end of their trains.

In a pinch, blocks B6, B6-2 and B0-1 could all be combined into one. But with three separate blocks more train movements are possible. For instance, while an engine is backing from the yard through B6-2 to reach the turntable, a mainline train can approach into block B6 to get closer to the yard before stopping.

Likewise, after the engine has cleared block B6-2, the train can move into the yard while the lone engine can still get onto the turntable after the table has come around.

Oval track plans

When you have ovals in your track plan (and this includes figure-eights and all other round-and-round schemes), you'll usually want two

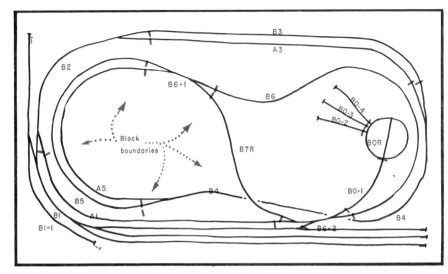

10-10 Add crossbars to a crude sketch to plan your blocks. Then number the blocks.

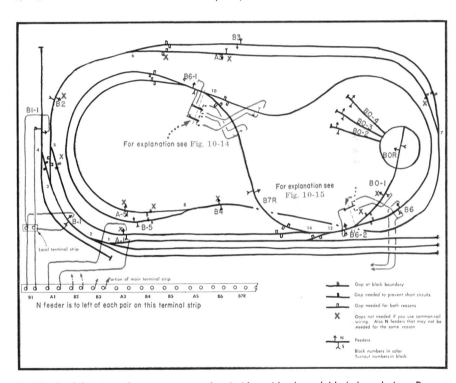

10-11 Final location of gaps pretty much coincides with planned block boundaries. Draw a terminal strip. You can add actual wires in color as shown if you wish, but block numbers beside strip make this optional. Solid black gaps near turnout 4 may not be needed; see text about switchback track wiring, page 43.

trains to follow each other in the same oval some, if not all, of the time. Then you need a minimum of at least four blocks, preferably six. This problem was illustrated in Fig. 10-7. For three trains, provide six to nine blocks in each oval, etc.

But many layouts are planned to run one train in one oval and another train in another oval. As long as the trains never pass from one oval to the other, each oval can be a single block. But usually there are crossovers, as in Fig. 10-12, and unless you provide at least three blocks in each oval, you cannot use the crossover without getting both trains in the same block. So

four blocks per oval is a pretty good minimum even in this case.

Passing on a single track

Where the line is single track with passing sidings, you can usually figure three blocks per siding. One block is the main line at the siding while another is the passing track. For example, see blocks B3 and A3 in Fig. 10-8. The third is the single track connecting to the next siding in either direction down the line. This third block includes the siding turnouts at each end of the single track, as in block B2 of Fig. 10-10.

If two operators will work at the

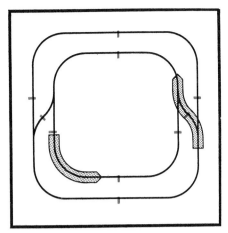

10-12 You might think you wouldn't need many blocks when two trains operate on separate ovals. But if either train takes a crossover, you'll have both trains in the same oval for at least a short while. Then you need three or preferably four blocks in that oval so the trains can run in separate blocks.

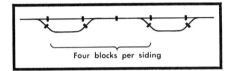

Four blocks per siding

10-13 Dividing the single track into two or more blocks facilitates unhampered switching moves at each station.

same time, switching operations at one siding will interfere with the next unless you divide the single track between them into two blocks, as in Fig. 10-13.

Very short trains

Sometimes a single locomotive is a train, for instance at the roundhouse or when pulling away from cars. So in some cases where a block is a "train length," it may be very short. For instance, the approach to a turntable might be made of several blocks, each

about as long as the turntable, so several locomotives can line up ready to turn. Special tracks for RDC cars, interurbans, etc., may also call for an occasional short block.

Interchange blocks

Short blocks are often likely to occur in your planning at places where several routes converge, then spread again. These interchange blocks were also discussed on page 34.

Another example of the interchange block is block B6-1 on the plan in Fig. 10-11. Here a train could be waiting in the siding for another to clear the loop. The short block will be needed in quick succession by first one train and then the other.

If a separate toggle were installed on the control panel for the short block, it would be an operating nuisance, so why not power the short block from one of the adjoining long blocks, depending on which train is using the short block. Contacts on the turnout or working with it (page 31) can automatically connect power properly when the turnout is thrown. Fig. 10-14 shows how this can be done with two break-make contacts.

Often only one contact is needed, as in Fig. 10-15, providing the N rails of both blocks can be tied together electrically. They can when you use the "common rail" type of wiring to be described later.

When there is more than one turnout fanning from an interchange track, add a contact (or pair if you use two per turnout) for each extra turnout as in Fig. 10-16.

When two crossovers are paired as in Fig. 10-17, an interchange block occurs on one main line as shown. But here the contact need be provided to work with only one of the four turnouts.

If an interchange track has more approaches from one end than the other, as in Fig. 10-16, you'll save on contacts by installing them at the entrance with the fewest turnouts. On the other hand, if there are the same number of turnouts at each end, it doesn't matter whether you borrow power from blocks to the east or west.

The role of selective control

I devoted a great deal of space in Chapter 8 to the difference between fixed- and selective-control turnouts. If you use only Snap-Track and other similar sectional track, you don't have any selective-control turnouts. On the other hand, you can convert any turnout into a selective-control turnout as is explained in that chapter and sometimes it is a good idea to do so.

A selective-control turnout is useful in just the opposite way from the interchange track idea. In the interchange track, we powered the block at the trunk of a track pattern from two or several branches by way of electric contacts. When you throw the turnout to line up a branch, that branch will send its power to the center area.

On the other hand, with a selective-control turnout you power the central area, and contacts associated with the turnout will send power to the proper branch.

This makes a good way to power blocks that are in branch relation to some other part of the track. Several examples were illustrated in Chapter 8, so they won't be repeated here.

In a way, the branches behind a selective-control turnout can be considered as separate blocks. But they are blocks with a limited sort of control since you can use them only one at a time.

The real difference is that while an

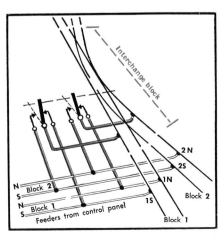

10-14 One contact switches the short S rail to connect with the S rail of either branch. The other contact switches power from the N rails in the same way. This simplifies the panel as extra toggle isn't needed for short block.

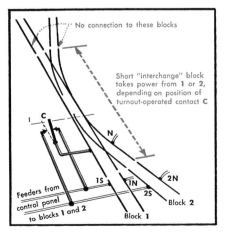

10-15 You need switch only the S rail when common rail wiring is used. Interchange block becomes a part of first one approach block, then the other, depending on throw of turnout.

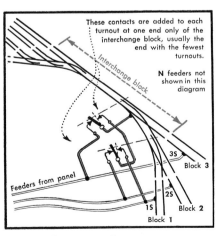

10-16 When more than one turnout approaches the interchange block, an added contact for S rail is needed for each turnout. Similar contacts are needed for N rail if you don't have common rail wiring.

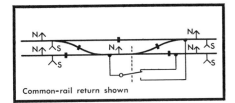

10-17 A single contact tied to one turnout handles interchange track between two crossovers by changing S rail connections.

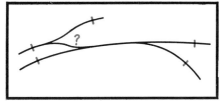

10-19 Is a boundary needed here?

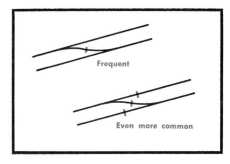

10-20 Boundaries cluster at crossovers.

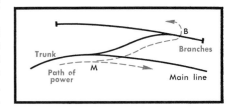

10-21 Switchback spur is fun to switch.

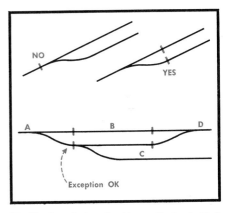

10-22 Boundaries should usually be behind turnouts, rarely near points.

ordinary block has its toggle on the control panel, the branch behind a selective-control turnout is a slave to the track in front of the turnout. If slave control is adequate, use one of the diagrams in Chapter 8 as your guide to wiring between turnout and branch block, rather than the general instructions for gaps and feeders that follow. Otherwise, create a new block for the branch so it can be operated independently.

Crossings

Most modern crossings are so wired that you can ignore them in planning blocks. The two tracks are in separate blocks. However, some of the crossing schemes of Chapter 9 were indicated as requiring extra gaps and feeders because the two tracks were tied together in the same block. With these crossings, it's a good idea to make this multiroute block a short one, perhaps only long enough so a train that approaches from the wrong entrance will stall without running into another train on the other track. Slip switches fall in this class too.

Checking your block plan

If you have planned wisely, most of the blocks you have created will resemble one of the figures in Fig. 10-18. There may be a different number of turnouts, but the block will usually be clipped short behind the turnouts to

each branch. An exception is a long dead-end branch used for a storage track, as this is usually made part of the same block as the trunk.

If you find two turnouts pointing away from each other in the same block, as in Fig. 10-19, it's likely that the block should be divided into two at the question mark. Crossovers will usually be dividing points, as in Fig. 10-20. If not, suspect that something has been overlooked.

An exception to this is the zig-zag switchback siding, Fig. 10-21. This can all be in the same block as long as you'll never get two locos in the area at the same time. But if you want to let the switcher get into the siding to let a mainline train pass by, then the switchback must either be made into a separate block or else you can use a selective-control turnout at M, fixed-control at B.

In our example plan, Fig. 10-11, there's a switchback siding at the left. This plan was made when all turnouts were selective control and that's why the gaps are needed in the crossover — not for block separation, for this siding is electrically joined to the yard at the local terminal strip. But those gaps were needed to prevent short circuits of the type mentioned on pages 33 and 34.

Be suspicious of any block boundary near the point end of a turnout, Fig. 10-22. Almost always the block boundaries should be behind the frog. One exception is the spur turnout on a passing siding. It would be better if the turnout was included in block A rather than C, but that might make block C too short to hold a train.

Gaps and feeders

Each one of the blocks you have now created will be separated from adjacent blocks by cutting gaps in the rails or using plastic rail joiners near the block boundaries. Also, each block will have feeder wires from it to the control panel. The details of installing these and how much freedom you have in locating them is discussed in Chapter 17.

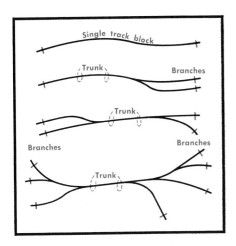

10-18 Typical block patterns. Sometimes they're wrapped around curves.

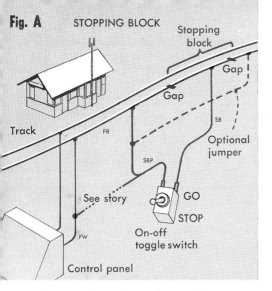

Fig. A STOPPING BLOCK

Stopping block

Gap

Gap

Track

FR

SB

Optional jumper

SBP

See story

GO

STOP

On-off toggle switch

FW

Control panel

SIX IDEAS FOR TRAIN CONTROL

MOST ARE SIMPLE TO USE

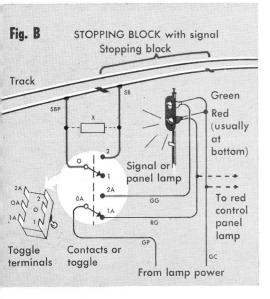

Fig. B STOPPING BLOCK with signal

Stopping block

Track

SB

SBP

X

Green

Red (usually at bottom)

Signal or panel lamp

2

O

1

2A

0A

1A

2A

2

OA

0A

1

1A

GG

To red control panel lamp

RG

Toggle terminals

Contacts or toggle

GP

GC

From lamp power

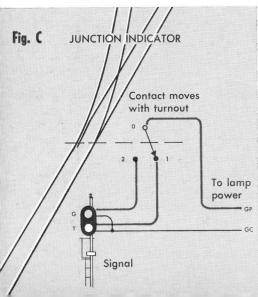

Fig. C JUNCTION INDICATOR

Contact moves with turnout

0

2

1

To lamp power

GP

G

Y

GC

Signal

STOPPING BLOCK — FIG. A

This arrangement stops a train automatically when it gets to a danger point or a station. But if you want the train to start or pass right through, flip the toggle switch on.

You provide insulated rail joiners or gaps (page 23) in the same rail far enough apart so the locomotive will surely come to a stop. You can do this in either the S or N rail. There's no need to gap both rails as one is sufficient to prevent current from passing through loco.

Use a simple on-off toggle, or *any* other kind of electric switch or contact you wish. Practically all contacts can handle the current and voltages used here. Connect wire SB to the isolated rail. Connect wire SBP to tap power from the same side of the track. However, if your toggle is near the control panel, it will save wire to connect SBP to the feeder wire FW instead of the feeder rail FR.

The optional jumper will be needed if the gaps you cut have severed the track beyond from its power supply.

STOPPING SIGNAL — FIG. B

Train stops if signal is red, starts on green. Signal can be controlled with toggle switch or by contacts on a switch machine or relay.

This circuit is the same as the stopping block, but with a signal added. Signal requires break-make contacts *in addition* to contact used for stopping block. Any dp. dt. toggle will do, or any switch with at least two poles and two live positions. Small numbers show how connections on a dp. dt. toggle correspond to contact connections on diagram. Also see Chapter 14.

Sometimes devices are added at X. A rheostat or fixed resistor here (about 100 ohms 2 watts) can be used so train gets a little power and stops more gradually. A simple rectifier can be added here so train can back away from signal even when red. This is also a big help because trains coming from the other direction can get past the stopping block. I suggest a radio type 1N91* or a larger type that will handle at least an ampere or two of current. Turn rectifier end for end if it favors wrong direction of travel.

---

*Avoid short circuits that might overload this size rectifier by using fast acting fuse or circuit breaker at the control panel.

JUNCTION SIGNAL — FIG. C

Signal shows green for main track, yellow for branch track. Other signals for trains coming in the other direction can be connected to the same contact.

Add contact to turnout throw rod or in other methods discussed on page 31. This selects proper lamp in signals. A lamp can also be put on control panel to burn when track is aligned for the branch. Added contacts can be used to stop train.

This is not correct railroad signaling practice as more lights are required for junctions in prototype practice.

TWO-TRAIN SECTION CONTROL — FIG. D

By keeping two trains on separate ovals, each can run from its own power pack

or you can use a two-throttle power pack. Disadvantage is that each train is deprived of operation over other track. This is one kind of "section control" and is fine for getting started, but it is not really railroading because of the great limitations on how you can operate.

JOINT TRACKAGE — FIG. E

Here some track is arranged so each train can use it, one at a time. Throw the toggle or other contacts to connect the block to either power pack, depending on which train is using the block. This is better than adding a third power pack. Use a center-off type toggle if you'd like to cut power from the joint block entirely sometimes.

A two-throttle power pack can be used in place of separate power packs. Be sure to cut gaps or use insulated rail joiners in both rails at each of the four or more block boundaries. Also, be sure that the outer-rail connections of each oval and the joint block are in the same row on the back of the toggle switch (all S rail connections in line).

If you make several parts of your railroad into joint blocks, using more toggles, you can greatly improve operations. When the entire railroad is blocked this way, you have the advantages of full cab control and you've saved money by using only two power packs.

AUTOMATIC TRAIN CONTROL — FIG. F

This is about as simple as you can go in having signals and train control work automatically. It's simpler, for instance, than adding contacts along the track. It prevents one train from overtaking another and also can operate signals of the red-green type as well as a train location light on the control panel.

The contacts are wired exactly as in the stopping signal circuit, Fig. B. These contacts are moved by a coil working against a spring. When a train moves through the protected block, a little of its power is used by the coil to move the contacts. Train speed is nearly normal. A fast train attempting to follow the first train will stop automatically at the red signal.

When first train leaves the protected block, no more current is drawn through relay coil; relay releases and signal changes to green. This also allows second train to cross the stopping block.

Use a relay with a few turns of wire of size 26 or larger. A Tru-Scale relay is fine. Weaken the relay spring if necessary so relay still works when train runs slowly.

This circuit won't protect a stopped train because then there's no current feeding to it through the relay. For full protection, use the Twin-T circuit described in *Model Railroader* in June, July and August, 1958.

Note that stopping blocks are on the N rail side of track but gaps for protected block on S rail side. This is often the most convenient combination but either could be shifted. Duplicate this for as many blocks as you wish.

You can add a rectifier at X, as we did before, so trains can back out of stopping section and are not stopped when running toward you past signals.

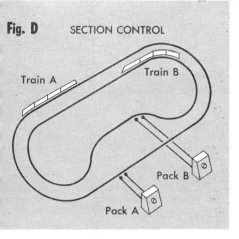

Fig. D SECTION CONTROL

Train A

Train B

Pack B

Pack A

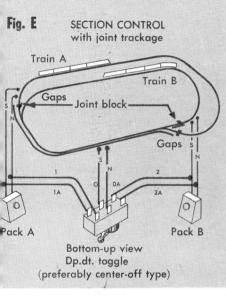

Fig. E SECTION CONTROL
with joint trackage

Train A

Train B

Gaps

Joint block

Gaps

Pack A

Pack B

Bottom-up view
Dp.dt. toggle
(preferably center-off type)

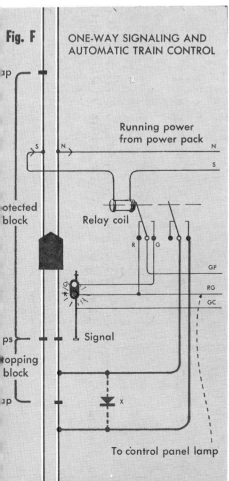

Fig. F ONE-WAY SIGNALING AND
AUTOMATIC TRAIN CONTROL

Running power
from power pack

N

S

otected
block

Relay coil

R   G

GP

RG

GC

ps

topping
block

Signal

X

To control panel lamp

11. Remote Control of Turnouts

SWITCH machines almost always work on the principle of a solenoid. This is just a coil with a hole in its center. When electric current passes around the coil, a magnetic field is concentrated in the hole and any soft iron or other magnetic material is attracted toward the hole. If there are two pieces of soft iron near each other, they are attracted toward each other as well as toward the hole. Thus, soft iron frames are sometimes added into a switch machine to increase the pull on the moving "armature."

Wires feeding current to the coils are often labeled NW and RW, standing for Normal sWitch and Reverse sWitch. Which way is normal is arbitrary, but usually the route most often used is called normal. The letter W is used in railroad signal departments to stand for switch because the letter S already has many uses. You might also label wires WC for sWitch Common, WP for sWitch machine Power, and the like.

Buying switch machines

When buying switch machines, you want to be sure you can install the machine easily and you want to be sure that the power will be adequate. But remember, any machine will develop more power if you can increase its voltage and perhaps stiffen the actuating springs.

You may want a machine with plenty of extra electric contacts built in for such uses as indicating lights, automatic coil cutoff, tandem operation (to be explained), or to have the advantages of selective control as described in Chapter 8. Lack of electric contacts has limited the usefulness of many an otherwise good machine.

You might think the throw of the machine should equal the throw of the switch points, but usually some overtravel is desired so you can use spring linkage between machine and switch. This reduces maintenance as the points don't get out of adjustment when track shifts slightly with the weather. When a simple rod or spring connects the switch machine to the turnout, a throw of ¼" as found on most switch machines is adequate. But the newer machines with ⁵⁄₁₆" or ⅜" throw are easier

to use when you have more linkage and cranks or when the machine is mounted under the table.

The pulling force of a switch machine depends on so many things that you cannot judge it by looks. Even the voltage and wire size make a difference. So the best way to be sure you get a good machine is to try one that looks good or is recommended. Some fellows have been badly disappointed because they bought and installed a lot of switch machines in blind faith without trying a sample in service first.

Since no one switch machine has all the desirable features — it can't — it may be a good idea to use two or even three types, each where it seems to fit your requirements best.

One-coil switch machines

Several types of switch machine have been made using only one coil, but since they are no longer available, or in very short supply, I won't go into much detail. An excellent early machine (Scale Craft) used a ratchet like a toy-train reverser but otherwise behaved like a two-coil machine and had cutoff contacts. Most one-coil machines use the coil to pull the points over and a spring to return them. This results in simple wiring and a simple mechanism, but has the fault that power must be left on all the time when the turnout is aligned for the branch. Power requirements go up as the number of machines is increased and most troubles with this type of machine can be cured by using a heavier power pack. D. C. must be used to avoid chatter, hum, and overheating.

The war surplus "rotaries" are very satisfactory, but differ in design from one lot to another. They usually have useful contacts mounted on top. Switch machines made along the lines of a pinball machine relay are more in the economy grade and suited mostly to small railroads where simple installation is important.

Two-coil switch machines

Double-coil machines, sometimes called "twin-solenoid," are the type that have been most universally used in model railroading despite their

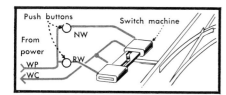

11-1 Power from wire WP passes through push buttons to reach each coil. Return power from both coils goes back to power source via wire WC. If machine has only three coil terminals, center is for WC.

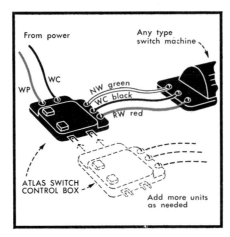

11-2 Atlas Switch Control Box can be used with any two-coil machine. It is the equivalent of two push buttons with added features, including simple way to fasten any number together in a line.

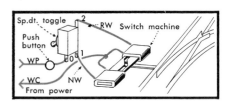

11-3 As on real railroad CTC panel, you flip a toggle first to select track direction, then push the button to operate the switch machine any time later. A good scheme for yard leads.

added complications. The coils are usually made rather small so they will not be so noticeable when mounted above the table. However, they must develop about five times as much power as a locomotive during the moment when they do their work. This is so much power that the coil would burn out in minutes if the power was left on.

In controlling a switch machine, you want to let power reach the coil only momentarily. There are many ways to do this.

Since the current is off most of the time, this puts another requirement on the machi..e:

It must not let the points gradually slide out of position (from vibration) and derail a train. In order to lock the points, a cam or a lever-and-spring toggle action is used. The latter is the more effective of the two methods.

Turnout control wiring

The most elementary way to control a two-coil machine is with two push buttons of the spring-return type — doorbell buttons, etc. See Fig. 11-1. Atlas makes a controller along this line that has the added feature of a window that shows which button was pushed last, Fig. 11-2. Several of these can be joined together for easy installation as you add more and more turnouts to the railroad. Also, nifty double push buttons in several styles are made in pairs just for model railroaders by Acme, Ideal, etc. The wiring for each pair of buttons is the same

as in Fig. 11-1. Use the red button for "reverse switch" and the green for normal.

A nice way to install push buttons on the control panel is to place them at their corresponding places on a painted track diagram. On the other hand, if panel space is tight, place rows of buttons below and number the places on the diagram to correspond with the buttons. More about panels in Chapter 15.

One of the disadvantages of ordinary push buttons is that you can't tell which way the turnout is aligned by looking at them. By combining a single push button with a two-position lever, you can select a position for the switch, then push the button to throw it. After this, the lever shows which way the turnout has been aligned; see Fig. 11-3.

Another way that's handy for switch machine control is the use of a special panel lever that sends current to the switch machine momentarily, but only while you are moving the handle. After the lever has been moved all the way over, the coil current is cut off again. Other regular type contacts may be provided on the same lever for lamps and track controls. One lever of this type is made for Walthers

(see Fig. 11-4), while other clever levers of this sort are imported by Austin and Pacific Fast Mail.

Cutoff contacts

My favorite method of controlling switch machines makes use of electric contacts attached to the switch machine to cut off coil current; see Fig. 11-5. These contacts can be arranged in many different ways, but there are always at least two, a "make" and a "break."

One of the big advantages of this is that the lever on the control panel need be just an ordinary two-position toggle or switch. Whichever way you move it, the turnout is sure to follow as long as power is turned on. Even if wheels start to jar a switch under a train, power will come on automatically and prevent a derailment. If you want to throw the switches by hand for awhile, turn off the switch machine power, for otherwise each turnout will snap right back to the way the control panel lever is set.

Suppose you flip the toggle in Fig. 11-5 over to position 2. This sends power from WP through wire RW to one coil of the switch machine. The current gets back to the power source

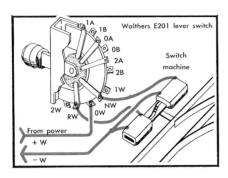

11-4 Walthers key has contacts NW and RW for momentary coil control. All other contacts may be used for lamps, etc. Contacts 0, 1 and 2 can be used for track polarity control, as illustrated in Chapter 8.

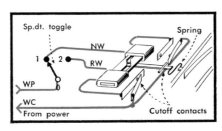

11-5 One make and one break contact actuated by throw rod converts any switch machine into cutoff type. Can be controlled by momentary or continuous type buttons or toggle.

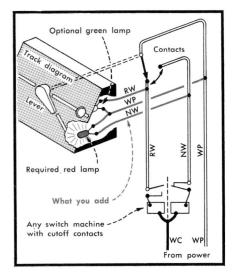

11-6 Lamps in control panel or wayside signals show which way turnout is aligned. Connect them to the same three wires as the control lever. Switch machine, lower right, is shown in diagramatic shorthand.

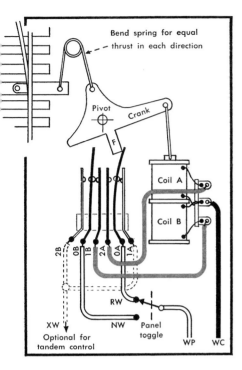

11-7 Kemtron and Tenshodo machines have contacts built in like this. Add the two colored wires to use these contacts for coil cutoff. See text for added features.

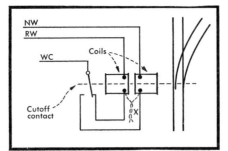

11-8 Separate return wires at X if you wish to use a single break-make contact for coil cutoff. Lamps of Fig. 11-6 will work with this arrangement as well as any other cutoff contact scheme.

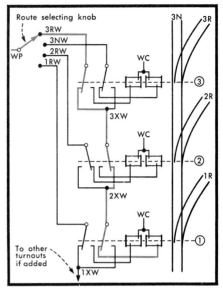

11-9 For tandem control, provide each switch machine with two break-make contacts. One half of each set is used in the usual way for coil cutoff and the outer halves are used to send power on to the next machine via wire WX. This drawing shows that the selecting knob has been turned to track 3R. Switch machine 3 has already operated and it then sent power to the normal coil of switch machine 2 which has also operated. (Follow the color.) However, switch machine 1 has not yet operated and the current is now going through its coil to operate it. This will be cut off as soon as all turnouts are aligned. Return power WC runs from each switch machine back to the power source.

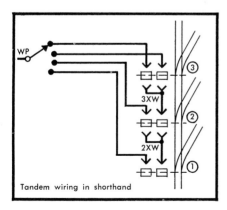

11-10 It's a lot of work drawing out all the contacts as in Fig. 11-9 and unnecessary since the contacts on each machine are wired alike. So why not use this shorthand in planning tandem wiring, together with one detailed sketch such as Fig. 11-7 for the particular contacts and machine you plan to use.

via a closed contact and the wire WC. But as soon as the coil operates the turnout, this contact opens and power is disconnected. Nothing more happens until you flip the toggle back to operate the other coil in the same manner. Coil burnout won't happen unless a contact sticks or a machine is jammed and can only move half way. Even this can be prevented with a slow-acting circuit breaker in the switch machine power supply.

Although it is usually an advantage to use the simple sp. dt. toggle or contacts to control power to a switch machine that has cutoff contacts, you can

still use push buttons or momentary levers instead, if you wish.

One advantage of cutoff contacts is that they can do double duty by controlling lamps to show which way the turnout is set on the control panel. They'll do this whether you move the turnout with power or by hand. In Fig. 11-6, you can see the circuit is very simple; just connect a lamp from switch machine power to either turnout control wire. Usually one red lamp is used so only turnouts in reverse position are indicated, but you can add green lamps for normal route too if you wish. Use both if you install the lamps in a wayside signal at a junction, as was done on page 44.

Notice that lamp current passes through the coil, but this doesn't interfere with coil operation because the lamp current is too weak. Suit the lamps to the voltage used for operating the switch machines.

You can arrange cutoff contacts on the switch machine or on the throw rod in a number of ways. The only requirement is that coil current is cut off late enough so the switch machine is sure to operate all the way over rather than stall midway. Usually it's better to move the contacts from some part of the action that has good leverage.

In Fig. 11-5 the coil current was interrupted in the return wires from the coils, but more often you will do it in the control wires as in Fig. 11-6. If you use Tenshodo or Kemtron machines, add the two wires shown in color in Fig. 11-7 to get cutoff operation. These machines come with adequate cutoff contacts, but you may have to adjust their timing a little. Sometimes a coil on these machines is accidently grounded to the frame during manufacture, in which case wrap a little cellulose tape around the longer contact springs so they don't touch the actuating finger F. Otherwise the coil may operate too long due to a current feedback at this point.

Switch machines with only one sp.

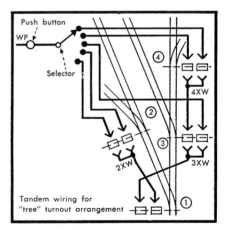

11-11 Here's how you can plan wiring of a tree-type yard throat in tandem shorthand. This illustrates another innovation, the combination of one push button with a multiposition contact on the control panel. This corresponds to the idea of Fig. 11-3. An advantage is that as you scan the rotary knob, switch machines that have nothing to do with the desired route will not be affected. If you wish to operate the same turnouts from several panels, for instance from any engineer's cab in cab control, or for another example the idea of being able to operate a group of turnouts both from a local tower and a master tower, then some kind of momentary contact such as this arrangement is necessary. Another scheme is to use a push button for each possible route instead.

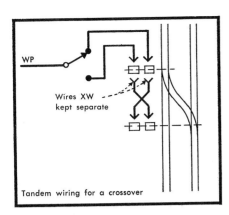

Tandem wiring for a crossover

Wires XW kept separate

WP

11-12 At a crossover, both turnouts are supposed to work in synchronism. So this time wires WX (contacts 1A and 2B of Fig. 11-7) are not joined together. Instead, each controls a coil of the other switch machine.

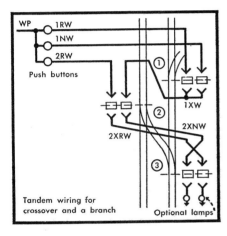

Tandem wiring for crossover and a branch

WP 1RW 1NW 2RW
Push buttons
1XW
2XNW
2XRW
Optional lamps

11-13 Here's a crossover combined with a branch. Only three buttons or a three-position selector knob are needed although there are six switch machine coils. If the shorthand is still hard to follow, check against Fig. 11-14.

two-position built-in contact can be converted for coil cutoff if you can separate the return power wire from both coils. The return power wires are usually twisted together and soldered to the center connecting terminal. Untwist them and connect the ends to the two fixed contacts as in Fig. 11-8. Connect the coil control wires to the other two coil leads.

Tandem or cascade operation

Another good feature of cutoff contacts is that they can be used to transfer power from one switch machine to the next. In a yard ladder, for instance, you may have several turnouts in a line. It's a nuisance to operate separate controls for several turnouts to line up a particular track. But if you send power only to the last coil down the line, that coil will operate, cut itself off, and then send your power to the coil of the next closer turnout. *Zip zip*, they go, like a row of tumbling dominos, and a whole route is lined up from one push button or multiposition knob on the panel. See Fig. 11-9.

If you use Kemtron switch machines, there are already enough built-in contacts to accomplish this. See Fig. 11-7. The two outermost contact springs are wired together (usually) and they go on as wire XW to control the coil of the next turnout. You can add extra contacts to the throw rod to accomplish this with other machines. In the case of the Tenshodo machine (which lacks the outer contacts), connect the wire XW from the main frame of the machine. The actuating finger F will provide the needed extra contact in an improvised sort of way.

When you plan wiring for tandem control, send your control line from the control panel to the turnouts farthest from the trunk of the block first, Fig. 11-11. Let the XW wires from each machine go to the next closer switch machine until you get to the first one. The XW of the first machine (last to operate) can be used to operate an "action completed" lamp or relay if you have use for such. See Fig. 11-13.

Since only one machine operates at a time, tandem wiring is very practical where you have many turnouts in a small area. No more current is consumed than for one machine.

Other contact uses

Contacts on switch machines or their throw rods may also be added for track polarity control (selective-control turnout) as described in Chapter 8, or for special purposes. Usually they should be electrically independent of the cutoff contacts.

If the turnout has a metal tie bar, be sure to use an insulating bushing or link somewhere in the rodding between the switch machine and the turnout. Otherwise electric current for train control and turnout operation is almost sure to foul things.

Power for switch machines

Most switch machines produce adequate pulling force when operated on 12 v., but once in a while a case comes up where 16 v. is needed, either because of machine design, a sluggish turnout, or a power source that doesn't deliver full voltage under the load of the machine.

One-coil machines require D.C., preferably from the largest size pack you have around the place. Some packs have convenient "Uncontrolled D.C." terminals for such use. Plus and minus make no difference.

The instructions that come with two-coil machines usually specify A.C., but this is misleading because

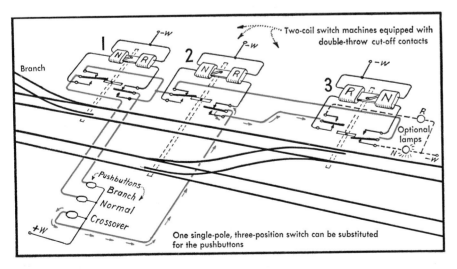

Two-coil switch machines equipped with double-throw cut-off contacts

Branch

1 2 3 N R

Optional lamps

Pushbuttons
Branch
Normal
Crossover

One single-pole, three-position switch can be substituted for the pushbuttons

11-14 Same circuit as 11-13 but shown in detail. Note also a new way to use lamps, this time powered from the WX contacts of the last turnout. They insure that all turnouts along a route have been aligned and operated. If push buttons are used, these lamps go out when the button is released.

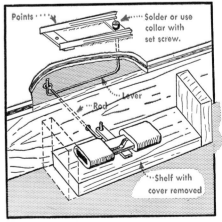

Points Solder or use collar with set screw.
Lever
Rod
Shelf with cover removed

11-15 Switch machines can be mounted on small shelves in front of the layout for convenient access.

D.C. will work just as well. The advantage of A.C. is that you can use a simple transformer rather than the more complicated power pack.

For a given voltage, A.C. may move a sluggish turnout a little better because of its vibrating force. On the other hand, D.C. is quieter.

Packs and transformers

On a small railroad it is adequate to use the accessory terminals on the power pack for operating switch machines. If you use several packs, power all switch machines from the accessory terminals of the largest of the packs (even though the control panel levers for some turnouts may not be near this pack).

If you use a variable transformer ahead of a pack for speed control, that pack cannot be used for accessories since all of its voltages are varied. Also, don't use train running power for switch machines. In either case, the voltage won't be adequate except when running a train at top voltage.

Operation is best when all switch machines are powered from their own transformer or power pack. If you have a big two-throttle pack and want to change over to running each train from a separate smaller pack, use the big pack for only one train (or no trains at all) and use its accessory terminals for lamps and switch machines.

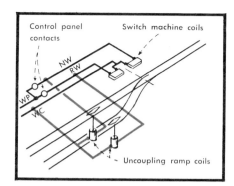

11-16 Uncoupling ramp coils can be operated by same switch or button that controls the switch machine. Control must be momentary contact type and it is better (but not required) to have cutoff contacts on the switch machine.

Special transformers are also sold just for model railroad accessories. You can also use an old toy transformer or a radio filament transformer for switch machines if the voltage is from 12 v. to 18 v.

The ampere rating of your power source isn't very important. Most units rated at 3 amperes or more will do well, but some units rated lower may still be able to furnish a full 12 v. when you operate a switch machine. This is the real requirement. Since the 3 to 5 amperes a switch machine might draw is for only a fraction of a second at a time, there's no likelihood of burning out a 1 ampere pack or transformer because the current is only momentary and the unit has time to cool off before it's overloaded again.

Wiring uncoupling ramps

While uncoupling ramps are usually wired with their own push buttons, you can save wiring and simplify control by using the same push button that throws a switch machine coil to power the uncoupling ramp coil of the same track.

Use switch machine control circuits that include a momentary contact, such as in Figs. 11-1, 11-3, 11-13, and particularly 11-11. When you push the button to throw the turnout to any selected track, the switch machine operates but the uncoupling ramp also rises. After throwing the turnout, any further pushing of the button raises the ramp as often as necessary for uncoupling operations.

To accomplish this dual control, merely wire the hot side of the uncoupling coil to the selector switch contact for that particular track, or to the push button for that track if there is no selector). Wire the cold side to WC. Cutoff contacts are desirable on each switch machine (but not absolutely necessary) so its coil doesn't continue to draw current during mere uncoupling operations.

11-17 This cab was in a Pennsylvania RR. steam locomotive. 1 is the throttle while the reverse quadrant, 2, is almost hidden behind the independent brake, 3. This brake has no effect on cars, but the automatic brake, 4, at engineer's hand, operates the cars as well as the loco and tender. The radio-phone overhead is used for talking to the caboose and sometimes to wayside stations and passing trains.

12. Control for Two or More Trains

THE practical way to control two or more trains on your model railroad is to divide the track into blocks as we did back in Chapter 10. Then you can send so many volts of electricity to one block to make a train go slowly, and at the same time you can send a different voltage to some other block to make another train run faster.

The obvious way to go about this is not the best way. The obvious way is to attach a power pack and throttle to one block and another throttle to the next block, then a third throttle to the third block, and so on. Whether all the throttles are attached to the same power pack or separate packs makes no difference here.

When throttles are permanently connected to the track in this way, you have "section control" wiring; all the track connected to a particular throttle is called a "section." Sometimes a section is divided into several blocks, but in any case the same throttle is always used to power the particular section. An example of a disconnected two-section railroad was shown in Fig. D on page 45.

Section control wiring used to be the standard way to wire a model railroad, and a big layout might be divided into half a dozen or many more sections. Today section control is little used except for test track or display railroads. This is because it offers limited flexibility in control and costs more to install than cab control.

How to improve your present panel

If you already have your railroad wired for section control, you can use your present control equipment and get still better operation. Just buy a few toggle switches and add them gradually between each throttle and the track. You can start with the idea in Fig. E on page 45 and then do this same thing with other parts of the railroad. In time you'll have full cab control at little cost or trouble.

The chief fault of section control is that you need many sections and many throttles if you want railroad-like operation. Even then operation is not always smooth. For instance, when a train crosses gaps into a new section it is momentarily powered through two throttles at once and it makes a sudden burst of speed until the gaps are crossed.

If, on the other hand, you use only a few large sections in order to cut costs, then two trains often get into the same section at the same time. Then you're helpless if you want to stop one and not the other, or if you want them to run at different speeds or in opposite directions.

Some commercial power packs are sold with the idea of using one pack for one block and another pack for the next. Two-throttle packs are sometimes even marked "Block 1" and "Block 2" opposite each throttle. This is a good way to sell a lot of power packs, but it doesn't result in good wiring. It's better to use the same power packs for a cab control wiring scheme.

Better wiring at less cost

There are two meanings to the words "cab control." One is a way to operate trains. "Cab control operation" is usually the best way to run trains when you have two or more fellows running trains together. On the other hand, cab control has met some criticism because when you run trains by yourself you can't handle more than about two trains at a time. Don't let this criticism of cab control *operation* mislead you. "Cab control *wiring*" is good whether you use it to run trains by cab control or by some other method. It is so flexible that you can run trains by many different schemes — some best for one-man operation, others for group operation.

With cab control wiring, toggles or some other type of switches are added into the wiring between the throttle units and the track. Enough toggles are provided so you can shift the throttle-to-track connections around to power *any* block from *any* throttle. There are no permanent throttle connections.

The result is that you can still operate by section control when you want to, plus many other methods, yet the cost is usually less than for section control because fewer throttles will be needed.

I'm going to explain cab control by starting with the control of a single block and working up to the whole system. In this way you'll see that cab control is not as complicated as it seems. This is because all the toggles for all the blocks are wired in exactly the same way.

Block control

Let's start out with a single power pack and throttle unit (they can be combined or separate) and one block isolated from the rest of your railroad. This block is powered through a single electric contact, perhaps an on-off toggle, as in Fig. 12-1.

Power to run the train starts at the power pack and comes out of the throttle unit at terminal S. On the way to the isolated block it passes through the toggle switch; if the switch is on, power can continue on to the isolated block. Thus a train won't know the difference when it crosses the gaps and it will keep going.

But if you turn the toggle off, the isolated part of the S rail will be dead electrically. This time when the train crosses the gaps it will stop. You could also use this toggle to stop the train when it is already moving in the isolated block.

Notice that we didn't have to put any toggle switch in the N feeder. This is because a motor cannot run unless electric current passes *through* it. Even though one side of the motor is still connected to the N side of the power pack, the motor won't run because there is no complete circuit until the toggle is turned on.

In the next diagram, Fig. 12-2, I've divided the whole railroad into blocks and furnished an on-off contact or toggle for each block. This is what we will usually do. When you do it with one throttle like this it's called "block control" and the toggles are "block selectors."

This block-control wiring scheme is a good poor-man's control system because it gives you some flexibility of operation. It can be used as is as the start of a cab control system.

When you run several trains with block control, you can flip the power off at any station or danger point and the trains will stop when they arrive there. You can keep two or more trains from overtaking each other, too,

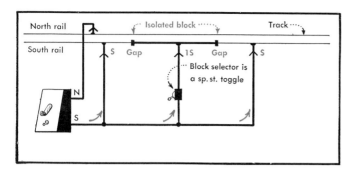

12 - 1 The stopping block (also see page 44) is the basic unit used in most control systems. You repeat this simple scheme many times over.

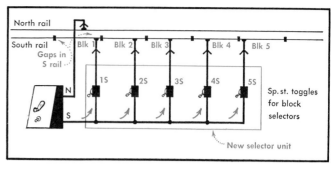

12 - 2 When all parts of the railroad are stopping blocks, a train can be stopped anywhere while other trains run. This is "block control."

but of course if you try to slow one train for a smooth stop with the throttle, all other trains will also slow to a stop.

Common rail wiring

Notice that no toggles were used in feeder wires to the N rail sides of each block. This wasn't necessary to stop trains for the reason given a moment ago. It also has the advantage of simplifying wiring and keeping costs down. When all blocks share the same power return rail, you have what is called "common rail" or more correctly "common return rail," and if you use a single return feeder wire it's the "common return feeder."

In more elaborate wiring schemes, we will want to use the common rail idea as much as possible to save on wiring and costs. Basic diagrams often show common rail wiring for the N rail because the diagrams are easier to read than those with contacts repeated for both rails.

Common rail not always possible

You cannot always have the advantages of common rail wiring. If you will recall our discussion back in Chapters 6 and 7, we divided the railroad into "mainline" and "return" sections. Common rail can be used in one or the other of these sections, but not both. Choose the section with the greatest number of blocks; common rail will then do you the most good.*

Back in Chapter 3, we discussed different kinds of power supply connections using one or several power packs. You can't use common rail wiring anywhere if you use the single power supply scheme, so be sure about what you're using for power before adopting common rail wiring for your mainline section.

You must use what is called "separate power return" or "doubled wiring" for all blocks of your railroad where the common rail isn't permitted. Doubled wiring is shown in Fig. 12-3. Notice that two-pole toggles

---
*If there are several mainline or return sections, only one can have common rail wiring.

must be used because both the S and N feeder of each block must be broken. Gaps must be put in the N rail approximately opposite the S rail gaps.

When common rail is permitted on the mainline section of your railroad, some toggles will be single contact (pole) and others double. In Fig. 12-4, a railroad plan is shown on which common rail is used. The loop block and turntable at the upper right, being return tracks, require doubled contacts in their toggles.

Common rail in practice

You can tie all N feeders in common rail territory to a heavy wire that runs the length of the table, as in Fig. 12-5. Sometimes bare wire is used for this "common return bus."

Another scheme is to jumper the N rail from one block to the next as in Fig. 12-6. This saves wire, but has the serious fault that one rail joiner with poor electric contact affects a lot of the track.

I prefer to wire N rails just like S

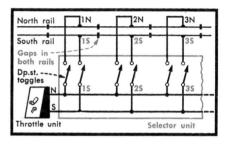

12 - 3 Sometimes both feeder wires and rails must be provided with contacts in the block selecting toggles. This doubled wiring is needed in all return tracks and also when you use only one power pack for several trains in cab control.

rails, as in Fig. 12-7, but then to tie the common N feeders together at the terminal strip only. This allows me to disconnect any individual N feeder to make wiring changes, or more likely to localize a short circuit that might otherwise be hard to locate.

These drawings show gaps between the N rails of adjacent blocks. However, you don't always need them. If

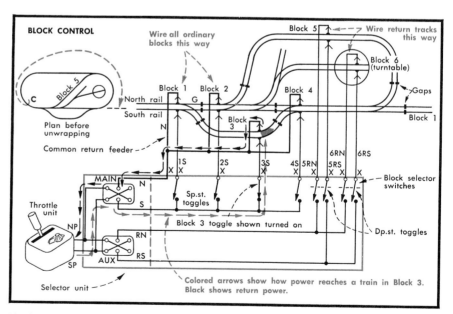

12 - 4 Practical wiring usually includes some blocks wired for common rail and others, as at the right, with doubled wiring for return tracks. This could be considered as a fragment of a larger plan, or as a complete oval railroad as in the tiny sketch. Often it's easier to plan wiring if you "unwrap" the oval as in this example. The oval was broken at C and redrawn in a more or less straight-line arrangement.

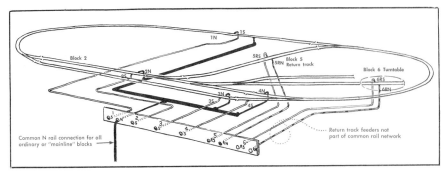

12 - 5   Common bus method of wiring common rail blocks together makes use of return feeder wire under table. N rail feeders in all blocks that can have a common rail are tied down to this bus. Often heavy bare copper wire is used for the bus.

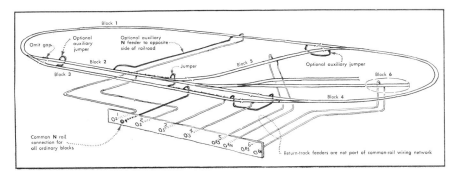

12 - 6   To save wire, jumpers are used from one N rail to the next and rails themselves serve as their own common bus in this method. Be sure to use separate N feeders for return track blocks as in the case of block 5 and the turntable in all three of these common rail diagrams.

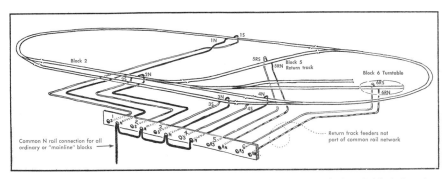

12 - 7   In this method, track is wired with separate feeders to the N rail of each block, but those that can have common return are tied together at the terminal strip. This method has the advantage of making changes easier and also it's easier to disconnect parts of the track if you want to localize wiring troubles later on.

the N rail on each side of a gap is connected to common, then you can leave the rail solid instead of cutting a gap. It is obvious that the gap marked G between blocks 1 and 2 in Fig. 12-4 is not needed. Some other N rail gaps on these plans would be needed only if selective control turnouts are used. If in doubt, gaps in the N rail will do no harm.

Basic control equipment

As you can see, block control panels consist of two main parts. There's the "throttle unit" for controlling the train and then there's the "selector unit" with all the toggles or other contacts to make sure you control only certain blocks. Between them are any direction control toggles that might be needed.

While both of these units can be built in many different ways, they are always distinct electrically, and you can use one design of throttle unit with other designs of selector panel.

The throttle unit is sometimes called a "controller unit" or a "cab unit." In most cases it's a power pack with throttle and reverse lever. The pack may be separate from the throttle if you want it that way.

The selector unit includes all the toggles or other types of electric contacts that are used to connect the throttle to various blocks. Sometimes lever or rotary type contact switches are used in place of toggles. Sometimes relays are used in automatic systems. But, in any case, all that really happens is that any combination of blocks can be connected to the throttle while other blocks remain disconnected.

Control for more trains

The throttle unit plus the selector unit or panel make up one "cab." When you use more than one cab in this way you have "cab control wiring," Fig. 12-8.

On a small railroad you usually will need only two cabs. That means two throttle units and two selector panels. But if your railroad grows, you may want to add more cabs. It's a good idea to provide as many cabs as you can run trains at one time. While this may sound like a lot of equipment, remember that you can add it a panel at a time, so there's little likelihood of building more panels than you need.

Ways to run the trains

In some train operating schemes, you set the cab toggles a certain way and leave them more or less alone. In other schemes you flip toggles more often. Here are the principal methods:

ONE-TRAIN CONTROL. Turn all the toggles on in one cab, off in all other cabs. Use this one cab to run a train

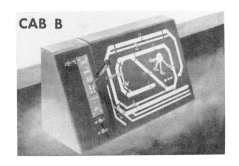

12 - 8   If you add a second block control panel identical to the first, you can use the two panels to run the railroad by any desired method — block control, section control, or cab control. When operating by cab control, the panels are called "cabs" and each cab is used to run only one train. The toggles are kept off except for the one or two blocks the train is actually using or about to use. You can add a cab control panel to any model railroad to get better operation without impairing the usefulness of any panel already installed.

anywhere. A variation is to turn just one toggle on in a second or third cab and use its throttle to run the train. Since all the toggles are on in the first cab, all blocks are connected together and power for one block from any other cab powers all other blocks by sneak connections in Cab A.

BLOCK CONTROL. Turn on all toggles in one cab, as before, and again use this cab's throttle to run all trains. Flip toggles off here and there to stop trains or to hold them back at a danger point. Stops will be sudden and jerky, but block control makes it easy for one man to manage many trains.

SECTION CONTROL. Turn on a group of blocks at one panel. Turn on another group at the second panel. You can have as many distinct groups as there are throttles. Each group is then a section as in section control wiring, only now you have the advantage of being able to change section boundaries just by flipping toggles. Also, you may isolate any train you wish for a smooth stop or start.

SPEED ZONE CONTROL. Set up sections as before, but group all blocks where you want a train to go slowly into one section (regardless of whether these blocks are close together or far apart). Assign other blocks to a medium-speed throttle, and if you have a third cab, add a high-speed group. At first you'd use high-speed blocks on uphill track and low-speed blocks on curves, downhill, and when approaching stations. Thus trains change speed without attention as track conditions change. If you want any train to slow and then stop, flip toggles so it is first transferred into a slow section and then flip a toggle off for the final stop. With this type of control you won't use the throttles much except for occasional speed corrections of a whole speed zone.

CAB CONTROL. This is the scheme that our modern methods of wiring were principally designed for. The object is to make running a model train as much like running a real train as is practical. Suppose you are the crew for Extra 377, a local freight. You sit at Cab A. No matter what happens at other cabs, you are primarily concerned only with your own train. You flip toggles on to send power from your throttle to your train and then you flip toggles off as soon as your train clears various blocks. This is essential so some other train can use the idle blocks without electrical interference.

Always turn the block toggle off as soon as your train leaves each block.

You make up your train in the yard while your yard toggle is on. Then

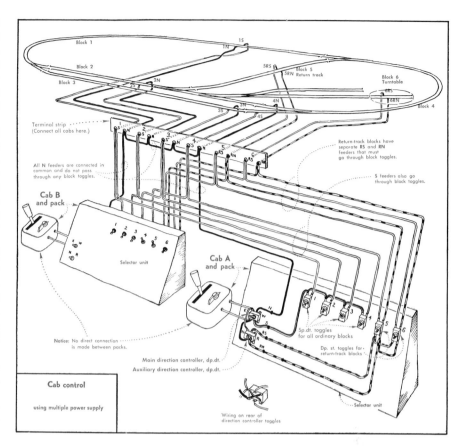

12-9 Each block control panel is connected to the terminal strip as though the other panel was not there. It's the fact that each block can be controlled from either throttle that makes this "cab control." Panel and track wiring is the same as in Figs. 12-4 and 12-11.

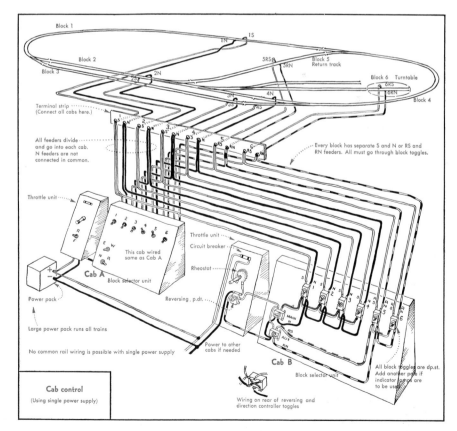

12-10 Same railroad with a single power pack requires doubled wiring (no common rail). While throttle units are shown as small assemblies here, a pack with two or more built-in throttles can be used in this same arrangement. In actual operation this scheme and Fig. 12-9 perform alike.

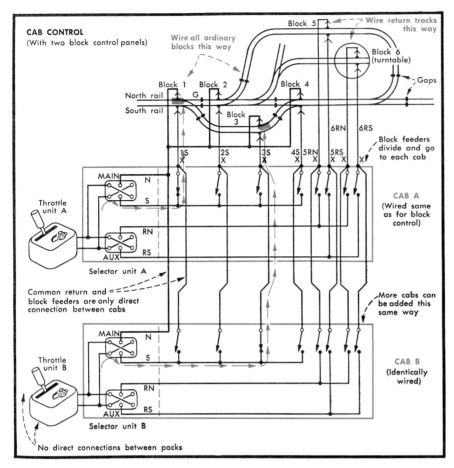

CAB CONTROL
(With two block control panels)

Wire all ordinary blocks this way

Block 5

Wire return tracks this way

Block 6 (turntable)

Gaps

Block 1   Block 2   Block 4

North rail
G

South rail

Block 3

6RN   6RS

Block feeders divide and go to each cab

1S   2S   3S   4S 5RN 5RS 6RN 6RS
X   X   X   X   X   X X X X

MAIN   N

S

Throttle unit A

RN

RS

AUX

Selector unit A

Common return and block feeders are only direct connection between cabs

CAB A (Wired same as for block control)

More cabs can be added this same way

MAIN   N

S

Throttle unit B

RN

RS

AUX

Selector unit B

CAB B (Identically wired)

No direct connections between packs

12-11 The pictorial diagram of Fig. 12-9 looks like this when drawn schematically. Any number of cabs can be added at places marked X, but no other connections are permitted between cabs and separate power packs are required for each cab (unless you use twin power supply). Compare this with Fig. 12-4 and you'll see that the second panel merely repeated the first.

Two-position switches

CAB A

X

CAB B

ETC.

(A)

Requires one toggle per block per cab

Engineer cab control (block control panels)

Three-position switches

CAB A

X

CAB B

ETC.

(B)

Requires one switch per block per each two cabs

Engineer cab control (dual throttle panels)

12-12 Wiring for a single block uses separate toggle in block control type panels, but one toggle serves two cabs in dual throttle scheme. Cab B is connected in each drawing.

when you have the right to leave the yard, you flip mainline toggles as your train proceeds.

Toggle flipping becomes so automatic with cab control that you don't think about it any more than you think about twisting a doorknob to enter a room. Instead, your attention is on the train, on the track ahead of the train, and on what you want to do next — just as in running a real locomotive.

Cab control can be very realistic because you can concentrate on smooth starting, precise switching movements, adjusting for grades, and so on.

Perhaps as you run along you must get into the siding to let the limited go past. You can do this with all the neatness of a real railroad train movement. As soon as the limited passes, you can open the gate and proceed onto the main to begin some local switching.

When you get to the end of the run,

you can use your same throttle to put your loco in the roundhouse, or if you have guests to help, you can have a "hostler" put the loco away for you. That's a good job for a new member if you work on a seniority system where veterans choose jobs before newcomers.

Cab control is at its best when you have a man for each train, but a few fellows are skilled enough to run two or three trains by cab control without help. Other fellows will use one of the other schemes we discussed when they operate solo. You can change from one scheme to any other instantly by flipping toggles.

Block panels for cabs

In Figs. 12-9 and 12-11, the block panel has been repeated, making a cab control system. Any number of additional cabs can be added in the same way. If you cannot use common rail wiring, then the scheme of Fig. 12-10 should be substituted. The page 53 drawings are a good place to study out the differences between common rail and doubled wiring.

Block control panels aren't the only kinds we can use for cab control, so a little later I'll tell how they compare

12-13 Dual throttle cab is really two cabs, but they share the same block selector toggles on a single selector unit panel. This is the best panel to start with for most model railroads. While homemade throttle units are shown, regular power packs can replace them at one or both sides.

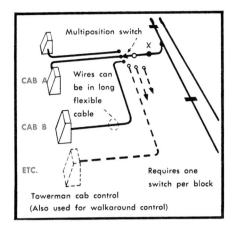

12-14 Multiposition switch for each block selects desired cab in this scheme. It's economical for clubs and for walkaround control where knobs are located near the blocks they control and you carry throttle on flexible cable.

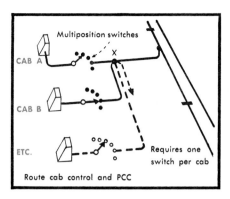

12-15 Turn multiposition switch the other way and you have route cab control. Connections to blocks are located consecutively around each engineer's selector. This results in economical semiautomatic control. Additional contacts are often added between selector and X to choose the route the selector will follow.

with others for our needs. In any case, you can connect cabs of different types to the same track at X locations in Fig. 12-11. Fig. 17-3 shows how several cabs can be connected to the railroad.

Building your control system

One of the nice things about our scheme of controlling trains is that it can start in a simple way and grow with your railroad. Here's a workable plan you might consider:

First, build a control box and panel with enough space on it to take a toggle switch for each block plus the controls for all turnouts that have switch machines. If you use Atlas controls, you just need a big mounting board for them.

Next, you install the actual wiring to switch machines. The idea is to get them in working order. The track is still one big block with a single throttle at this stage.

Dividing the track into blocks comes next. Do the paper work one night and you'll know how many toggles to buy the next day. If you are production minded, wire the whole control panel on your workbench and attach it to the railroad later. Or you can put toggles into the panel and wire them a block at a time. Building a block at a time prevents mistakes.

In either case, you needn't cut gaps in the track until the toggle and track feeders for each new block are installed. In this way you can always have trains running if you have to lay down the tools for a day or two.

If you make this first panel along the lines of the dual throttle control panel I'm about to describe, it will be just right for handling two trains at the same time and also well suited to test runs, electrical trouble shooting, etc. Later on you may need more

panels for more trains, but we'll talk about that after the dual throttle panel.

Dual throttle cabs

The dual throttle cab is so versatile, simple to wire, and inexpensive, considering what it can do, that I feel it is the best design to use for the main control panel on almost every model railroad. This goes for big railroads as well as small ones.

Actually it is two cabs in one place. Fig. 12-13 shows a dual throttle panel. Notice that there are two throttles but only one set of block selector toggles. These toggles are of a type we haven't used previously. They move from the left to the right to connect a block to either the left-hand or right-hand throttle. The toggles also have an off position in the center so any block can be made dead. This type of panel is easy for one, two or three people to operate at the same time. Let's talk about operation with two people first.

Assume you have a guest at the panel. The guest isn't familiar with your railroad, so you want to make it easy for him. You use the left-hand throttle and everywhere your train goes, you throw the toggles over to the left so you get power to the blocks where your train needs it. How about the toggles for the other fellow? Well, if you just throw your toggles to the extreme right each time your train clears a block, all of the blocks you don't need will be connected to the other fellow's throttle, so no matter where he runs his train he has it under control. Sometimes I've called this "father-and-son" control because it's a good one for Dad and Junior.

Of course, whether the other fellow is your son or a guest, sooner or later he's going to learn how to handle the

toggles for himself. Then, instead of throwing the toggles all the way over, you throw them only as far as their off positions and the other fellow will operate his train in the same way you do, throwing the toggles back to the center off position when he's through with them.

When you want to use this cab for three people at the same time, one fellow can handle the toggles while the other two handle the throttles.

For solo railroading, you can handle both trains by cab control methods or you can throw some of the toggles to the left and others to the right and operate by section control.

If you operate by speed zone control, you have the advantage that two speeds and stop can be controlled with a single toggle for each block. Another scheme is to set one throttle unit for forward and the other for reverse. Then every toggle on the panel becomes a reversing switch for its particular block.

This versatility of the dual throttle panel is one of its great assets. The other big assets are its simplicity and cost. Since only one set of toggles is used, the panel doesn't cost as much as the two cabs of the plain type that it replaces and less wiring is required.

Cab switching schemes

Where the block control cab uses a two-position (on-off) toggle for each block, as in Fig. 12-12A, we can accomplish the same result, at least for our purposes, by using a three-position (double-throw center-off) toggle or switch, Fig. 12-12B. This toggle can be moved to either side to connect either throttle to the track or it can be left in the center where no connection is made.

Since the handle will go only one way or the other, we have the added advantage that you cannot connect the block to both throttles at the same time — it's self-interlocking. This is the difference between the block control cab and the dual throttle type. Both are "engineer cab control" because the engineer can do his own block selecting.

Let's digress a moment to two advanced techniques. In Fig. 12-14, we again see the wiring for one block to several cabs, but now using only one multiposition "cab selector" switch per block. Usually these switches are located in groups at various "towers" around the railroad but could be in a central "power dispatcher's panel." Towermen (or a power dispatcher) then connect each block to the proper cab as the trains come along. This system has been used in many clubs and is economical to install. It has the

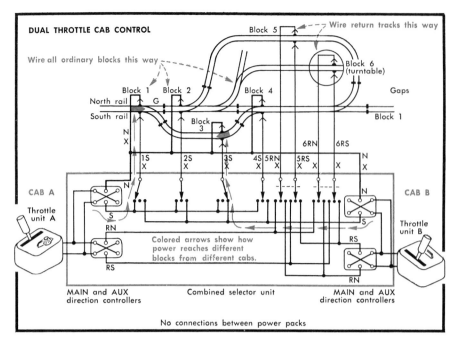

12-16 Dual throttle cab economizes on toggles and gives best type of one-man and good two-man control. Toggles at right, blocks 5 and 6, have doubled wiring to serve return blocks. Mainline tracks can have common rail as shown if two packs are used.

fault that towermen are likely to connect the block to the wrong cab occasionally.

A wonderful use for this scheme on a home railroad is for "walkaround control." You put your controller unit at the end of a long flexible cable and walk around as you run the train. You turn these cab selectors to connect each block to your cab as needed.

Locate the cab selectors near the actual track on the railroad, or in groups on localized panels.

In Fig. 12-15, the multiposition switch is reversed so the engineer can connect to one block after another with the same knob. This is route cab control, and it can also be done with radio-tuning push buttons or relays.

If you like more than one of these

schemes, you can wire some cabs each way and run trains with both kinds of cabs at the same or different times. Just connect all cabs to the same blocks at places marked X. In these drawings the wire from each cab will also connect to other selector switches, depending on number of blocks.

You can even use the same throttle unit with two differently wired selector units at different times because there's no real reason to always associate the same throttle with the same selector. Put a switch between a throttle and several selector panels if you wish.

Dual throttle wiring

Fig. 12-16 shows the dual throttle cab complete in diagrammatic form while Fig. 12-18 is a semipictorial of the same thing. These are practical wiring diagrams that you can copy for your own railroad. All you need do is change the number of toggles to fit the number of blocks on your own plan. The group of four toggles on the left is shown as wired for the common rail part of your railroad. Those on the right have doubled wiring for return tracks. Of course, you don't have to mount the toggles in this order. You can locate them in the order of actual occurrence of blocks on your railroad or you can mount them right in their places on a track diagram, as in Fig. 12-13.

If you want to use the dual throttle panel, but with a single power pack, make the following modifications:

Connect the pack to throttle units as in Fig. 12-10. Add MAIN and AUX direction controllers as usual. Run the wires from AUX direction controllers to return track toggles just as in Fig. 12-18 for blocks 5 and 6. Now use dp. toggles for blocks 1, 2, 3, 4 (all mainline region blocks). Wire them as 5 and 6 were wired, but powered from the MAIN direction controller. Draw this out a step at a time and you won't go wrong. There will be no common rail or feeder.

You can build a dual throttle cab quickly with Atlas control devices. You need at least one Atlas controller or more if you have several return track blocks. However, one Atlas selector handles four blocks. Instead of flipping toggles to each side to select cab A or cab B, you move the selector slides up and down. The center is off.

The Atlas controller is peculiar in operation. Slides A and B are MAIN direction controllers for each throttle unit. Slide AB connects a particular return track to either cab so this is really the block toggle for the return track or turntable. Slides marked 5 and 6 are AUX reversing switches for the return tracks. After a little

12-17 Dual throttle wiring for same railroad using Atlas components. Get one Atlas controller for direction control. It also handles one return track. Add another for each additional return block. These must be placed at left regardless of actual location of blocks on railroad. Plug in Atlas selector unit for each four blocks in common rail territory. Devices are handy for economical, quick and simple wiring, or for temporary control while you build permanent panels.

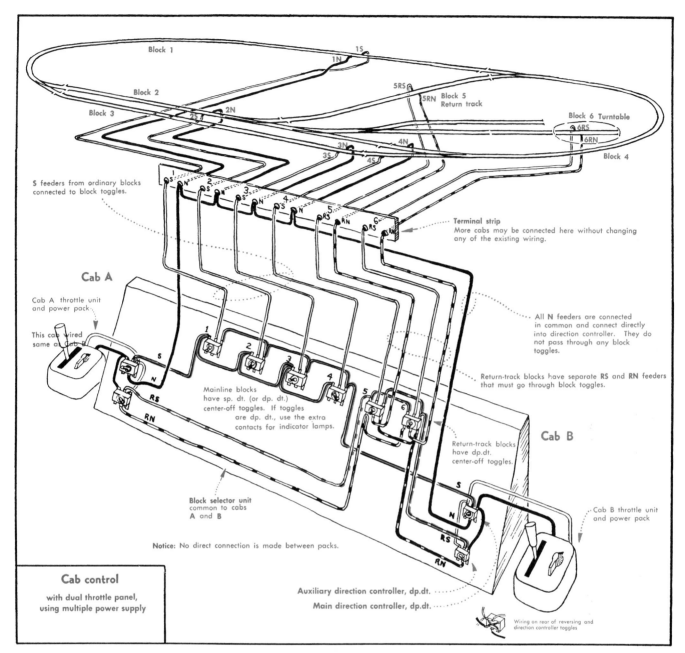

Block 1

1S
1N

Block 2

5RS
5RN Block 5
Return track

Block 3

2S 2N

Block 6 Turntable
6RS
6RN

3N 4N
3S 4S

Block 4

S feeders from ordinary blocks
connected to block toggles.

Terminal strip
More cabs may be connected here without changing
any of the existing wiring.

Cab A

Cab A throttle unit
and power pack

This cab wired
same as Cab B

S

N

RS

RN

1
2
3
4
5
6

S
N

RS

RN

All N feeders are connected
in common and connect directly
into direction controller. They do
not pass through any block
toggles.

Return-track blocks have separate RS and RN feeders
that must go through block toggles.

Mainline blocks
have sp. dt. (or dp. dt.)
center-off toggles. If toggles
are dp. dt., use the extra
contacts for indicator lamps.

Return-track blocks
have dp.dt.
center-off toggles.

Cab B

Block selector unit
common to cabs
A and B

Cab B throttle unit
and power pack

Notice: No direct connection is made between packs.

Cab control

with dual throttle panel,
using multiple power supply

Auxiliary direction controller, dp.dt.

Main direction controller, dp.dt.

Wiring on rear of reversing and
direction controller toggles

12 - 18 While toggles are shown in a line here, they can be arranged on a track diagram as in Fig. 12-13, providing you can afford to make the panel larger than otherwise. Most common error in building this panel is for a fellow to run wires from one pack to the other. Don't!

practice you can get on to the system, but visitors may be confused.

Atlas components are designed to work only with multiple power supply and common rail track wiring.

Three and more trains

When your railroad outgrows the first master panel, you can add any number of cab control panels of any type by connecting each new panel to the feeder wires at the terminal strip, at places marked X. Now it's a matter of what types of panels to choose.

If you will operate mostly by yourself and occasionally with guests, adding more dual throttle panels will be an economical and practical way to expand the control system. Put the panels at one location or else on cables

so they can be close together when you operate alone.

If you will always have guests operating, and you have enough space, add block-control type panels. They offer the advantage that each man gets a panel all to himself. This advantage goes for route cabs and other one-throttle types as well.

Lamp indications

When you have several control panels, and especially if they are not close together, some special problems in wiring come up because each man must know when he might interfere with what another man is doing.

If you install block indicator lamps on each panel, they will help prevent two fellows from turning power into

the same block at the same time. Place one lamp for each block on each panel. All the lamps for a particular block are wired in parallel so if any man turns a block toggle on, he will light the lamp for that block not only on his own but every other panel.

When you buy toggles or other switches for block control, get them with one extra moving contact or "pole" and use this extra pole to light the lamps. See Figs. 12-19 to 12-21.

Notice how the scheme in Fig. 12-20 makes the lamps go on no matter to which side you turn the block toggle of a dual throttle panel.

Power for a system of panel lamps can come from any one, but only one, of the various power packs or a separate lighting transformer can be

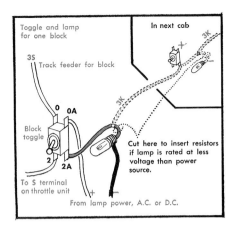

12 - 19 This indicator lamp will shine to show when a block is in use by any operator at any cab panel. All block toggles for the same block must have an extra pole to handle the indicator circuit (since lamps operated from the running power wouldn't protect stopped trains). Thus sp. st. toggles would be replaced by dp. st. and dp. st. (for doubled wiring) by 3p. st. toggles or wafer switches. The wire 3K must connect to the block 3 lamp in every cab panel. A similar indiKator wire is provided between the cabs for every other block. The plus and minus for all the lamps for one block must go to the same power source, but if you want to split the load you can power one block's lamps from one pack and another block's lamps from another.

used. This is discussed in the next chapter.

In addition to having a lamp near the block toggle on each cab control panel, you might want to have an "illuminated track diagram" with another set of lamps up where everyone can get a picture of all operations at a glance.

Some men like to have panel lamps show where trains actually are, not just where power toggles are turned on. The lamp circuits for this are the

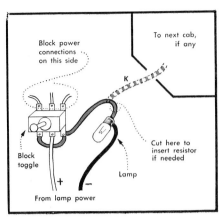

12 - 20 Indicator lamps for dual throttle cabs are wired the same as in Fig. 12-19 except that the indicator wire (shown in color) must reach two places on the toggle. Thus the light will burn when the switch is thrown to either side. Use a 3-pole switch for return track blocks.

same, only instead of using an extra contact on the block toggle, you use a contact on a track relay. This was indicated in the signal circuit on page 44 and the same idea can be used with more advanced signaling relay circuits.

Turnout control from cabs

When you don't have the manpower to use towers at each junction or to have a dispatcher control all turnouts from a CTC panel, the next best scheme is to have duplicate turnout controls on each cab panel. Just as your power must be disconnected from the blocks you are not using on a cab control panel, so it must also be disconnected from turnouts you aren't using lest turnout controls on your panel interfere with the turnouts in another train's territory.

Any of the momentary contact schemes for turnout control are suitable, including push-button schemes. This is because power reaches the machines only when the button is pushed. At other times the button might be pushed on some other panel. The scheme in Fig. 11-11, shown in a variation in Fig. 12-29, is good for cab control panels. Repeat the button and route selecting switch on each cab panel. You can select a route anytime, but don't push the button until the

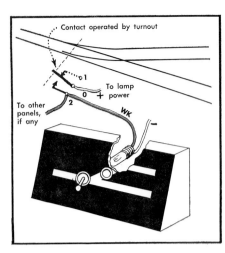

12 - 21 This lamp, installed on each cab panel, shows all engineers when a particular turnout isn't lined up for the main line by burning red. The controlling contact can be on a control lever, but one on the switch machine or throw rod is more certain to give a correct indication. The lamps on panels can also be powered through coil cutoff contacts as we did in Chapter 11, providing the lamps don't draw so much current that they tend to operate the coil and weaken the force of the machine. Four to six grain-of-wheat lamps can be powered through most coils without trouble.

track is clear lest you derail someone else's train. Cutoff contacts are optional, but are handy for the lamps as well as for coil protection.

In order to see which way remote turnouts have been thrown, turnout indicator lamps can be placed on each cab panel as in Fig. 12-21. The actuating contact can't be a panel lever because some cabs will have turnout control levers set one way and other cabs another way at the same time. The contact must be either on the

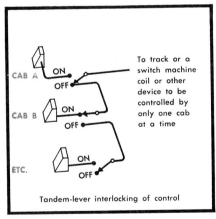

12 - 22 By connecting the moving pole of one lever to the off position of the previous one, any number of levers can be connected in tandem so only one cab at a time can possibly reach the controlled device. Cab A has priority over all others. Use this for interlocked block control from cabs or duplicate it for each coil of a switch machine that is provided with cutoff contacts. You should have an experienced man at Cab A.

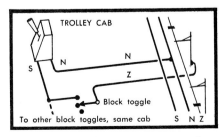

12 - 23 A block selector can connect a cab to a trolley wire instead of an S rail if desired.

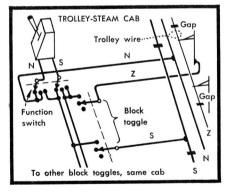

12 - 24 More elaborate cab has three-way function switch above, shown in position for running steam and diesel trains. Middle position operates trolley equipment without fouling S rail so steam or diesel can come into same block. Third position also operates trolley equipment but uses the S rail for return power in case trolley equipment has turned around a loop and must use S rail for its grounded wheels. The block toggle is shown as for a dual throttle cab with three positions but it could be any other type.

turnout throw rod or on the switch machine.

The tricky ways we used to light lamps through the coil cutoff contacts back in Chapter 11 can be used here, providing there aren't too many panel lamps in the circuit. This is because each lamp will pass a small current through the coil of the switch machine and if there were more than about six lamps, the current might be great enough to interfere with switch machine operation.

Tandem lever wiring

The scheme of Fig. 12-22 has been used occasionally to interlock the control of block toggles between cabs and can also be used to control coils of a switch machine

As shown, Cab B is operating the turnout or block at the moment. It is impossible for Cab C to control the device until Cab B lets go. On the other hand, Cab A can take over control at any time. While this requires an experienced operator at Cab A, the man at C can't do much wrong for it is impossible to connect two cabs to the device at the same time.

In using tandem control, it is a rule that a man must turn his toggle to the off position after each use, otherwise the men farther up the cascade are helpless.

Many kinds of cabs

You may not want to build a duplicate of the master panel for the third and fourth trains, etc. You may want to build more specialized types of control panel.

In specially designed panels, the cab control circuit is really the same. You still disconnect and connect power to any block, but you may use special types of electric switch to do the connecting, or you may build a limited service panel that has toggles for only a part of the railroad. The limited service panel saves space, wiring, and is easier to use when you can justify it. Here are several types of limited service cabs:

BRANCHLINE CAB. This cab has toggles for every block in the branchline territory, but it also has mainline toggles as needed so the branchline train can run from the junction point on into the main terminal. Toggles for other branches and remote parts of the mainline are omitted from this panel.

MAINLINE CAB. This cab would be one designed primarily for mainline train operations. We would have toggles for all blocks along the main, but toggles for branch lines, yards, industrial sidings, etc., might be omitted.

SUBURBAN CAB. This cab can be used for suburban passenger trains or for industrial switching near the main

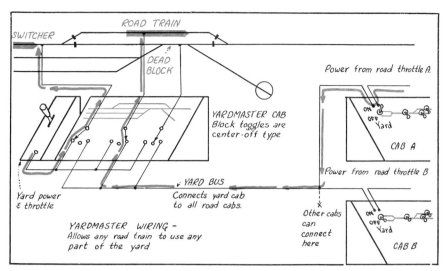

12-25 Only one toggle on each engineer's cab, right, is needed to allow engineer to pull road train in and out of any yard track. Yardmaster sets up desired track on his own panel, left, and can do switching on any other track simultaneously.

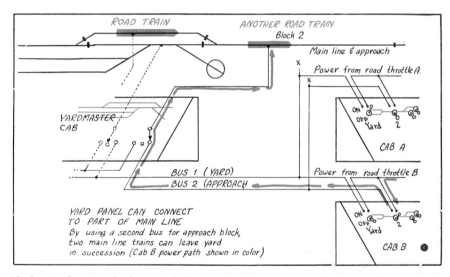

12-26 Yardmaster cab idea extended to control of shared mainline block as well as yard. This is really a development of tandem control scheme of Fig. 12-22.

terminal. It has toggles for most blocks around the terminal and for some distance, but not all the way, along the main line. If you have electrified the suburban district, this particular cab could be connected to the trolley sections instead of the S rail if you like; see Figs. 12-23 and 12-24.

YARD CAB. This cab would be one designed only for yard switching and would have toggles for all yard blocks plus those mainline blocks that are used in yard switching. A dual throttle cab here will allow you to switch in two places at once, but most often a block-control type cab will be adequate.

YARDMASTER CAB. This is a special type of yard cab that is particularly helpful on railroads where there are quite a few tracks in a yard. The scheme is shown in Fig. 12-25 and it involves the design of both the yard cab and the mainline panels.

The idea is to put all detailed controls on the yard panel only. Then only one "yard toggle" would be placed on the road cabs. This would save a great deal of space on road cabs and simplify operation as well.

The yardmaster cab is wired like a dual throttle cab but only equipped for the blocks in the yard and nearby approach tracks. There would be only one throttle. If any block toggle is flipped to the left, it connects this part of the yard to the throttle. In operation, a yardmaster would switch a train in this manner and then place it on any convenient track ready for departure. Next he would flip the toggles of that track to the right, which would connect the rails to the "yard bus" shown in Fig. 12-25.

When a road engineer wants to pick up the waiting train, he flips his yard toggle. This connects his throttle to the yard bus and through the yard

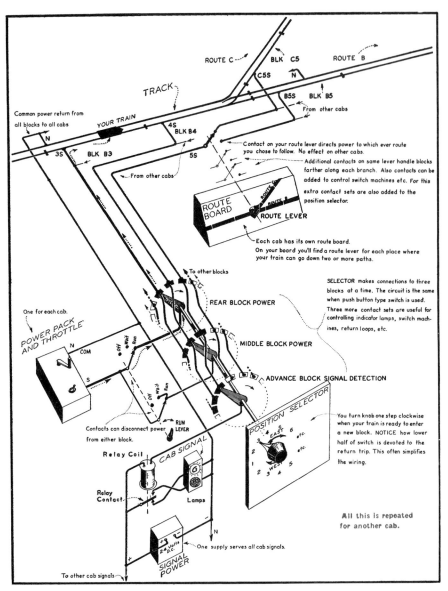

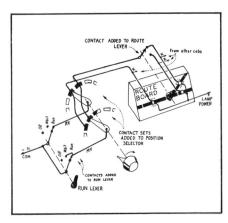

12 - 28 Two extra wafers on position selector can control block indication lamps in route cab and can be tied to other cabs as was done in Fig. 12-19.

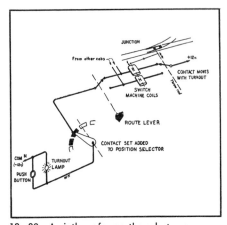

12 - 29 A sixth wafer on the selector can connect you to switch machines along the route. Lamp shows if they need to be thrown and push button will throw them.

12 - 27 Elaborate route levers can transfer many of the contacts around the position selector to as many blocks on a branch line in place of the main. Here only one block is transferred by the remote lever for purposes of illustration. All wiring is repeated to control another train.

cab to whatever blocks the yardmaster has set up. Thus the road engineer can take his train out of the yard, yet he needs only one toggle to represent all possible yard tracks.

The scheme in Fig. 12-26 shows how this idea can be repeated for an approach track so a different road cab can have access to it. Two bus wires are used.

If you want to do switching in two parts of the yard simultaneously, you can use any idle road cab for a second throttle temporarily. If the need is frequent, a permanent second yard throttle can be connected to the yard bus. Leave the reversing switch at center off position to disconnect this throttle when road cabs use the bus.

Route cab control

When you use some kind of a switch with many positions to switch train running power to one block after a

another in sequence, you have one kind of route cab control. The germ of this idea is shown in Fig. 12-15, showing the wiring from three cabs to one block. Other contacts on the same three selectors serve all other blocks along the route. You can see that if you need only one selector switch for all the blocks for one cab, you're going to save money. Also, it is nearly like automatic control since you turn the selector one notch at a time to make power follow your train around the route. Block power is cut off behind the train automatically.

Fig. 12-27 shows more of the detail of a simple route cab, including how you can send power to blocks on both sides of a gap to prevent jerking and how a working cab signal can be installed. It gives you signaling all around the railroad with only one relay. Figs. 12-28 and 12-29 show other features that can be added with

extra wafers on the rotary block selector.

Progressive cab control

When you make the rotary selector of route cab control turn by itself, you have "PCC," or progressive cab control. (Sometimes relays replace rotary stepping switches in PCC just as a row of radio tuning buttons may be used in route cab control instead of a rotary switch.) PCC has two main advantages. It makes model railroad operation more realistic by eliminating most or all toggle flipping, leaving you to run the train without unrailroadlike devices of any kind. The other advantage is for a man running many trains solo. A PCC "pilot" can read its own cab signal and run the train at various speeds and stop it accordingly. Thus you can have several trains run around the railroad by themselves, while you run another train or do switching by hand control. Some PCC information is included in the cab control articles just mentioned.

13. Lamps and Lamp Wiring

THE grain-of-wheat sized lamp bulb has almost entirely replaced the radio dial lamp and other miniature base lamps in scale model railroading. Popular prices plus their small size account for this revolution.

Grain-sized bulbs come in many voltage ratings, several colors, some variations in size, and some special shapes. Some bulbs have special bases to fit the sockets in signals or locomotives, but most grain bulbs have two pigtail wires which you solder into the circuit. Use care with these pigtail bulbs as the tiny wires are easily broken at the place where they enter the bulb. A little Ambroid or similar type cement dabbed at the bulb end of the wires will help to protect them.

While lamp bulbs are individually inexpensive, you can use a great many of them to light buildings, cars, yards, streets, beacons and the like around the railroad, so avoiding burned-out bulbs becomes important if only for maintenance reasons.

Usually model railroad bulbs should be operated at somewhat below their rated voltage, as this means both a longer life and a wider margin of safety against momentary flashes of too high voltage.

If you start at a very low voltage, a bulb will begin to glow an orange red at only a fraction of its rated voltage. As you increase the voltage the glow becomes gradually brighter and more orange, then yellowish.

At somewhere around its rated voltage, the bulb will burn light yellow or white in color and quite bright. Increase the voltage just a little more and the whiteness and brightness become intense and soon the bulb will burn out.

Normal bulb voltage is not an exact thing. Some bulbs burn normally with a little more, others with a little less, than their rated voltage. The color is a good gauge, for you can soon recognize a yellowish bulb from a white one. Fortunately, if necessary it is easy to adjust individually the voltage for each bulb you use, as we'll soon see.

While you increase the color temperature of the bulb, two unseen things are happening. One is a change in electrical resistance. Most devices have a nearly constant resistance, but not those which change temperature radically. While a 12-v. grain-of-wheat bulb might have a resistance of perhaps 100 ohms at its normal light yellow temperature, the resistance when cold may be only 25 ohms.

The other temperature effect is a change in the life expectancy of the bulb. As temperature increases, the metal of the filament in the bulb tends to boil away, but the amount of vaporizing isn't important until you approach the rated voltage. At somewhat below rated voltage — orange yellow color — lamp life is a matter of years. At normal voltage it is a matter of days or weeks, depending on how the rating was determined. At something above the rated voltage, when the filament is very white, the life may be a matter of minutes or only seconds.

Lamp voltage ratings

Both grain-of-wheat and the larger "miniature" bulbs are sold with voltage ratings from around 1½ v. up to 16 v or 18 v., and this is a general guide for you in selecting bulbs along with data on their sizes (which varies a lot) and mountings.

It is a good idea to buy bulbs in batches and then test them yourself, say on a moderate voltage, to see which will burn white and which yellow on that same voltage. Then use the whiter bulbs in places where you can replace them more easily, or else use dropping resistors so they don't burn as brightly You'll find imported bulbs particularly will not be standardized in color temperature for their rated voltages.

Danger, rheostat in circuit

Ordinarily, only bulbs of 16-v or 18-v rating should be used in trains. This size will usually be bright enough for operation at 8 to 12 volts and yet can stand the sudden surges of voltage, up to as high as 18 v., that might occur. Such surges can easily happen if you run trains with a rheostat. You may remember that a rheo-

stat controls trains by wasting voltage that's in proportion to the current passing through it.

When you run a train at 9 v., you waste about 7 v. in the rheostat (because a pack without load furnishes about 16 v. total). Well, suppose the locomotive reached a dead section or suppose there was a defect in the motor wiring and suddenly only the lamp is left in the circuit. A grain-of-wheat lamp draws about $\frac{1}{12}$ a., which is only one sixth as much as the motor draws. Therefore, the voltage lost in the rheostat is only one sixth of the former 7 v. or about 1.2 v., leaving about 14.8 v. across the lamp bulb. Poof! Burned out!

Variable transformer speed controllers usually do not create this particular hazard, although if turned on full, more than 12 v. will reach a bulb with any speed controller

I have some locos that run fast enough at only 6 to 8 volts, and a 16-v or 18-v. bulb is too dim for these locos. Then I use a bulb of lower voltage, but of course at the risk of a burnout if a greater voltage should somehow reach it.

In general, you want to select a bulb of somewhat higher voltage rating than it is likely to be used with.

You might think from this discussion that it would be best to use 16-v. or 18-v. bulbs everywhere. Fortunately, there are several ways to operate low-voltage bulbs safely on 12 v and higher voltage circuits safely. The first is to string two or more bulbs in series.

Bulbs in series

In the series string, Fig. 13-1, two or more bulbs are arranged so the same current passes through all of them on its way around the circuit. The voltage across each bulb will then be proportionate to the resistance of each bulb and the voltages of all bulbs will total the supply voltage. Thus if three identical bulbs are connected to a 16-v. supply, each bulb will get 5.3 v. In this way you can use three

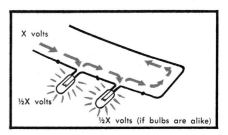

13-1 Bulbs in series share the voltage. If the bulbs are alike, the voltage will divide half and half. If the bulbs are different, one will draw more voltage than the other. This is all right if they still burn at a safe color temperature.

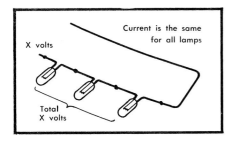

13 - 2 Any number of bulbs can be connected in series. Bulbs should have same current rating but can have any voltage rating as long as total is at least as much as supply voltage. Since current is the same through all bulbs, one burned-out bulb will cut current from all the others until it is replaced.

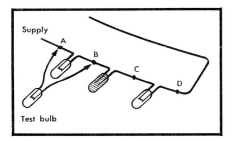

13 - 3 To find which bulb in a series string has burned out, connect a good bulb of the same current rating across one bulb and then the next. When you bridge the defective bulb, the test lamp will light along with all the others.

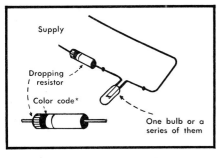

13 - 4 Radio resistor wastes voltage by producing heat so lamp bulb or bulbs don't burn too brightly.

Resistor Color Code

Resistors of ¼-w. to 2-w. sizes are marked with color bands to indicate their value. The first two bands from the end are digits and the third band indicates how many zeros follow them. The colors are:

0	Black	5	Green
1	Brown	6	Blue
2	Red	7	Purple or Lavender
3	Orange	8	Gray
4	Yellow	9	White

Thus Orange-White-Red would be 3900 ohms. A fourth band of gold means 5 per cent accuracy, silver 10 per cent; otherwise 20 per cent.

8-v. bulbs safely on a 16-v. supply or two bulbs on 12-v. supply.

In actual practice, bulbs will vary slightly from each other, but if no bulb burns too white, your series string is safe. It is even quite safe to burn bulbs of different voltage ratings together on the same string, providing no particular bulb is too white. See Fig. 13-2.

When installing a new string, try it on somewhat less than final voltage first to check relative brightness. Replace any bulb that's quite a bit brighter than the others. Use the disqualified bulbs somewhere else. You can get less than normal voltage for testing by putting a loco on clean track and running it at a slow speed. Temporarily connect the string of bulbs across the rails. Then try them at the full 12 v. or 16 v. or whatever the final voltage will be.

If one bulb in a series burns out, the others will also go out. Connect a spare bulb across each bulb in the string in turn, Fig. 13-3. When you come to the defective bulb, the string and the test bulb will light up.

Series strings are particularly useful for locos with two headlights (see Chapter 5) and for groups of buildings.

Dropping resistors

Another handy technique for operating bulbs on a higher voltage than they are rated for is to use a resistor in series with the bulbs. A resistor is a tiny heater that wastes some voltage. Like the rheostat, it wastes it in proportion to the current passing through it. Radio resistors usually look like firecrackers with a fuse at each end and with colored rings around them to indicate the resistance value.

In Fig. 13-4, a resistor is shown in series with a bulb. It doesn't matter whether current passes through the resistor first or the bulb first. Again, the voltage is divided in proportion to the resistance of the bulb and the resistor. Since the grain-of-wheat bulb draws $\frac{1}{12}$ a. (caution, this varies), the resistor will waste about 1 v. for each 12 ohms of its total value. So if you want to use an 8-v. bulb on 16-v. supply, you want to waste another 8 v., and you choose a resistor of about 96 ohms. To play safe, start with a somewhat higher resistor ohms' value and work down until the bulb is bright enough to suit you.

Since the yellow or white color of the bare filament is a good indication of bulb life expectancy, you don't need voltmeters and other technical devices to select a dropping resistor. Instead, get the first few or perhaps all the resistors in the following list

from a hobby shop or radio parts store. Then try one resistor after another, starting from the top of the list, until you find the value that burns the bulb just brightly enough. Buy more resistors of this same test value to use as your dropping resistors for the particular size bulb.

Ohms	Watts	Color code
220	½	Red-Red-Brown
150	1	Brown-Green-Brown
100	1	Brown-Black-Brown
68	2	Blue-Gray-Black
25	5	None for large resistors
15	10	None for large resistors

Should one value make the light a little too dim and the next too bright, you can select a resistor of intermediate ohms' value but with the larger of the two watts' ratings.

If a whole series string of bulbs burns too brightly, you can use dropping resistors with the string just as well as with a single bulb.

Miniature bulbs

Sometimes you may want to use radio dial lamps or other bulbs with miniature screw or bayonet base. These come in many voltages and sizes and usually the current rating is 0.15 a. or 0.25 a., about double that of grain-of-wheat bulbs. The same things we've been saying about series strings also can be used here and dropping resistors can be selected from the same list.

If you have any old-style series string Christmas bulbs, they are about 16 v. rating and are especially handy for test lamps as used in Chapter 18.

Lamp power supply

Lamp bulbs work equally well on either A.C. or D.C., so if you have only half a dozen or so lighted bulbs around the railroad, you can power them from the accessory terminals of any power pack. The voltage here is usually 16-v. D.C. or perhaps 18-v. A.C. (but sometimes higher).

As soon as you have about a dozen street or building lights, it's a good idea to consider using a separate transformer to power the lighting system. When you get to this point will depend on the size of your power pack, and you can figure that about 12 grain-of-wheat lamps or 12 series strings* of them draw an ampere of load from the pack. This is in addition to the train-running and car-lighting loads.

Any low-voltage transformer can be used for lamps. Some are made just for scale railroading or you can use an old toy transformer. Another

---

*All the bulbs in a series string use the same current, so they draw no more current than a single bulb. When figuring load on a power source, add the current for one bulb only for each string. The way the other bulbs in a string get extra power is from the added voltage each requires in the string.

transformer that's popular is the radio filament transformer which comes in many different voltage sizes.

A transformer or pack delivering 12 v. or more may be used both for switch machines and lamps at the same time. Figure the current rating primarily for the lamps, as the machines will be used only momentarily. If the pack or transformer is small, the lamps will flicker whenever machines are thrown.

Lighting wiring

The same basic circuit that we've used for train running and switch machine power is repeated for lamp wiring, but this time it's simpler than ever. If you wish, you can connect two wires to the lamp power supply and run them to all places where you want lighting around the layout. Connect the terminal wires of each lamp or series lighting string to the two main feeders and you have it. When you turn on the transformer, all lamps light up.

On a larger railroad you'll probably want to use more than one such lamp circuit, each branch circuit having its own on-off toggle, Fig. 13-5.

Sunset and night

You can achieve a very nice changing scene with one or more of the ideas that follow. Arrange all the lights in your scene in random fashion on at least three different circuits. Then a few minutes after "sunset," you can flip on the first toggle. Here and there a few lights come on. When you flip the next toggle, perhaps a minute later, more lights come on mixed among the others. In this way, the countryside and city are lighted in helter-skelter pattern as in real life. Of course, all the street lights on a particular street or parking lot should come on at the same moment because in real life they are controlled to work that way.

You can dim the room lights gradually by powering them through a variable transformer if you wish. Have a few small blue bulbs (grain-of-wheat will do) up high to give a little moonlight. Visitors won't notice that they are lighted until room lights are down.

Motor-operated accessories

Small motors to operate windmills, oil wells, conveyers, and other accessories can be powered from the lighting system if the voltage and current (A.C. or D.C.) are right. Provide a toggle or rheostat to turn them on.

If the power is not the right kind, add another power pack or transformer as required, but otherwise wire the accessories in the same man-

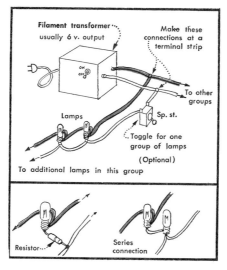

13-5 Any number of lamp and accessory groups can be added to a power pack or transformer and each group can have any number of bulbs. The limit is when the current drawn by all devices equals the current rating of the transformer or power pack. Low-voltage lamps can be connected with resistors or in series to match a higher voltage supply.

ner as a lamp system, using a toggle switch to turn each accessory on.

Most small motors of low-voltage rating run on D.C., but don't hesitate to consider a motor of, say, 24-v. rating even though your pack furnishes only 12 v. If the motor will run at all it will be safe; it just won't run fast.

Lamp and accessory feeders

The same sizes of wire you use for track feeders will be about right for lamp systems too. Note the current ratings in the wire table on page 74 and allow about 12 grain-of-wheat or five miniature bulbs to the ampere.

Common return for accessories

You can save wiring by using a common return feeder from lamps, switch machines, and accessories. The common return will work well even if some accessories are powered from different packs or transformers than others, Fig. 13-6.

This common return may have to be separate from the track common return, but sometimes it can be combined with still more saving in wiring.

The two common returns must be

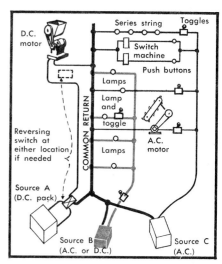

13-6 Even though several power sources might be used, all lamps and accessory devices can share the same common return feeder wire as long as no circuit breaker, fuse, switch, or other device is cut into the wire. In some cases this can also be the common rail of the track (see story). Common return should be able to carry entire current of all devices.

separate if a train-running power pack happens also to be used for accessory power in the single or multiple power supply schemes, page 9.

On the other hand, in twin power supply on the same page, either of the power packs can be used for accessories or lamps, and with the same common return. This makes the twin supply a very handy scheme for large model railroads.

Gap polarity indicators

One use for lamps is to bridge them across gaps between blocks, or more often to show polarity differences at the entrances and exits to a return track. The lamp may be mounted in a signal beside the track or on control panels. The one-lamp scheme of Fig. 13-7 lights up when the turning track polarity is properly aligned. In Fig. 13-8, a red and yellow or red and green lamp can be used similarly for a two-aspect signal.

These lamps depend on running voltage and will dim and go out as a train is stopped.

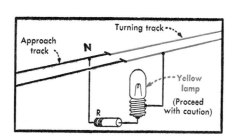

13-7 One-lamp return track polarity indicator lights when train may pass.

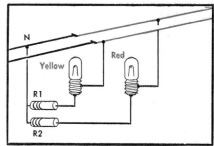

13-8 Two-lamp indicator can be used in signals beside track.

14. Toggles, Switches, and Contacts

A CONTACT consists of two pieces of metal that you can pull apart to open an electric circuit or touch together to complete the circuit again, as we saw back in Chapter 4. Contacts can be added to mechanical devices, coils, thermostats, etc., so they close when something else happens, or you can add a handle so the contact becomes a manual switch. But no matter what the arrangement for operation, the contact does the same thing electrically. Thus in any circuit you can substitute many kinds of switches and contacts, one for another.

I think it might require a 10-page index in fine print just to list the kinds of contacts that could be used on a model railroad. What I'm going to do here is to help you distinguish the useful switches and contacts and give some pointers in making good use of contacts.

Contact ratings and care

Some fellows are confused by the voltage and current ratings on switches and contacts. The marked ratings are maximums. On a contact rated at 125 v. 10 a. you can use any voltage up to 125 v. and any current up to 10 a. The switch will work equally well at 12 v. or 2 v. or 125 v.

Too much voltage burns the contact when it is opened with a flame-shaped, brighter-than-normal spark. Too much current burns the contact both when opening and closing and may cause the contact to weld together. Too weak spring tension allows the contact to spark and overheat or weld shut even while closed. Also, too much voltage, too heavy a current, or too weak a spring tension can cause a contact to burn at the surface and roughen. You can dress it with a file or emery cloth, but the permanent cure is to stay within the contact rating.

Homemade contacts and cheap switches are often overloaded because they don't have silver or other special metal tips. I have found that they give better service if wetted with No-Ox fluid, which is sold for contact treatment in radios. No-Ox is also an excellent treatment for oxidized rail or wheels and a drop will go a long way.

Some contacts are rated for A.C. or "non-inductive load." This is merely a warning to you about the effect of coils. These contacts can be used on D.C. or A.C., regardless of these markings, and most coils used in model railroading do not damage such contacts. However, a coil does produce an unexpected high voltage at the moment when its current is cut off. If the coil has many turns of wire, as in some relays, then a coil in a 12-v. circuit can produce well over 100 v. for a moment and possibly create an arc at the contact. Our motor and switch machine coils usually do not give this kind of trouble.

Contact terms and mechanics

There are many names for the same things in electric switches because they've come to us from many different industries. When a contact is "closed" it is the same as "on," "made," "connected," "active." Likewise, when it is "opened" it is the same as "off," "broken," "disconnected," "interrupted." The moving part of a contact is called "pole," "wiper," "finger," or the like, depending on the kind of switch and on who's talking. Usually the word pole is understood.

This pole is always able to move to at least two "positions" but one of these positions is sometimes only an "off" position. Some switches, particularly the rotary types, may have 12, 18, or even more positions. This means you can turn a knob to connect the central pole to any of 12 or 18 different circuits.

The word "throw" usually means exactly the same as "position," but there are two very important exceptions. A "single-throw" switch is a two-position switch with one of the positions an off position. A "double-throw center-off" switch is a three-

14-1 The most-used switches for control panels are toggles, upper row. These take a medium amount of panel space and are available at most hobby shops. Often we need more contacts than are available on toggle switches so wafer-type switches, lower row, are beginning to appear in hobby shops. Metal encased single gang switch, lower left, comes in many contact arrangements, such as 6p. dt. or sp. 17t. Two samples of "multigang" switches are shown. These are similar to the single gang except that they are made up of from one to six decks, each deck having as many contacts as the single gang. Lever-action switch, lower right, is a wafer switch mounted on edge to take less panel space. Its handle is moved up or down like a toggle while gang switches are twisted to left or right with a pointer knob.

position switch with the middle position off. Except for these, two throws means two positions, and so on.

Many switches have several poles arranged to move at the same time so several circuits can be switched on and off at the same time. Insulation between the poles keeps the circuits separated electrically. We used switches with an extra pole to switch a lamp on at the same time with block power in Chapter 12. The separate pole allowed us to use different currents for the lamps and trains.

Buying switches

In catalogs, you might find switches listed with various abbreviations for pole, circuit, etc., and for position, throw, etc., but usually the poles are listed first. Thus these are the same:

6 ckt. 11 pos. 6 p. 11 t.

Not all manual switches stay put when you operate them. You already know about push buttons for switch machine control. Then there are toggles and levers of the "momentary" contact type. They have a spring that restores them to normal as soon as you let go. You can use them for looks or when push buttons don't furnish enough poles.

If a particular circuit calls for a contact set or switch with x number of poles and y number of positions, you don't have to get a switch with exactly this number. Any switch with at least as many as x and y will do. The excess poles and positions will do no harm and sometimes you'll find a use for them later on.

Of course, you can substitute any 2 pos. switch for a "single throw" and and 3 pos. for a "double throw," in each case leaving one position unconnected if you still want it to be off.

Diagrams of contacts

Professional wiring diagrams usually show contacts in a "normal" position, which is usually the at rest state. Then a contact that will make when you operate it is called a type A or "make" contact. Here are the three most common types as you might find them on diagrams:

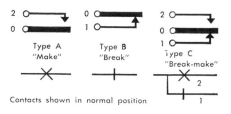

Type A "Make"   Type B "Break"   Type C "Break-make"

Contacts shown in normal position

The symbols shown below the words are an alternate way to draw contacts when you doodle shorthand electrical diagrams. They save a great deal of time.

Sometimes you want a transfer contact to close at 2 before it opens from 1. You can do this by bending the outer springs inward; then it's called a "make-break" contact, or type D. In professional practice, special contact arrangements are used for type D

Useful types of contacts

TOGGLE SWITCHES come only in simple contact arrangements up to 4p. 2t. They mount in ½", or more correctly ¹⁵⁄₃₂", holes and should be fastened tightly or cemented to prevent loosening. It is customary to mount on-off toggles with handle downward for off.

ROTARY, WAFER, or MULTIGANG SWITCHES offer the widest variety of contacts from simple up to as many as 6 poles and 20 or more positions. Unfortunately, there are too many

kinds for hobby shops to stock all, if any, so you may have to order through a model railroad mail order house or from a radio parts supplier. The most useful lines are the metal-encased single-wafer 3200J series by Mallory and the PA series by Centralab. Parts are also sold separately for making up your own PA switches.

In the PA series, a single wafer may be had in any of these arrangements:

4p. 2t.   3p. 3t.
2p. 5t.   1p. 11t.

And more than one wafer may be stacked to multiply the number of poles. The handle turns 15° for each position and a stop can be adjusted to limit the number of positions.

Get "non-bridging" or "non-shorting" switches unless you especially want the circuit to the next pole to be made before breaking the former circuit. Rotaries mount in a ¾" hole and should be anchored so they won't twist in their holes.

LEVER-ACTION SWITCHES are like a single wafer of a rotary, but turned on edge with a togglelike handle passing through a slot in the control panel. See lower right in Fig. 14-1. They are not easy to mount but otherwise quite attractive, and come in contact arrangements up to 2p. 4t. and 4p. 3t.

KEY or ANTICAPACITY SWITCHES are lever switches but with spring-type contacts; see Fig. 14-3. Some mount in a ¹⁵⁄₃₂" hole but most require a rectangular opening and additional holes for screws. Some are imported by PFM and Austin; others are made for telephone switchboards. These have the advantage that you can rearrange their contacts for special arrangements.

SLIDE SWITCHES are usually an economy grade of switch but are also

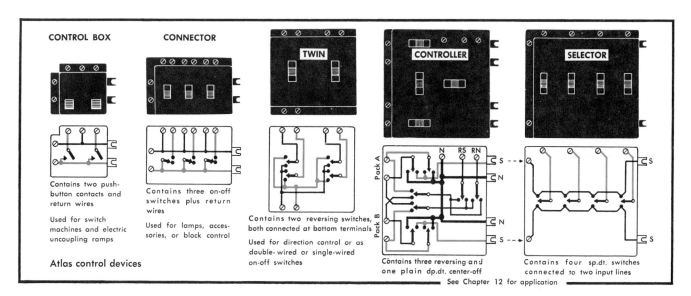

CONTROL BOX

Contains two push-button contacts and return wires

Used for switch machines and electric uncoupling ramps

Atlas control devices

CONNECTOR

Contains three on-off switches plus return wires

Used for lamps, accessories, or block control

TWIN

Contains two reversing switches, both connected at bottom terminals

Used for direction control or as double-wired or single-wired on-off switches

CONTROLLER

Contains three reversing and one plain dp.dt. center-off

See Chapter 12 for application

SELECTOR

Contains four sp.dt. switches connected to two input lines

14 2 Atlas control components are printed circuit slide switches designed for particular tasks on the railroad, but when you know their circuit you can use them for other purposes. Chief advantages are availability, low cost, and quick assembly without soldering or drilling

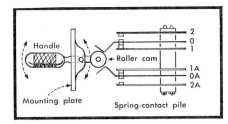

14-3 A typical key switch has additional sets of type C contacts on the far side or perhaps an entirely different arrangement. Note that only the upper sets move when the lever is pushed down. The lower sets move only when the lever is pushed up. So this is more than a center-off switch; it's two separate contact sets that can be operated alternately.

found in the Atlas line; see Fig. 14-2. They are available in about the same contact arrangements as toggles but may take less panel space.

PUSH-BUTTON SWITCHES, familiar for tuning radios, come in various arrangements. The most common is one in which only one button at a time remains depressed. They are handy for switch machine or block selection, but less versatile electrically than multi-gang rotaries.

PUSH BUTTONS are not always of the simple doorbell sort. Some are made with type C contacts or even more

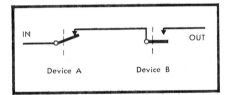

14-5 Contacts in series.

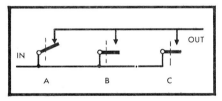

14-6 Contacts in parallel.

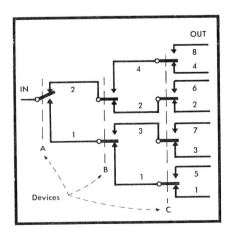

14-7 Contact tree, an expanding series.

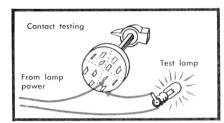

14-4 Any lamp bulb with suitable power supply can be used to check connections inside an unfamiliar switch.

than one set of contacts. Some are adaptations of toggle switches. Any momentary contact type switch will do the same job as a push button.

CONTACT SPRINGS are used on relays, in key switches, and you can use them at turnout throw rods, drawbridges, turntables, and other places where you want contacts to tell when a mechanical operation is started or completed. Separate spring parts are sold for revising relay contact arrangements and the Guardian Series 200 Contact Parts kits are the most available. They come in a miniature size about 1¾" long and a 2½" normal length. You get springs, silver contact rivets, and spacing insulation.

SNAP-ACTION SWITCHES, including the well known "Micro-Switch" brand, are simple, encased contacts that move decisively when an actuating pin is moved only a small distance. They are handy for contacts you want to have either closed or open when something moves to a certain exact point.

How to make substitutions

You can substitute any kind of contact or switch for any other as long as the new one has enough poles and enough active positions for the circuit. If it has more, that's okay.

If you mark the moving poles 0, 0A, 0B, etc., for both the old and new switch, you can keep track of where the old wire connections go on the new switch. Then mark the first position contacts corresponding to these same poles 1, 1A, 1B, etc., and the second position contacts 2, 2A, etc. I've marked the terminals this way in many drawings in this book.

When you don't know the contact arrangement inside a switch, turn it to its first position and check it out with a test lamp, Fig. 14-4. Find all

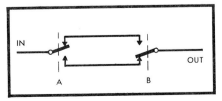

14-8 Two-way series contacts.

contacts that are connected together at this position. For each pair, one will be a 0 and the other a 1 contact. When you turn to the second position you'll know which is which for the 0 contacts will still be active, but now touching the 2 contacts. Keep this up until you've tested out all positions and all terminals.

Contact logic

You may think of contacts just for turning power on and off, but they can do many thinking jobs for you too. For instance, two or more contacts can be wired in series as in Fig. 14-5; then power can get through only if all contacts are made. One use for this is as an emergency power circuit so that a man at either A or B can cut power from all trains.

Contacts arranged in parallel will pass current if any one of them is operated, Fig. 14-6. This circuit is used in our cab lamp indicators so a toggle on any panel will light block indication lamps on all panels.

In Fig. 14-7, you can select either of two circuits with contact A. Add the pair B and you can select any of four circuits depending on which way you throw both A and B. Add the four contacts C on a third lever and you can select any of eight outputs with only three switch handles or other contact devices. This is called a "contact tree." In Fig. 14-8 you can turn a circuit on or off from either place. This is the familiar upstairs-downstairs circuit used in house wiring.

Relays

Don't be afraid of relays. You already know a little about switches and contacts. A relay is only a coil to make these electric contacts move. When you buy a relay you are interested in the contact combination and rating. Besides this you have a choice of voltages A.C. or D.C. for the coil. This is usually just a matter of suiting the coil to the available power. The simple relay on page 44 worked on a very low voltage (about ¼ v. taken in series with the loco). Relays are also sold with 12-v. coils and in model railroading the 24-v. coil relay is often the best choice. This is because it draws less current yet can usually still operate on 12 v. if you adjust its springs carefully.

Here's how to design a relay circuit: First figure out how to make a lamp bulb light at the time you want something to happen. Then replace the lamp with the relay coil. Finally, connect other devices to the relay contacts — signals, switch machines, motors, etc. Then when your lamp would have come on, the devices will operate instead.

15. Building Control Panels

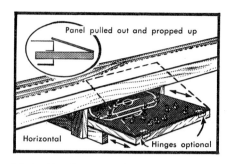

15-1 Flat frame panel can be slid under table. If hinged, it can be propped to a more convenient angle when pulled out. Hinges also allow you to tip the panel up for operation or forward for easy maintenance.

CONTROL panel fronts can be built at any angle from the horizontal. A horizontal panel can be slid out from under the table like a drawer, and thus be out of the way for sweeping or when running trains in some other part of the room; see Fig. 15-1.

A slope of around 30° from horizontal is more comfortable to use as it allows you the largest panel space within easy reach and at a natural angle for operating either sitting or standing, Fig. 15-2. Unfortunately, both these schemes take up a good deal of aisle space so more nearly vertical panels are usually necessary. I usually end up with a panel 60° from horizontal as a compromise, Fig. 15-3.

The lower front edge of the panel must be high enough for you to get your knees under it when operating while sitting on a chair or stool, but preferably high enough so you don't have to droop a shoulder to reach the bottom row of levers when operating while standing. For me, a height that puts the lower edge of the panel 33" above the floor is about the best, but if you're tall, put it a little higher. Usually the upper limit of the panel is determined by your ability to see trackage beyond the top.

You can make a control panel quite wide, up to 60", and still reach all parts of it while sitting. A nice idea for super panels is to build them in L or U arrangements, Fig. 15-5.

Control boxes

The framing behind the panel can be simple, as in Fig. 15-6, and then merely mounted at the desired angle, or if you don't mind the extra carpentry, you can make a box with tri-angular ends as in Fig. 15-7. This not only looks designed for the job, but also furnishes useful "floor" space inside for a power pack or other devices.

Small panels for one or two controls are occasionally needed, particularly at remote areas where switching is done locally or around a railroad where walkaround cab control is used. Little or no framing is needed for these. Sometimes toggles or other controls are merely mounted in the front board of the railroad itself, but a separate small panel usually pays for itself in convenience when making changes in track or wiring.

For larger control panels the all-wood construction is easiest for most fellows to use. Use hardboard, such as Masonite, no thicker than ³⁄₁₆" for the panel front. This material is better than plywood for panels because of its smooth front surface and thinness combined with strength.

Aluminum panel fronts are nice and not much more difficult to cut if you get the type of aluminum sold in hardware stores, but the thickness limits the over-all size to smaller panels. For large panels, say more than 12" in either direction, aluminum or steel of at least 1/16" thickness should be used.

If 115-v. wiring will enter your control panels, for instance to reach un-cased power packs or variable transformers, the high-voltage portions of the control box should be protected from other wiring by being encased in metal. You can use fruit cans, lunch boxes, or you can bend up neater compartments with hardware store aluminum. All-metal control panels

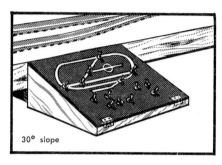

15-2 Low slope is easy to reach when sitting or standing.

can also be made to order for you by a tin shop or heating firm. Use rubber grommets to line holes where wires pass through sheet metal.

Hinges and fastenings

Panel fronts can be screwed down with No. 4 or larger screws about every 6" to 12" around the border. However, it is a good idea to use only hinges along the bottom edge (not the top) of a panel so you can remove the upper screws and then swing the panel front toward you to install, check, or change the wiring. If you put the hinges on top, you have a very awkward situation trying to hold the panel open while working. When you install hinges, check carefully to see that the panel will be able to open all the way without jamming or tearing out the hinge mounting screws. Don't worry about the wiring as it is easy to arrange it for a big zig-zag hinge action.

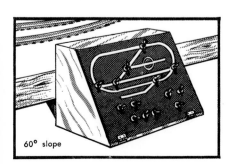

15-3 High slope saves aisle space.

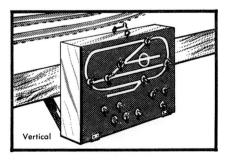

15-4 Vertical panel takes least aisle space.

Console desk on casters

15-5 Any panel can be put on caster cart.

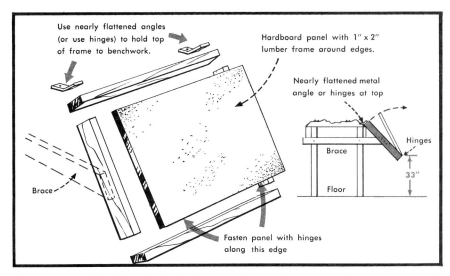

Use nearly flattened angles (or use hinges) to hold top of frame to benchwork.

Hardboard panel with 1″ x 2″ lumber frame around edges.

Nearly flattened metal angle or hinges at top

Hinges

Brace

33″

Floor

Brace

Fasten panel with hinges along this edge

15-6 Frame of 1″ x 2″ lumber is simple support for panel and can be braced at any angle. Screws at sides and top can be removed so panel swings down on hinges for maintenance.

Planning the panel

It is usually better to build a separate small panel for standardized things, such as the throttle units, and then arrange the specialized wiring, such as selector units and towers, on either one large or several medium-size panels. The idea is to preserve the standardized part of your work so you don't have to do it over again if you change track around or move to another house. Also, it's usually easier to wire two medium-size panels than one big one.

I like to put my most-used throttle units at the left so my right hand is left free for flipping toggles and doing other things that take thinking or agility. Throttles in real locomotives are usually left-hand devices.

Things you must look at are usually arranged more toward the top of a panel and rows of toggles or levers toward the sides or bottom. You can use colors, offset position, spacing, or the shape of a handle to help find things quickly.

In using colors, it's usually more satisfactory to associate several blocks in a group with one color rather than to use a different color for every block. Consider how colors and other aids can be helpful for guests who are not yet familiar with your railroad. One suggestion is to assign a group of blocks at a low level a red color, then make other groups cooler colors — orange, yellow, green — with sky blue for the highest level. If you explain this, a guest has an easier time of it because he can see the level of the track and guess the appropriate group color for it.

I've already mentioned that the map-type track diagram with toggles in their proper places is simplest for beginners to use. However, this panel takes up the most space.

When it comes to saving space, a better idea is to unwrap the track plan (Figs. 15-8 and 15-9) and arrange the controls in a straightened version of the plan. This takes a wide panel, but not a very deep one. If you put the plan in two lines, one above the other, the plan is shortened.

You can save still more space by putting toggles in straight rows below the plan and numbering the plan to show where each block and turnout is located. Colors also help on this kind of board so you can quickly relate a lever to its position on the plan. As a compromise, you can place all lamps and certain controls on the diagram, and leave others in a row at the bottom. Finally, to save space to the utmost, you can omit the track diagram and just have a row of controls. A separate track diagram can be hung against the back wall for reference.

Another idea to save panel space is to put the terminal and yard details on a separate control board or else in an open space at the middle of your track diagram.

Toggle spacing

Toggles and other controls will have to be spaced far enough apart so they don't interfere and so you can mount them conveniently. Putting the hex nuts on the front of the panel and using long wires behind controls* allows you to take out any toggle no matter how close it is to others. Wire it before pushing it into its hole. In Fig. 15-9, an imaginary panel layout shows how toggles might be spaced if their outer dimensions were about 1″ x 2″. The track lines are drawn to fit the toggle spacing, not the other way around.

Whether you make a map or straight row panel arrangement, it's a good idea to make a full-size paper panel plan. Then you can lay parts on it to see if they will fit and if they clear the inner sides of the control box. With scissors and tape, you can take out excess panel space where it isn't needed and add strips of paper to make more room somewhere else. Then the final mockup can be used as a drilling template if you fasten it to the panel with rubber cement.

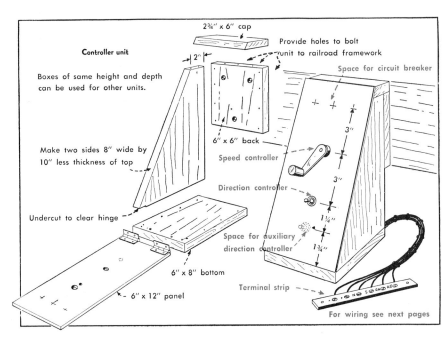

2¾″ x 6″ cap

Controller unit

Boxes of same height and depth can be used for other units.

2″

Provide holes to bolt unit to railroad framework

Space for circuit breaker

Make two sides 8″ wide by 10″ less thickness of top

6″ x 6″ back

Speed controller

3″

Direction controller

3″

Undercut to clear hinge

1¼″

Space for auxiliary direction controller

1¾″

6″ x 8″ bottom

6″ x 12″ panel

Terminal strip

For wiring see next pages

15-7 Height of this panel and box are a near minimum, but width can be increased as desired. Instead of screws, storm-window hooks and latches can be used to fasten box to railroad table.

*Another good reason for leaving rather long wires connected to each toggle is that you can bore new holes and shift toggles to new places should you have to move things around to provide for track or turnout additions.

Now, just a reminder that you have the option of putting turnout controls on one master tower panel, in separate towers near various junctions, on engineer's cab control panels, or in all these places at the same time. Maybe some engineer's cabs will have all controls; some not; some could be map style for visitors, or some row style for your own private use. It all depends on how you want to operate, how much space you have for panels, where the space is located, and how much you want to spend on duplicated controls.

Panel painting

If you use hardboard such as Prestwood for your panel, give it a coat of shellac, or perhaps several coats, so paint won't sink in later on. Then paint the entire panel with the color you want to have for the lines and detail work. Yellow is very attractive for this, but white is just as popular. Use paint in a self-spray can if you don't have a spray gun, or have an auto-body shop do the painting.

Next, add strips of tape across the panel to represent track lines. You can lay them all across, then cut out the places where you don't need tape, more easily and more neatly than to put the tape down in small pieces; see Fig. 15-10. Use tape only ½", ¼", or even ⅛" wide for main tracks and only half that width for side tracks. This difference in width will help to emphasize routes; see Fig. 12-13 in which ½" and ¼" tape was used. Narrower tape gives a less cluttered look to the panel.

Even at this late stage you can move tape around a little for visual improvement if you have not yet drilled the holes. To represent the ends of blocks, cut gaps perhaps ¹⁄₁₆" wide across the tape lines.

Now push the tape down at all overlapping edges and spray the panel dull black or dull Pullman green. This background color will cover everywhere until you pull the tape off. Add decals for numbers and letters (Walthers has a wide variety) and when dry, spray the whole panel with a dull varnish finish.

Interior panel wiring

Your first control panel wiring will probably be done in some haste. Some of the things I'm going to suggest may seem useless right now, but in time you'll find that a little extra care in the proper "dress" of your panel wiring will save a lot of time later on if you must look for trouble, replace a part, or if you want to revise your panel. So don't take the following suggestions too lightly.

1. Choose an adequate but flexible

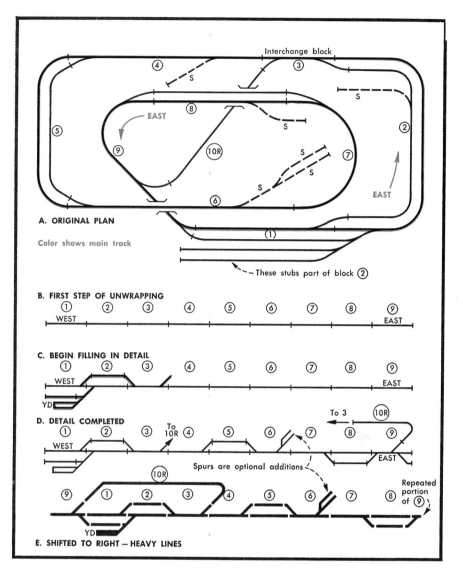

A. ORIGINAL PLAN

Color shows main track

B. FIRST STEP OF UNWRAPPING

C. BEGIN FILLING IN DETAIL

D. DETAIL COMPLETED

Spurs are optional additions

E. SHIFTED TO RIGHT — HEAVY LINES

15-8 A. To develop a straight-line control panel diagram, start with a sketch of the railroad with main route emphasized. At B, a horizontal line has been divided into as many blocks as happen to occur along the main route. Next, at C, details of one block, then another, are filled in. Start at the west entrance to block 1 on the plan and move eastward to one turnout after another. In this particular block, there's only one turnout on the main track at the east end and it branches to the north. Fill in this turnout and also the parallel track on the south side of the main track, then go on to block 2. If you keep in mind eastbound travel, you won't have trouble when blocks on the plan go in some odd actual direction. At D, all blocks are filled in. No attempt was made to join the tag ends that make the return track at block 10R. Just label where any diverging route rejoins the straight line again. In this particular example, we do rejoin these lines in step E, but sometimes you never do. Also in step E, the whole pattern has been shifted one block to the right so the major part of block 9 now appears at the left. You can shift any amount you wish for convenience. This instance allowed convenient rejoining of the return loop and perhaps a better location for yard area controls. You may want to provide for adding industrial spur toggles on your panels

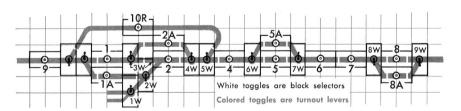

White toggles are block selectors
Colored toggles are turnout levers

15-9 Paper mockup of control panel front might look like this. Diagram E from Fig. 15-8 was redrawn, a toggle at a time starting from the left. The diagram was compressed just as much as possible, limited only by the width of toggles turned one way for blocks, the other way for turnouts. Black rectangles show assumed size of toggles behind panel; ruled colored lines might be a help in planning if all toggles have uniform size such as these, which were twice as long as they were wide. Be sure to allow extra panel length at left and right ends where panel laps over sides of control box.

15-10 Tape is stretched all the way across the panel to get straight lines, then unwanted parts are cut out. Diagonal or curved tape can be used for curved track at corners of space and for return loops, but minor curves in track plan are usually straightened on the panel. Fig. 12-13 shows finished panel.

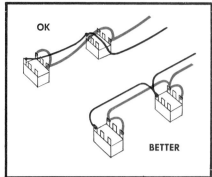

15-11 Wires routed directly from one toggle or other device to the next may save a little time, but the scheme at the right is much more convenient for maintenance as well as original wiring. Wires run around, never across, parts.

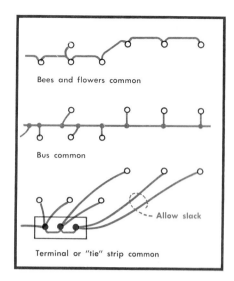

15-12 Compare these common connection schemes with the common rail wiring schemes illustrated on page 52.

type wire that's easy to strip (remove insulation) and easy to fasten to screw or soldered terminals. See Chapter 16.

2. Don't scrimp on wire length. Extra length won't hurt operation but will help in wiring and later in maintenance. On the other hand, you don't want excessively floppy wires hanging in the way either.

3. Don't use more than one or two short, direct wires between toggles or lamps behind the panel as they make parts replacement difficult, Fig. 15-11. For the same reason, leave slack in any wires that pass behind mounted parts so the wires can be pushed aside to get through to the parts.

4. Likewise, keep wires reasonably close to the panel front or box sides so they aren't easily snagged by tools. If many wires run in the same general direction, keep them loose enough so you can tie them into a bundle with scrap ends of wire or masking tape.

5. When the same wire is common to many toggles, bulbs, or other devices, you have a choice of ways to

route it. At the top of Fig. 15-12, the wire flits from one terminal to the next like a bee visiting flowers. This is the easiest to install and is satisfactory if only one or two such wires reach each device.

The bus method is only slightly more complicated. The bus is usually a bare wire located in a nearby but out of the way place. The third method is also simple and is the best for maintenance. Each device has its own wire to a tie point on a suitable terminal strip and as many tie points as necessary are bridged together. How many tie points? Well, a good general rule for all wiring is not to join more than three, or at the most four, wires at any one terminal post. Obviously you can combine these methods.

Methods for soldering wire or at-

taching terminals are discussed in Chapter 16.

Connections to the railroad

In Chapter 17, we'll talk about table wiring and other installation problems. Usually it is not good to run wires from a control panel directly to the track, switch machines and accessories, but rather to a terminal center near the control panel. I find the simplest way to do this is also very effective. It's illustrated in Fig. 15-13.

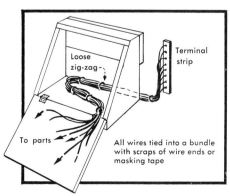

15-13 Fasten a bundle of wires into a zig-zag bend so panel opens easily.

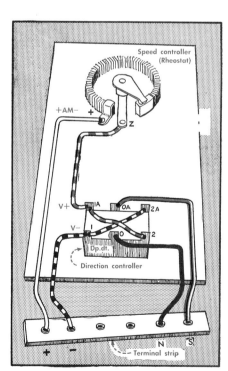

15-14 Be sure wires to terminal strip are 18″ to 24″ long for mounting convenience.

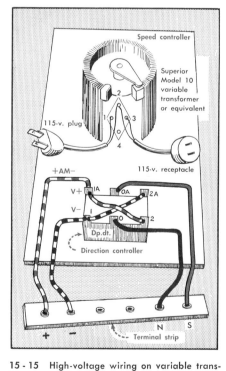

15-15 High-voltage wiring on variable transformer panel has no connection with low-voltage wiring and should be separated by metal case. Connections shown are for the particular make of variable transformer (on which terminal 4 is not used). Check diagrams of other makes for 0 to 120-v. range.

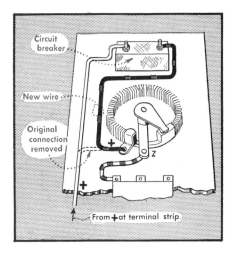

15-16 The proper location for a circuit breaker is in either wire from a transformer or power pack, but ahead of rheostats or reversing toggles. Return power wire to pack is uncut.

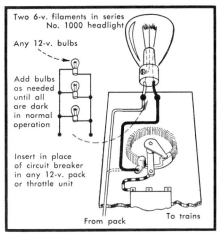

15-17 A headlight bulb or a group of bulbs can be used to replace a circuit breaker. Choose lamps of same voltage rating as the power supply, but add enough bulbs so normal train running current, etc., will not light them. Two 6-v. filaments of headlight bulb, in series, are just right for most HO operations.

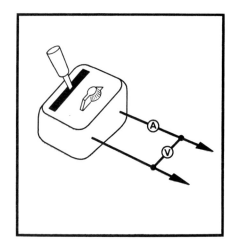

15-18 Ammeters are always cut into one wire of a circuit while voltmeters are bridged between supply wires. If you deduct starting voltage, voltmeter tells you about motor speed. Ammeter, on the other hand, shows how hard loco is pulling or if circuit is open or shorted.

The idea is to route a group of wires to either lower corner of the back of the panel and then turn them back the other way for 8" to 12" in a tied bundle. From here they go as far as necessary to reach a terminal strip. The wires are fastened to the terminal strip in some logical order; if you wish you can trim excess length of any individual wires at this end conveniently if you do it just before soldering or screwing to the terminals. The zig-zag bundle makes a sort of hinge that allows you to open the panel front without any binding. If there are more than 30 wires, start a second bundle.

Plan of action

You can wire all the control panel on the workbench if you are sure of your methods. This will save time.

On the other hand, if you wire the panel in place for one block, then the next, and so on, you can find mistakes more easily because you can try each new toggle and block as you complete its wiring. In either case, you need not cut rail gaps until the toggle wiring is completed for the block.

Home-built throttle units

You might want to build your own throttle unit, either to add a second throttle to a power pack, to use a pack that has no throttle, or merely to incorporate features you don't find in commercial packs. Essentially you need either a rheostat or a variable transformer for speed control, plus a reversing toggle. The basic diagram for the rheostat version is in Fig. 15-14. The + and − terminals connect to the uncontrolled D.C. terminals on any power pack and the N and S go either to the track on a simple pike or to the MAIN and AUX direction controllers, if you have a return track. (If you wish, the MAIN and AUX toggles can also be added to the throttle unit instead of placing them at one edge of your selector panels.)

Rheostat sizes were discussed on page 15. If you prefer to use a variable transformer, it can be mounted in place of the rheostat, preferably in a metal can, and wired as in Fig. 15-15.

Circuit protection

It's a good idea to add a circuit breaker or current limiter so your power pack will not be damaged in case there's an undetected short circuit. The circuit breaker comes with two terminals. Cut the wire at +AM− in either diagram and insert the circuit breaker turned either way around. Fig. 15-16 shows how this might be mounted above a rheostat.

Simple circuit breakers are bimetal strips that mount in fuse clips on the front of the panel. These cost a dollar or perhaps less and do well for a while. In time they should be replaced as they tend to become less sensitive or weld shut with age. More de luxe circuit breakers are made that look like oversize toggle switches. A rating of 3 a. is about right for HO or 5 a. for O gauge, but the rating is not critical.

Thermal circuit breakers are usually better than magnetic just because the magnetic types may pop off too quickly and stop trains more often than necessary. However, a magnetic type with a built-in time delay, such as the Heinemann breaker, is excellent.

Current limiter bulbs

A lamp bulb makes one of the best current limiters and many model railroaders prefer it to a circuit breaker because it protects your power pack automatically and doesn't need resetting. It works on the principle that a hot bulb has a much higher resistance than a cold one. You select a bulb that is large enough so it remains cold when train-running current

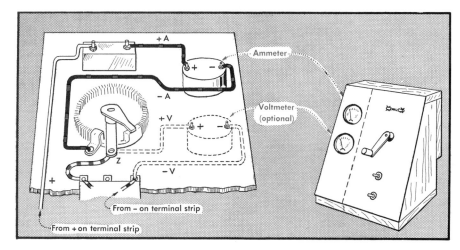

15-19 How built-in meters may be added to homemade controller unit or commercial power pack.

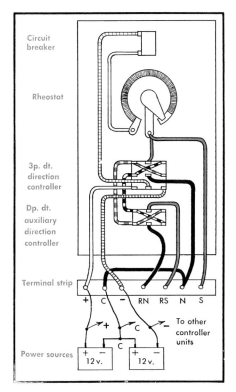

15-20 Special throttle unit wiring for use with twin power supply makes it unnecessary to flip two toggles at once.

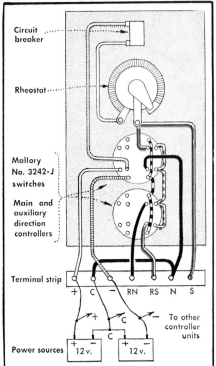

15-21 Wiring is same as in Fig. 15-20, but using Mallory 3242J rotary switches which have four poles each. Not all poles are needed here.

The popular center-zero meter is not so good for this very reason, because it gives you only half the scale length to read at a time. It's a meter scale only half as big as it should be. (Sometimes it's the only kind you can use or would want for other reasons.)

A meter rated at 3 a. or 5 a. won't tell you much about a train drawing only ½ a. For HO a small meter should be rated at 1 a. or not more than 1.5 a. and a long-scale meter at perhaps 3 a. This is because what you want to know is how much current the train draws while running. The amount of current drawn during a short circuit is of little importance and any meter will swing violently to the right to tell you when you do have a short.

For voltmeters, the ideal scale is probably 15 v. Even though some power packs will push the needle beyond the scale to the right when there's dirt on the rails, higher voltages aren't often used in running trains. Again, it's the voltage during normal operation that you want to know about.

Perhaps a good plan is to install cheap meters, or just an ammeter, beside each throttle. Then arrange a plug or some other way to connect a pair of high-quality test meters into any throttle unit for testing or de luxe readings while operating. (Good meters cost about $12 each for the 4″ size.)

An ammeter reads current only if you pass the current through the meter. The meter causes no appreciable voltage loss. You can cut any wire and connect the two loose ends to the meter.

Since the current around a simple (one train) circuit is the same all the way around, you can cut the wires anywhere. But the usual place to cut them is ahead of the reversing switch, at +AM- in the drawings on page 70. This is because polarity doesn't change in the wiring until after passing through the reversing switch. The meter will work following a reversing switch only if polarity is right or if you use a center-zero meter.

You can add a meter to any power pack this way just as well as to build it into a throttle unit. See illustration in Chapter 3.

Connecting a voltmeter is all the easier because you don't cut wires. You just connect it between any two places and read the voltage difference. If you connect ahead of the speed controller, you get the power supply voltage; if after the speed controller, you get the voltage sent to the train (including any voltage lost in the feeders).

The usual place to connect a voltmeter is at V+ V- in the drawings,

passes through it. However, if a short circuit occurs, the extra current makes the bulb hot, which in turn limits the current to a relatively safe value. The bulb lights up at the same time, warning you of the short.

Use any bulb rated at the operating voltage, but for four to eight times as much as normal operating current. You can use several 12-v. bulbs in parallel to protect any model railroad circuit. Keep adding bulbs until none of them glow when passing normal current. Thus you can protect accessory circuits as well as train-running circuits. If you can still get one, the size 1000 automobile headlight bulb is just right for train-running circuits, Fig. 15-17. It has a resistance of about

¼ ohm when cold, but limits short circuit current to 3 a.

Ammeters and voltmeters

Meters help you run trains, but more important they help you find troubles. I have operated for months on end without any meters so I know you can get along well without them. On the other hand, when you once use good meters you'll always want them.

Most meters I've seen around model railroads are rather poor because they have an unsuitable scale. Low-priced meters have to have a rather small scale, so it's important that the needle travels as far across the scale as possible so you can see small changes in voltage or current more easily.

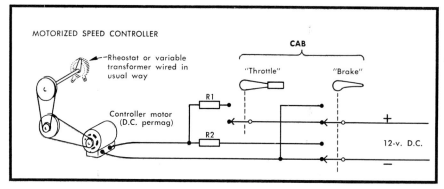

15-22 Easy way to control motorized throttle makes use of single contacts for throttle and double poles for brake. Resistors R1 and R2 may be added to adjust rates of acceleration and braking separately. A more elaborate scheme might substitute a rheostat for the throttle contact and a multiposition switch for the brake, so several rates of braking plus emergency can be used.

again because polarity is always the same. If you connected to points beyond the reversing switch, you'd sometimes have wrong polarity for a reading or again have to use a center-zero meter.

Usually we use D.C. meters, but some A.C. types are usable, if not accurate, on both A.C. and D.C. Generally the wrong kind of current won't hurt the meter if it is of about the usual voltage or current value. The needle just won't give a reading or may vibrate.

Be careful not to connect an ammeter between any two points, for it has such low resistance that it will act like a short circuit through itself, possibly damaging itself or other equipment. Connect an ammeter only into normal current paths by cutting wires.

On the other hand, a voltmeter is not damaged by wrong connections unless connected into circuits of rather high voltage.

It doesn't hurt a meter to connect it with the wrong polarity into the circuit; the needle just tries to go the wrong way harmlessly. Also, a meter can take quite a bit more voltage or current than it is rated for, at least for a short time. The most common damage that occurs to any meter is the bending of the needle if it moves too suddenly on over-voltage or over-

current. With care, the case can be opened and the needle bent straight again, but watch out for hair-size wires that are easily snagged and ripped.

A throttle unit with built-in meters is shown in Fig. 15-19.

Twin power throttle units

Special wiring is used in throttle units for use with twin power supply. In the example on page 9, a simple toggle was shown for reversal and this is adequate for any railroad without return tracks. However, when you have a return track, this ordinary wiring scheme becomes awkward to use. This is because in shifting from one power pack to the other in preparing to go the other way down the main line, you inadvertently reverse the train in the loop as well. This requires taking your hand off the throttle and flipping both the MAIN and AUX toggles at the same time.

The scheme in Fig. 15-20 overcomes this by using a 3 p. dt. toggle or switch for the MAIN. Fig. 15-21 shows the same using a Mallory rotary switch, as this may be easier to obtain than a triple-pole toggle. In these examples, there is no plain reversing switch, just the MAIN and AUX, and perhaps we have things complicated enough without adding the third switch.

De luxe throttle units

You can build a miniature engineer's seat and arrange the cab like the cab of a real locomotive if you wish, Fig. 15-23.

Some model railroaders have enjoyed operation with a throttle with a "flywheel" effect, or what might be called "controlled acceleration." The idea is to have some kind of delayed action between the throttle lever and the performance of the loco. This has been done with pneumatic time-delay devices, motors, vacuum tubes, and more recently with transistors. I'll present only one such idea here and that only in a rough sketch.

In Fig. 15-22 the speed controller, whether a rheostat or variable transformer, is operated by a meter. In the control cab, a throttle lever can wind the throttle motor up while a brake lever winds it down by reversing polarity. If neither lever is pulled, the motor leaves the speed controller alone.

In operation, you pull the throttle and the motor moves the speed controller which begins to increase track voltage. Soon the train starts slowly It gains speed only gradually but continues to accelerate as long as you pull the throttle. If you release the throttle handle, the train continues to run at the same speed, much like the drifting (coasting) of a real train. The only way you can stop the train is to pull the brake lever and then it stops only gradually, like a real train.

If your track is clean the effect is wonderfully realistic. It has the advantage of making operations much more like real railroading. You have to plan ahead to stop at a station or else you'll overshoot it just like a rookie engineer. In yard switching, it will drive your guests batty. It's a wonderful way to increase the fun of operation.

This scheme also fits well into walk-around control systems. You can carry the throttle and brake levers (or use multicontact push buttons for them) at the end of a four-wire flexible cable. Then as you walk around with the train you can make it accelerate or apply its brakes. Two more wires would be needed to control reversing, or else you could save wire in the cables by making use of relays to operate the controls.

To keep the centralized motor-driven rheostat in contact with your particular train, you can add selector switches at each block around the room, wired according to the scheme shown in Fig. 12-14. As your train approaches a new block, turn the cab selector to pick up your individual rheostat or "cab."

15-23 Ed Spinney of Wauwatosa, Wisconsin, built this cab to simulate a real railroad cab.

16. Wire

ELECTRICAL "hookup" wire is a type of wire well suited for model railroad purposes. Although I shall tell you the types I use and why, your dealer may have other varieties of wire that are equally good. However, don't just use wire because you have it around the house or can get it at a bargain. Old wire and bargain wire may be brittle, hard to strip, untinned, or so badly oxidized that it is difficult to solder.

Wire size is graded in AWG (American Wire Gauge) numbers; the lower the number, the larger the wire. A size of wire three numbers higher than another means wire half as big in cross-sectional area and thus able to carry only half as much current safely. Size 23 wire can safely carry only half as much current as size 20.

In the chart below, you can see that small copper wire can carry the currents we use in model railroading. We don't often use wire smaller than about size 26 because smaller sizes lack mechanical strength.

Solid wire is useful when you don't want to solder because it fits nicely under screw terminals. It is also used where you want rigidity. I prefer it in size 22 or 24 for the wiring from one part to another on the back of a control panel where the flexibility of stranded wire isn't needed. The fault of stranded wire is that it tends to fray at the ends, especially if you try to use it under screw terminals. You can touch solder to the wire end before shaping it, but then you might as well add a terminal lug or use solder for the entire joint.

In spite of this fault, stranded wire is best for most model railroad uses because you must often shove wire this way and that and stranded wire is not harmed by this.

Stranded wire has the same amount of copper as solid wire, but divided into many small wires in a bundle within the sheath of insulation.

The insulation on wire must be reasonably flexible, too, but most important, it should be easy to strip off at the ends for making connections. The most commonly used wire has thermoplastic insulation, a rubberlike colored plastic that strips easily. It has the fault that if a hot soldering iron accidently touches it, the insulation peels off and sticks to everything else around. So where this might be a bother, and where you might need a little more resistance to mechanical wear, such as in the zig-zag of Fig. 15-13, I prefer what is called lacquered cellulose braid. This is a harder plastic with a cloth braid under the shell. It is quite flexible but not what you'd call limp.

Wire size

If a wire is too small for the current it handles, it can overheat, burn, or melt its insulation. This causes a short circuit that makes things all the worse. Small wire does this more easily than large wire because it has more resistance per foot and thus wastes more heat per foot for the same current.

In columns five and six of the chart below, safe currents are shown for wires in free air and unventilated quarters. As you can see, quite small sizes of wire are adequate for model railroad needs on this safe-heat score.

Larger wire may be needed for its mechanical strength. On long lines large wire is needed to reduce the voltage loss. This is because small wire wastes more voltage per foot than larger wire carrying the same current. But the voltage lost in small wire is insignificant for short lengths of wire, such as between parts around or inside a control panel or from a terminal under the table to the rail above it. For this reason, it is good practice to use small wire in tight places where its ease of handling is important, but to use larger wire for the long runs to distant locations.

I'll describe the types of wire I use, but you may substitute other kinds. Depending on your railroad, you can limit yourself to one size of wire, or use several sizes. You can substitute one size of wire for another within wide limits.

For any purposes up to an 8-foot total length (two wires running up to 4 feet from the control panel) the wire called "indoor antenna wire," such as Belden No. 8014, is handy. This is size 25 AWG stranded and so flexible you can use it between locomotive and tender or to a power truck. I also use it from the side of a rail to a connection with larger wire under the table, Fig. 17-13, and for much general wiring for short distances. It is low in cost and has a gray "chrome" thermoplastic covering. It sells in 25-foot and 500-foot spools.

From part to part within a control panel you can use this same wire, or you may prefer size 22 or 24 solid wire, which is perhaps the easiest wire to solder as well as to fasten under screw terminals.

I've already mentioned the use of

Wire Sizes and Characteristics

Wire size AWG	Diameter Inches	Copper Ohms per 100 ft. 68°F	Copper Feet per Ohm	Copper Safe current in amperes In free air	In closed space	Nichrome Ohms per Foot
12	0.080	0.16	625	30	15	0.092
14	0.064	0.25	400	25	13	0.146
16	0.051	0.40	250	20	10	0.233
18	0.040	0.64	156	15	8	0.370
20	0.032	1.02	98	10	5	0.589
22	0.025	1.61	62.4	8	4	0.936
24	0.020	2.57	39.9	5	3	1.49
26	0.016	4.08	24.9	4	2	2.37
28	0.013	6.49	15.5	3	1.5	3.76
30	0.010	10.3	9.7	2.5	1.3	5.98
32	0.008	16.4	6.20			9.52
34	0.006	26.1	3.98			15.1
36	0.005	41.5	2.48			24.1
38	0.004	66.0	1.52			38.3
40	0.003	104.9	0.96			60.8

AWG wire sizes   22 20 18 16 14 12

cellulose braid insulation from control panel parts to the terminal strip. This can be either 20, 22, or smaller stranded wire. Size 18 is a little big for this because you will have greater difficulty in soldering large sizes of stranded wire in close quarters.

Distance is important when you choose wire to run from the terminal strip to the blocks, switch machines, and accessories. You can select the wire size to fit the greatest distance from control panel to a block and use this same size for all other feeders as well. Then a train in the farthest block will get only ¼ v. less voltage than a train at the control center.

Wire sizes for various distances

Assuming a 1 a. current and two feeders, one coming, the other return.

Distance from panel in feet	Copper wire size, AWG
3	26
4	25
5	24
8	22
12	20
20	18
30	16
50	14

This table is conservative, for your rail joiners will give you more voltage loss than many feet of wire. The ¼-v. loss in a distant block might slow a low-geared or rubber-band loco perhaps 10 scale miles an hour below its speed near the control center. Higher geared locos will hardly be affected. You could use the same wire sizes for two or three times the distances with reasonably good results.

However, you can completely eliminate this speed change by using the table a different way. Use different wire sizes as shown according to the distances to each block and speed will then be the same everywhere because the voltage loss will be constant.

Extra-large wire

While you might use heavy lumber on a model railroad to make it sturdy, you don't always want to use this same logic with wiring, for wire that's too heavy may mean poorly made connections at terminal strips or mechanical troubles from expansion and contraction. Use large wire only where heavy current requires it.

Wires that will carry from 3 a. to 6 a. should be selected four AWG numbers lower (larger wire) than shown on the table above. This would be for common return feeders from track, and perhaps from switch machines and lamps too. Also, use large size wire on any long power feeders from power packs or batteries.

If you need only a few feet of wire in a size larger than you have, run two smaller wires side by side.

17. Installation

YOU are often advised to read an instruction sheet completely before starting to build a car or locomotive. Can you do it? Even if you can, I'll bet it isn't easy reading and that some details of construction remain hazy. But after you build the kit you could build another without any instructions.

Well, that goes for wiring too. You may or may not read all of this book before starting, and you'll certainly have no better than a hazy idea of some things anyway. But it will all clear up *after* you have installed the actual wiring and run some trains.

Therefore, go ahead in blind faith. Nothing very serious can happen and any wrong connection you make can be corrected in three minutes.

I've suggested that first you wire the railroad so one train can go everywhere (no blocks, but with return tracks if necessary). When you get good one-train operation, add one block toggle as we did back in Fig. 12-1 and make sure it works properly. As you add more toggles, cut the gaps for the additional blocks one by one. Then you can find any mistake you make and correct it right away. If you were to wire 10 toggles before checking, you might need 30 minutes to fix the mistakes instead of only three minutes. Of course, after you know your way you'll save time by wiring groups of toggles all at once — that's what veterans do.

Cut your first block gaps in some remote place where the wiring problems are simple, then work toward the yards and complicated junctions, reaching them last. When you do get to them, the basic scheme will be familiar so tackling special problems will be easier.

Control panel location

We talked about the shape of control panels but not their location. Most model railroaders put the master control panel within easy reach of the main yards so they can see congested track more easily and be within reach in case of derailment. If you add other cab panels, you can place them nearby so all engineers work near each other,

or you can put the cabs at some place chosen for a good view of most of the main line. I like this last idea better.

Another scheme is to put some or all engineers' panels on long cables so you can change their locations. In clubs, the favorite place for cab control panels is on a balcony where the entire main line can be viewed. Usually towers for turnout control should be close to the track they influence.

Labeling wires and feeders

The next thing I will tell you about is a master wiring diagram. To help you read the diagram, first let's talk about labeling wires even though we're a bit ahead of need.

You will want to develop some kind of a system so you can find any wire at a terminal strip. You may be able to accomplish this just by arranging the wires in some logical order on the strip. More often you'll want to use colors or written symbols to identify each wire. In a printed book we have to use the written label system so I'll tell you a bit about it. The idea is to name each wire briefly, but not so briefly that you can't understand it. For instance, you won't have much trouble remembering that wire COM is a common power return and 9RW the wire to the Reverse coil of sWitch machine 9, but you'd have more trouble if these same wires happened to be labeled 349X and KJ9V because these last codes are not in any way suggestive.

Generally it's good to use few digits and letters for the most-used wires, such as B for block or WP for switch machine power. Then use longer codes of three-letter "words" for wires you don't use so often because three letters per word will help you a good deal in remembering, such as DBR for drawbridge or SCJ for Scoville Junction.

The table on page 77 shows a code used in some of the drawings in this book. To these letter codes you can add a number or other letters to show which of several like wires you are labeling. Again, try to use number systems that are simple. We discussed some of these back on page 40.

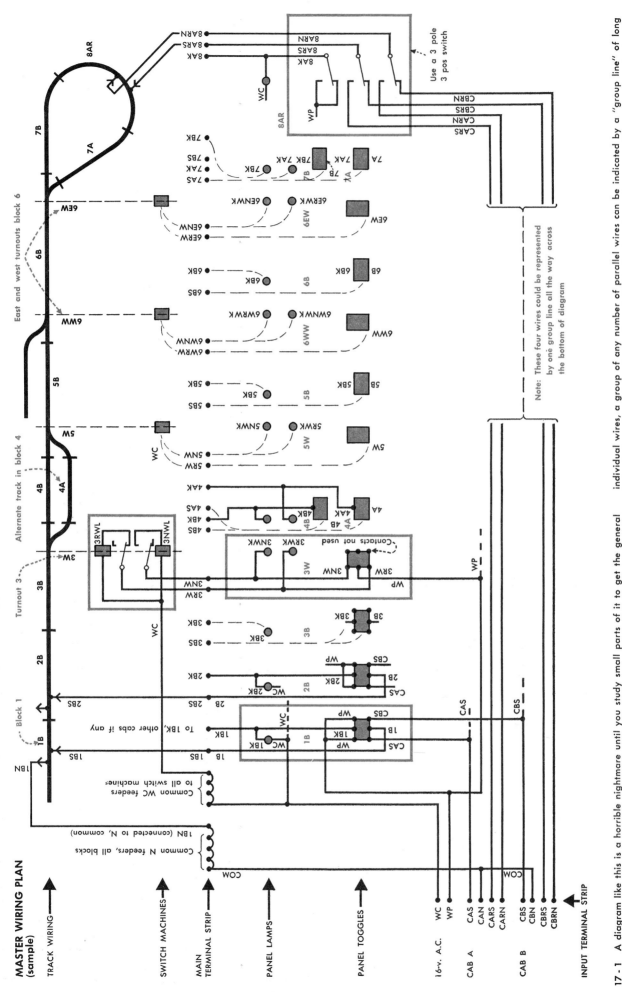

MASTER WIRING PLAN (sample)

Note: These four wires could be represented by one group line all the way across the bottom of diagram

17-1 A diagram like this is a horrible nightmare until you study small parts of it to get the general scheme in mind. In the left-hand colored rectangle, all wires associated with one block toggle and its lamp are detailed. However, block toggle 2B has a simplified drawing with control wires shown but not power connections merely labeled. The diagram can be simplified still more if you assume the power connections to be repeated and merely label the control wires as in block 3. Instead of showing individual wires, a group of any number of parallel wires can be indicated by a "group line" of long light dashes. The labels show where individual wires leave the group line at each end. In the central rectangles, turnout lever, lamp, and switch machine control wiring are shown in detail but are not repeated at other turnout levers to the right. At the far right is a three-pole switch for a return track plus its panel lamp. This would be repeated if there were other return tracks on the railroad.

Color-coded wires

Since you can get wire in many colors and you can also add dabs of model dope to color the ends of plain color wires, color is often a help in identifying circuits.

You can use color in many ways, but it makes more sense to use it mostly to tell similar wires apart. For instance, it is usually rather obvious that a wire is a switch machine wire and not a block feeder because of where it starts and ends and because it might be in a group with other switch machine wires on a terminal strip. You don't need color to tell wires in different function systems apart as much as to distinguish individual wires within a system.

Thus, red might be used for both S rail feeders and reverse switch machine coils. Black might be common return in each case, and green might be used for the normal switch machine coil.

Master wiring plan

One of the most important things you need is some kind of plan that shows which wires connect to where. Perhaps your wire coding alone will do it for you, but most fellows like to have some kind of record on paper.

You can draw a master wiring diagram on paper showing every wire everywhere if you wish. This is a lot of work and it can introduce some mistakes, but it does help you understand the whole job ahead of time. It takes a very big sheet of paper if your railroad is more than medium sized.

If you merely label track feeders on the track plan you have already sketched, you need not draw the track plan again on your master wiring diagram. That's up to you.

In order to save time, you may want to take some short cuts in making up the master wiring plan. This is a matter of abbreviating any details that are obvious. In Fig. 17-1, I have drawn a master wiring diagram for several blocks, switch machines, plus their indicator lamps using common power return, and combining circuits we used for dual throttle cab control in Chapter 12. However, since much wiring is a rubber-stamp repetition, detailed wiring is drawn only where necessary. At the left in a colored rectangle is complete detailed wiring for one block. In the center, complete wiring is shown for turnout control; at the right, for a return track with indicator lamp. You'll see by the caption how much of a drawing can be omitted, providing you can still understand it. If you can't, draw in more of the details.

If the circuits are reasonably clear

to you, you can make an even more simplified master plan. Just draw the circuits I've shown in the colored rectangles and then draw the terminal strips complete with all connections labeled. Omit all else.

If you can get along with an abbreviated diagram, you will have fewer chances of making a mistake in the drawing and then wiring the mistake into the railroad.

The role of terminal strips

On any but the smallest railroads, a terminal strip or several strips should be provided with at least one terminal for every wire going in and coming out of the control panel. The terminal strip is a sort of oasis along the line of a wire. It helps keep wires organized so you can identify them; it protects parts in the control box from being bent or broken if a wire should be snagged; and it allows you to do the work in two steps, track to strip first and then terminal strip to control box.

The terminal strip is essential if you are going to connect more than one panel to the same blocks or switch machines. The most important of all uses is for testing. You'll be able to run down wiring troubles quickly if you can touch your trouble light to one terminal after another all at one location. If you must disconnect a wire to find a short circuit, here's the place to do it.

I like to use terminal strips in pairs or sets behind control panels as in Fig. 17-2. Then if I must disconnect the control box, I just cut the bare jumper wires between the strips rather than to disconnect every wire. When the strips are replaced beside each other, I merely renew each jumper wire. If I had used only one strip here, I would have had to identify and reconnect each wire individually. With two strips their proper order is preserved.

You can put any number of strips side by side in this manner and that's a good way to plan to add more cab control panels. See Fig. 17-3.

See page 40 for block number code.

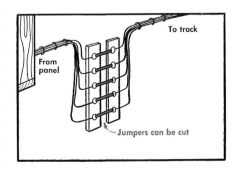

17-2 Siamese-twinned terminal strips make it easier to install and revise control panels.

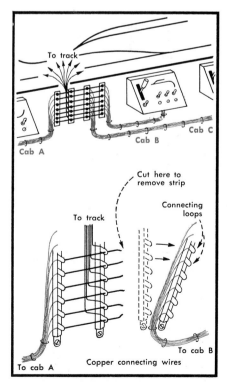

17-3 Several terminal strips wired alike are mounted side by side to join cabs to track.

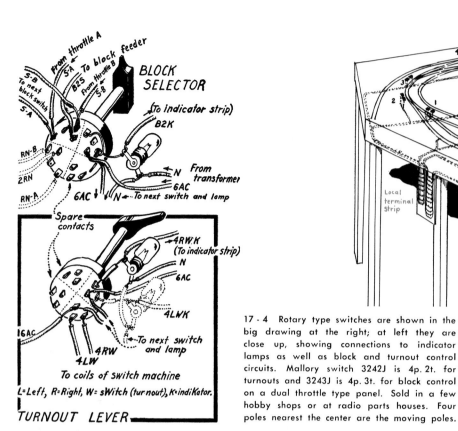

17 - 4 Rotary type switches are shown in the big drawing at the right; at left they are close up, showing connections to indicator lamps as well as block and turnout control circuits. Mallory switch 3242J is 4p. 2t. for turnouts and 3243J is 4p. 3t. for block control on a dual throttle type panel. Sold in a few hobby shops or at radio parts houses. Four poles nearest the center are the moving poles.

Types of terminal strips

The most economical terminal strips are designed only for soldered connections, such as in Fig. 17-5. More expensive strips have one or even two screw heads per terminal, Fig. 17-6. The advantage is that you can connect and disconnect without soldering. Disconnecting soldered terminals is easy enough, but you may not always want to wait for the iron to heat up.

Terminal lugs

If you use solid wire under screw terminals, you can bend it into a small hook like a backward question mark, preferably with wire bending pliers. Stranded wire isn't so well behaved and it is better to touch the wire end with solder before bending, or to use a terminal lug. Spade-tongue lugs slip under terminals quickly but ring-tongue lugs stay in place better because you must remove the screw to take them off. I buy ring lugs and snip

out a side for the few times I want a spade tongue. See Fig. 17-6.

Ordinary lugs are soldered to the wire but solderless lugs are being used more and more. These are made in the A-MP and the Lynn lines, each requiring a special crimping tool. The tool is also a wire stripper, cutter, and in the case of the A-MP tool, also a handy screw cutter that doesn't ruin threads when you shorten screws. See Fig. 17-12. Recently special toggle switches have been made with slip-on crimp terminals so an entire control panel could be built without either soldering or screws.

Assigning terminals

When you have several wires to connect together, there's a limit as to how many can be conveniently attached to one terminal. Perhaps three or four wires is a limit to strive for at each terminal, but the size of the wire will affect this. When a terminal becomes overcrowded, you can assign

several spaces side by side for the same purpose. In Fig. 17-1, several spaces were allocated for common returns at the left end of the horizontal terminal strip. It's also a good idea to plan spare terminals for expansion.

There is no rule as to where to put things along the terminal strip, but it helps a lot to have some system. Putting common terminals together is usually more practical than spreading them, but you might want to put each three terminals for each switch machine in a group, including a common return connection. Each idea has its merits. In general, it's just as well to keep all switch machine feeders entirely separate from blocks. Lamps would be in a third grouping and power from power packs in a fourth.

In any case, be sure you have some way of telling which wire is which, either by color, location, a letter-number code written beside the terminals, in a notebook, or on a card tag attached to the table nearby.

Feeder routing

Feeders can be slung into hooks made from excess coat-hanger wire and fastened to the back side of the front board of the railroad table, Fig. 17-8. This is just about the best location for them. Then as you string feeder wires from the central terminal strip to other locations, you go as far as you can just slipping the wire up into the hooks. When you come to a point opposite the final terminal of the feeder, you crawl under the table for the first time.

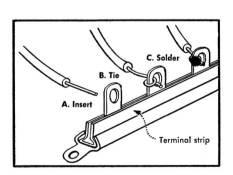

17 - 5 Wrap wire a half or full turn through a terminal before soldering for a secure joint.

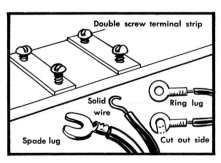

17 - 6 Use lugs on stranded wire under screw-type terminal strips. Limit: three lugs per screw.

Control Panorama
How your complete wiring installation might look.

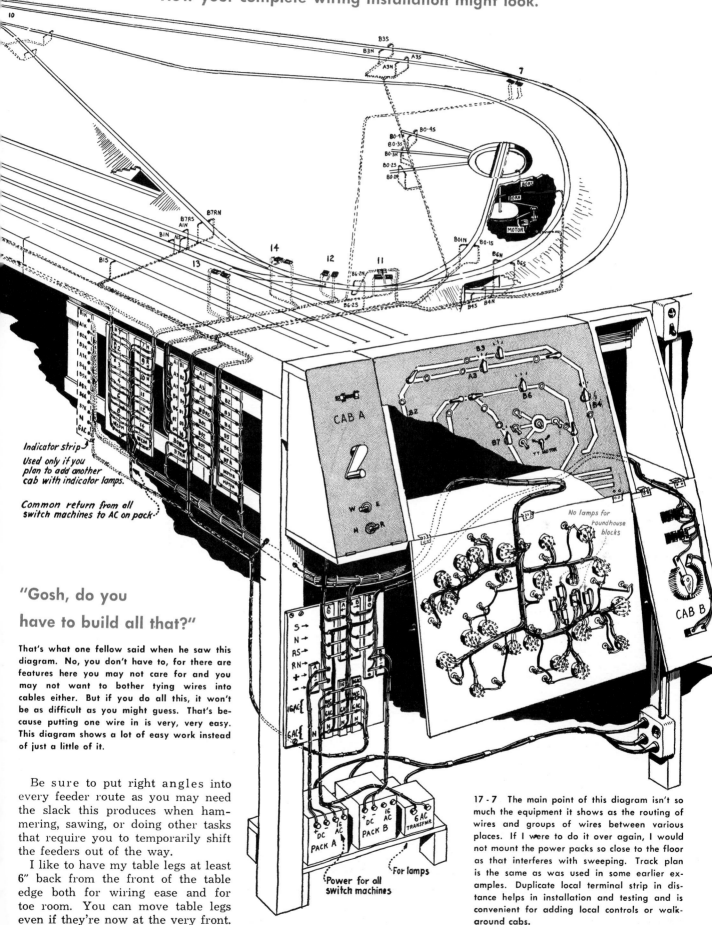

Indicator strip
Used only if you plan to add another cab with indicator lamps.

Common return from all switch machines to AC on pack

No lamps for roundhouse blocks

CAB A

CAB B

Power for all switch machines

For lamps

"Gosh, do you have to build all that?"

That's what one fellow said when he saw this diagram. No, you don't have to, for there are features here you may not care for and you may not want to bother tying wires into cables either. But if you do all this, it won't be as difficult as you might guess. That's because putting one wire in is very, very easy. This diagram shows a lot of easy work instead of just a little of it.

Be sure to put right angles into every feeder route as you may need the slack this produces when hammering, sawing, or doing other tasks that require you to temporarily shift the feeders out of the way.

I like to have my table legs at least 6" back from the front of the table edge both for wiring ease and for toe room. You can move table legs even if they're now at the very front.

17-7 The main point of this diagram isn't so much the equipment it shows as the routing of wires and groups of wires between various places. If I were to do it over again, I would not mount the power packs so close to the floor as that interferes with sweeping. Track plan is the same as was used in some earlier examples. Duplicate local terminal strip in distance helps in installation and testing and is convenient for adding local controls or walk-around cabs.

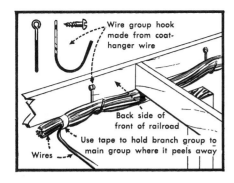

17-8 View of feeders supported in hooks as seen from rear through table top.

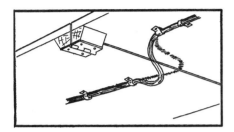

17-9 Wires across hinged portion of railroad should make offset bend and have some slack.

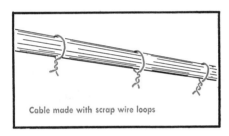

17-10 Loops of scrap wire or even masking tape can tie wires into cables quickly. Below, Henry Stange of South Bend devised this cart for working under the railroad table. You can make back support hinged for adjustable height.

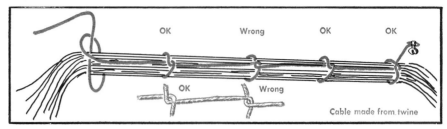

17-11 Professional way to lace a cable starts at a firm anchor. String or special waxed cord is looped around bundle of wires every 4" to 6"; make sure the string runs under each loop as this keeps it tight if you let go. Use hard, smooth wrapping string about twice as long as the length of the cable. Branch cables can use main cable as anchor for twine.

Our drawings often show feeder wires tied into neat "cables," but you don't have to make a practice of this sort of thing. Cable lacing does help to prevent damage and makes things look less disorganized if you bundle feeder wires, but you can do this with a small length of paper masking tape or even a leftover scrap of wire. Space the ties only as close as is necessary to keep individual wires from wandering.

When you tie wires into a cable, you'll find some wires are longer than others. The excess slack can be tolerated at the ends farthest from the main terminal strip. If you wish, you can retrim all wires to obtain even length.

Estimating wire needed

When you estimate feeder lengths, measure laterally, longitudinally, and vertically and add the three, rather than taking diagonal measurements. You can measure for all feeders individually and get a precise total, but you can get an accurate total more easily if you merely add the length of the shortest feeder to the longest, then multiply this by one fourth of the total number of feeders. This will come out just right if the feeder lengths are evenly distributed between the long and short limits.

In any case, allow 12" per feeder for scrap and terminal bends or 24" for those feeders that must make a zig-zag hinge bend, as in Fig. 15-13.

Inside the panel, you'll need about as much wire as the height of the panel plus its width times ⅔ of the number of wires entering the panel, more or less depending on how you route the wires.

Stripping wire ends

Many kinds of tools are helpful in removing insulation from the ends of wire and in general the price of the stripping tool is about in proportion to its convenience. See Fig. 17-12 for a de luxe and a medium price example.

Usually only ¼" of insulation need be removed. In any case, try to avoid nicking the wire or scraping the metal part of it with the stripping tool; weakened ends may break off later.

Soldering tools

Soldering wire and rail is about the easiest kind of soldering you can do. If you've shunned soldering up to now, this is a good place to try it.

You'll probably need only one soldering iron, a midget rated at 25 w. or a little more. A big iron would be needed only if you have joints with lots of metal around them. Of course, if you can afford two irons, you'll find a trigger type very handy. In any case, your wire joining will be easier with a tip about ⅛" in diameter.

If the tip of the iron gets black, file it clean and retin it with fresh solder. Wipe off the excess droplet of tin, using a rag or paper towel.

Much of the beginner's dislike for soldering can be blamed on the solder and flux he uses. Some dimestore and hardware store solders are poor alloys and some of the fluxes sold are a swindle. For instance, one commonly sold soldering paste is labeled to sound like it won't corrode metal, yet it's one of the worst offenders of all with stranded wire. It is a petroleum jelly with acid in it and acid should never be used around stranded wire.

Use only resin core solder of a top brand, such as Ersine Multicore, Kestor's Resin 44 or Kester's Resin 5.

Resin is an acid too, but only when hot. When cold it's an inert plastic that causes no harm to tin, lead, copper, etc.

Normal soldering

Let the iron heat a little longer than enough to melt the solder. Fasten the wire to the terminal so it holds on a little mechanically without solder. Touch the tip of the iron to the wire on the terminal. Touch the solder to the terminal itself nearby. When hot enough, the solder will flow onto the terminal and from there to the wire. If both wire and terminal have been wetted by the solder, remove the iron, but don't disturb the wire until the solder freezes. This should take from two to ten or more seconds.

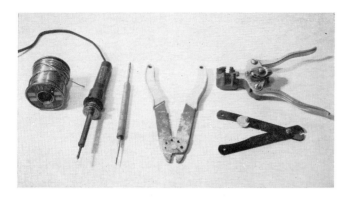

17-12 Midget soldering iron and resin core solder are best for many model wiring jobs. Pointed tool is radio repairman's "soldering tool" for holding wires or for removing them from terminals. Solder won't stick to its alloy points. At center is A-MP terminal crimping tool which also strips, cuts wire and screws. At right are de luxe and plain wire strippers. Wire forming and cutting pliers are also handy.

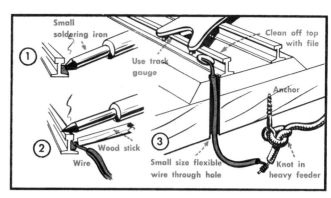

17-13 Tin the rail side, then wipe off soldering iron and place it on top of rail for final joint. Hold tinned wire in place with small wood stick. If ties are plastic, use metal track gauge on each side of solder location so rail stays in gauge if ties soften. The hotter the iron the less the ties will soften because job goes faster. Tie heavy feeder to screw eye, bent nail, or solder it to a local terminal strip to anchor is well.

If the solder freezes quickly, perhaps forming a puddled dimple or icicle point where you removed the iron, the iron is not hot enough or perhaps not big enough for the job. (Maybe you're working in a draft.)

If the solder has a frosty crystalline surface, you moved the wire before the solder was frozen. Melt it again for a stronger joint.

If the solder didn't wet the surfaces everywhere easily, you may have an old or oxidized surface. Scrape it clean.

If the joint is a rounded blob, remove excess solder so you can see the general shape of wire and terminal better. You can remove excess solder from the iron by first flinging it down toward a newspaper spread on the floor (don't let go). This throws excess solder off. A wiping rag can also be used, but don't burn it. Then touch the iron to the work and much of the excess solder will flow onto the tip of the iron. You can take as much off the joint as you like this way for the solder needs only to make a metal

bond electrically; you don't depend on it for strength.

A "cold joint" looks properly done but really has a film of undisturbed grease or oxide between the metals. This may eventually insulate the wire and still look like a good joint, so don't depend on your eye. A cold joint is due to wrong flux, dirty metal surfaces, or to the terminal surface not being as hot as the wire, for instance if you touched the iron only to the wire and not for long enough.

Acid flux and most pastes corrode wire slowly, causing trouble after several months or even years, depending on humidity.

Soldering to rail

New rail is usually clean enough for soldering but a scraper or abrasive cloth wheel will remove oxide or corrosion. Tin the side of the rail with resin core solder. If you use steel rail you may have to use acid flux, in which case mop all remaining traces of flux several times with a rinsed sponge. Use metal track gauges to

absorb heat and hold rail in place if you solder Atlas Snap Track or other track with plastic ties. See Fig. 17-13.

Fling excess solder from the iron toward a newspaper spread on the floor, or wipe with a thick cloth. Hold the end of the wire against the side of the rail with a small stick and touch the top of the rail with the soldering iron. After wire attaches to tinned rail, hold it with the stick until solder is frozen.

If solder sticks to the top of the rail, it can be scraped off with a sharp screw driver or small file. This method should allow you to solder wire to either side of rail with no interference between wire and car wheels.

Where to connect feeders

Published plans usually show symbols for track feeders at the trunk of each block, and of course this is a safe place to make your feeder connections. However, if it is more convenient, you may shift feeder connections anywhere along the feeder rails that flank the block. See Fig. 17-14.

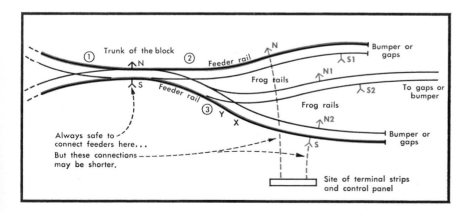

17-14 You can connect feeder wires anywhere along feeder rails that flank the block (shown in color), not just where symbols are drawn. When auxiliary feeders are added for better power distribution, they may also connect anywhere along these rails. Connections to frog rails are permitted only if turnouts between connecting place and the trunk of the block are of fixed-control type of wiring. In this case, connecting at N1 or S1 requires turnout 2 to be fixed control. Connecting at N2 or S2 requires both turnouts 2 and 3 to be of fixed-control type.

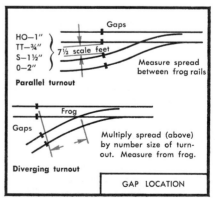

17-15 The best location for block boundary gaps is where car wheels stand when equipment on adjoining track can pass in the clear. These dimensions are a compromise meeting both control and signaling requirements. Usually exact location isn't so important.

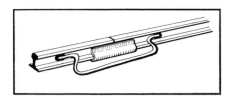

17-16 Rail bonds are short flexible wires that jump around rail joiners to insure good electrical continuity. Be sure bond has bends to allow for thermal and mechanical expansion.

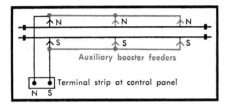

17-17 Auxiliary booster feeders strung parallel to the track, usually under the table, can be conveniently connected to rails at many points. Some model railroaders feed every length of rail individually and may not even use metal rail joiners.

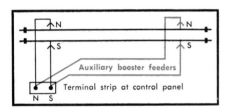

17-18 When distance isn't too great, booster feeders may run from terminal strip to several places along track or just to both ends of the block, depending on the need for them.

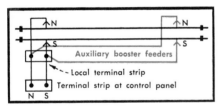

17-19 Local terminal strip provides easy connections for any number of booster feeders.

Any attempt to connect feeders to frog rails behind kit type or Tru-Scale turnouts would cause trouble unless you were using the interchange block idea of pages 34 and 42, or unless you used gaps and jumpers behind the frogs as in Fig. 8-1 at B.

Gap location

We saw how to cut gaps on page 23 and we've also learned many reasons for needing gaps. Often gaps can be located at existing rail joiners, and you can cut them by sawing through a metal rail joiner if it isn't convenient to raise the track to install plastic joiners.

Gaps can be opposite each other or staggered a little. The only rule to keep in mind is that you usually don't want to have gaps located where trains often stand. For instance, if you get the gaps at each end of a passing track too far from the turnouts, the train in the siding might have to be a car length shorter in order not to stand across either set of gaps.

The best place for block boundary gaps behind a turnout is either at the fouling point or at any convenient place between the fouling point and the frog of the turnout.

The "fouling point" is the place where a car can stand on one track and not be sideswiped by a car on the other branch track. Just where this is depends on the curve of each branch and the overhang of the cars, but on parallel turnouts like those at a passing siding, the fouling point is at about the place where the frog rails have spread 7½ scale feet. See Fig. 17-15. On a diverging route a good general rule is to measure the distance from the frog rather than the spread. Make it equal to the frog number times the 7½ foot (or what you decide to use) spread. Thus the fouling point would be 4″ from the frog of a No. 4 turnout in HO.

As I said, control block boundary gaps could be anywhere between here and the frog. On the other hand, if you ever install track circuit type signaling, the gaps for signaling should be at the fouling point or a little *farther* from the frog.

If you use the same gaps for signal and for control blocks, the fouling point is the only place that fulfills both requirements.

Auxiliary booster feeders

Rail joiners are rather poor electrical joiners because oxide and dirt often interfere with their all-metal path from one rail to the next. You can add small, flexible wire "rail bonds" as in Fig. 17-16 if you wish, especially around joiners known to give trouble.

After current passes through several lengths of rail, there may be enough voltage loss from joiners so that a train runs more and more slowly as it gets farther away from the track feeder connections. If this happens it is a good idea to connect feeders near the middle of a block rather than one end. However, an even better scheme is to connect extra "auxiliary" or "booster" feeders at two or perhaps several places along the block. This can be done in several ways starting with Fig. 17-17.

Warning! If you ever have to hunt for wiring troubles, the presence of booster feeders makes it much more difficult to find the exact trouble spot. Either provide for an easy way to disconnect *both ends* of every added booster or else get the railroad into perfect shape electrically, no shorts, no wiring mistakes, before you add any booster wiring.

Common rail wiring

Schemes for feeders from the common return rail, if used, were shown in Chapter 12. Booster feeders can be used here as well since rail joiners can behave just as badly in either rail.

Gaps are not needed in the common rail side of the track except behind selective-control turnouts and at boundaries of return sections. However, cutting gaps in the common rail opposite each S rail gap is a help in trouble shooting since it enables you to disconnect any portion of the common return rail for testing. I cut them but you can suit yourself. I also need them for signaling purposes.

Emergency cord

It's a good idea to arrange a master switch with a cord running around the room where you can always reach it. Then if a train derails, two trains get into the same block, or other emergencies occur, you can pull the cord and cut power to all trains at once. Usually this switch can be the main 115-v. switch for the railroad or else one for train-running power packs but not lighting.

High-voltage wiring

The 115-v. wiring to your railroad should pass through a master switch so all power can be turned off at one place when you leave the room. You can arrange a heavy-duty extension cord with a switch this way if you want to keep things on the simple side. However, if you use extension cords, keep them in sight and off the floor. Check them at least every six months to see if they need replacing. Around the model railroad they can become a shock hazard or even a fire hazard.

A more ambitious scheme is to use house wiring equipment fastened to the underside of the railroad to distribute power to utility outlets near each power pack and transformer. If this wiring starts from a main switch fastened to the railroad table, and you use an extension cord from this box to the nearest wall outlet in your house, you may not need a license to do the extension wiring. Of course, permanent wiring connected to the house lines requires electrical inspection and should follow your local code. A booklet sold in the electrical department of Sears Roebuck & Co. stores is very helpful in showing you how to install high-voltage electrical boxes, wire, and switches.

18. Finding Troubles

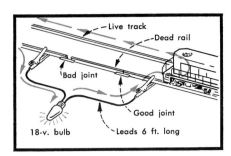

18-1 Power from live track doesn't reach loco because of defective contact in rail joiner. But test lamp completes the circuit if it bridges the joint even though both clips are on same rail. Light shows bad joiner is between the clips. Moving a clip between them will show which one is the offender. Loco is needed to provide path of lamp current to opposite rail.

WHEN lamps don't light when they should, when switch machines are dead or trains don't run properly due to electrical failures, you must become a detective, using various clues to locate the cause of the trouble.

When you hunt for trouble, be sure you do it methodically. If you just guess and check over and over again it might take you more than an hour to locate a trouble spot. But if you use a method we'll soon discuss, you can find the failure that might be in any of 64 different places with only six one-minute tests.

Test indicators

The most-useful testing tool is an 18-v. lamp (or a lower voltage lamp with a dropping resistor) equipped with long flexible wire leads and a miniature alligator clip on each end, Fig. 18-1. This is your voltage tester. You can connect it between *any* two places in your wiring and if it lights you'll know there is a voltage difference between the selected points. The bulb works equally well in low voltage A.C. and D.C. circuits and will glow on as little as 3 v. For very low voltage testing use a 6 v. bulb which will glow on as little as 1 v.

The voltage-tester bulb gives you a rough idea of voltage by its brightness and color. You can connect it across motor brushes to see if voltage is reaching them. You can connect it across rails or feeder wires or the power pack or transformer terminals the same way. You can also connect to two points along the same wire or rail. For instance, if there's a bad rail joiner, the bulb will glow if you connect to two places and the bad joiner is between these places. If the bad joiner is somewhere else, the lamp will not light.

A voltmeter is the professional voltage tester because specific voltage

readings are more helpful and because (together with ammeter readings) you can use Ohm's law, Watt's law, etc., to figure out the mathematical things about wiring and control. Use the meter in the same way as a test lamp. But before you buy a voltmeter, be sure to get an ammeter for it is much more essential.

The ammeter is just about a must in trouble shooting because it is important not only to know that current flows through a circuit, but to know whether it's the normal amount of current or something else. Plan to purchase at least a cheap ammeter with a scale of 1.5 a. or 3 a., or in O gauge 5 a. or so. Choose a scale reading suited to one or two motors rather than a meter that measures all the current of all the trains. The ammeter should almost always be connected at the same place, Fig. 18-2, or built in as on page 72, so there is little need to equip it with flexible leads.

Lacking an ammeter, you can connect an 18-v. test bulb in the same place temporarily as a "continuity tester." This bulb will light as long as current can find some path around the circuit. It will help you locate short circuits, but since the bulb doesn't pass enough current to run the train, it is useless for tests where you want to know how much current the train uses.

An excellent way to wire in a permanent continuity tester bulb is to connect it across the terminals of your circuit breaker. This serves two purposes: If the circuit breaker should pop off, indicating a short circuit, the lamp will light up to tell you about it and it will continue to glow as long as current passes through the circuit.

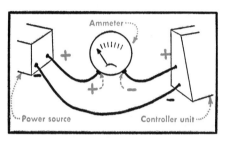

18-2 Connect ammeter here for temporary testing. Polarities should be observed to get a reading but reverse polarity won't hurt meter.

If you lift the loco or any lighted cars from the rails and the lights go out, the trouble was in the cars or loco or in the way their wheels touched the rails. But if the test light still glows, you can assume the short circuit is in other wiring. The light will go out when the short circuit has been removed.

Watch the indicators

When a train jerks or spills, a novice often says, "I guess there's a short circuit somewhere."

Or he may think a sluggish train has a "weak magnet." Well, I wish I had a nickel for the times he is wrong. Your indicators will show what the real trouble is.

Keep the voltage indicator, whether a lamp or a voltmeter, connected across the power pack terminals for awhile. (A voltmeter in its built-in location is already properly wired for this.) Then watch the indicators and

Continued on page 86

18-3 OPEN CIRCUIT. First test lights lamp, showing break is somewhere in the upper feeder wire route. Second test does not light lamp so you know the break is between first and second test points. Additional probing soon locates exact place to be a defective solder joint at the feeder connection to the rail.

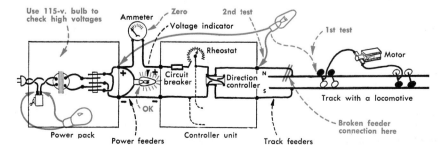

QUICK DIAGNOSIS CHART

Look for test results in color.
Read analysis below in black.

POWER SUPPLY FAILURE

Power unit is quiet.
House fuse is not blown.

OPEN CIRCUIT somewhere in house or power unit wiring.

Power not turned on.
Plug loose in house receptacle.
Broken connection in cord.
Broken wire or connection in high-voltage wiring inside power unit.
Broken connection or wire in transformer primary coil.

Power unit is quiet.
House fuse is blown.

OVERLOAD or SHORT CIRCUIT in some unit on same house circuit. Not necessarily the railroad power unit.

Defective insulation in any power cord.
Loose wires in any appliance plug.
Defective insulation or loose wires in power unit.
Too much load for the house circuit rating of 15 a.
Overheated transformer has burned wires that touch each other. Replace the transformer.

Power unit hums.
Unit remains cool.

OPEN CIRCUIT in low-voltage wiring of unit.

Loose connection or wire broken inside insulation.
Poorly soldered connection.
Defective reversing switch.
Circuit breaker or fuse blown in unit.*
Burned-out rheostat, rectifier, or wire in transformer.†

_____

*This indicates a short circuit or overload has occurred previously or that circuit breaker trips off too easily.

†This would take some time to occur and should have caused heating and burning odors previously.

No operation.

Ammeter reads above normal.

Voltage normal or low at power terminals.

SHORT CIRCUIT

Current decreases to zero when train is removed from track.

SHORT CIRCUIT in a loco, a car, or because of manner in which their wheels touch the track.

Wheels touch rail of opposite polarity at a turnout, crossing, or gap.
Wheel insulation defective.
Wheels and axle turned wrong end around in truck.
Truck turned wrong way around on metal frame of car or locomotive.
Short circuit occurs to next car through uninsulated couplers.
Pickup truck touches main frame or has defective insulation.
Both motor brushes grounded.
Tender touches locomotive.
Wheel flanges touch metal frame.
Loose wire touches frame.
Metal body touches motor brushes.
Wire is pinched or worn by gear until it shorts.
Coil in motor grounded to shaft.

Current decreases to zero when certain power or block toggle is turned off.

SHORT CIRCUIT in feeder wiring or terminal strip or track.

Wires have a wrong connection.
Adjoining bare wires touch.
Feeder wire touches scenery screen or common return bus, etc.
Frayed wire at terminal strip touches another.
Power wire and return wire connected to same side of lamp, coil, or track.
Solder blob joins terminals on strip, coil, or back of lamp bulb, etc.
Wires, terminals, or rails touch metal framework or other path for short circuit.
Spikes touch inside wood below gap, closing the gap.
Switch machine frame is connected to rails via metal throw rod.
Insulation failure in turnout.
Coin or other metal object bridges rails — watch your friends on this one.
Rail gap not cut or has closed up.
Another cab is connected to same block in cab control.
Contacts stuck together on switch machine.
Turnout not properly insulated.

Current remains high regardless of toggles.

SHORT CIRCUIT in wiring between power pack or transformer and the toggles.

Wires have wrong connection. Check toggles and terminal strip connections especially.
Direction controllers not wired properly. Check to see if they have some unusual contact arrangement as explained in Chapter 14.
Check other possibilities as listed in columns at left.

No operation.

No current at ammeter or continuity test lamp.

Voltage normal or above at power unit terminals.

OPEN CIRCUIT

Power unit hums.*
Unit shows signs of overheating.
SHORT CIRCUIT in the low-voltage wiring of the power unit.

Bare wires crossed.
Bare wire touches case.
Fiber washers dislodged at terminal screws.
Rectifier short-circuited due to previous overload.
Coil burned out due to rectifier burning out previously and overloading it.
Reversing switch wired incorrectly.

---

*The hum itself is normal, and assures that power reaches the transformer.

Full voltage appears between rails where loco stands or at wires beside lamp or coil.

OPEN CIRCUIT in loco, lamp, coil or other device.

Dirty wheels, oxidized rail.
Poor connection between wheels and truck frames or to main frame at bolster.
Poor wire connections.
Motor brushes worn out.
Wire pulls brushes away from commutator.
Brush springs loose.
Body shell touches brush holders.
Motor, lamp, or coil wire broken.
Dirt, weak spring, oxidation, or burning of switch machine cutoff contacts.
Wheels lifted off rails due to lack of nod or rock in trucks.
Wiring not completed.

No voltage between rails where loco stands or between wires to lamp or coil.

OPEN CIRCUIT in control wiring, panel, terminal strips, feeders, or rail.

Poor connection or poorly soldered joint.
Wire broken inside insulation.
Wire missing or fallen from connection.
Defective toggle switch.
Poor rail joint contact.
Metal rail joiner has slipped off or is missing.
Rheostat or transformer slider loose or wire broken.
Gap cut at wrong place in track. Part of rail not connected to any feeders.

Poor operation or stalling.

Ammeter reading below normal.*
Voltage indication normal or above normal.

POOR CONDUCTIVITY

If voltage at the load is the same as at power pack or transformer, the trouble is poor conductivity in the load. Otherwise voltage tests made along the feeder lines and rails will show a voltage drop somewhere where it shouldn't be. Test the same as to find an open circuit, but looking for this abnormal voltage loss.

Oxide on wheels.
Dirty or oxidized rail or any other metal where contact should be good.
Paint interferes with connection, grease, etc.
Poor soldered joint.
Poor rail joiner.
Contact to lead is die-cast metal, iron, etc., rather than copper or silver.
Feeder wire very long and small.
Too many unbonded rail joiners.
Current passes through steel or iron where copper would be better.

---

*Continuity lamp not useful in this test.

Ammeter normal.

Voltage below normal with throttle full on.

HALF-WAVE POWER

If locomotive runs sluggishly or makes buzzing or rattling sound, you may have left the pulse power switch on. A rectifier with one leg disconnected in the power pack will cause this unexpectedly.

A partial short circuit in power pack can cause similar symptoms but power pack will eventually show more than normal heating if this is the case.

Ammeter above normal motor current.*
Voltage indication normal or below.

OVERLOADED MOTOR

If motor seems to turn freely in fingers but runs fast and hot without load, the magnet may be weakened.

If mechanism is tight, the motor may be overworking and overheating.

If load the motor pulls is too much for it, it will also become hot and draw excess current.

If ammeter needle swings with each turn of motor or wheels, look for binding gears, etc.

If some current shows with loco removed from the track, there is a partial short circuit somewhere or another train on the track, etc.

Locate it in same manner as a full short circuit.

Motor armature may be clogged with iron filings; remove with help of slips of paper.

---

*See page 18 for motor ratings.

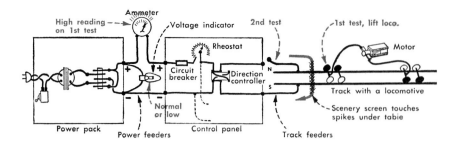

High reading on 1st test — Ammeter — Voltage indicator — 2nd test — 1st test, lift loco.

Rheostat — Circuit breaker — Direction controller — Motor

Normal or low — Track with a locomotive

Power pack — Power feeders — Control panel — Track feeders — Scenery screen touches spikes under table

18 - 4 SHORT CIRCUIT. Scenery screen happens to be a short circuit path. Lifting loco shows loco is not to blame because meter still registers abnormal current. However, disconnecting feeder at terminal strip does break the circuit, proving that the short is beyond the strip. If you open the circuit at several other places you can localize the trouble.

be familiar with their brightness or readings when trains run normally.

Usually the ammeter will show from 0.3 a. to 0.7 a. per motor (HO operation values) depending on the motor, gearing and load it must pull. The voltage when a train just starts may be from 2 v. to 6 v., or even higher with some rubber-band locos. When a train runs at 60 scale miles per hour (which is a foot a second in HO), it will rarely require the full 12 v. from the throttle.

Once you know the normal indications, you can quickly determine the kind of troubles that occur by noting abnormal indications.

The chart on pages 84 and 85 shows the ammeter and voltage indications that occur and the kind of trouble they indicate. You can tell instantly whether you have a short circuit, dirty track, or a poor connection.

Locating trouble exactly

If the place causing trouble isn't evident at once, don't guess. There's a good trick you can use to locate the trouble very quickly. The idea is to divide the offending circuit in two parts and test each separately. One shows OK, the other shows a fault. Now divide the faulty half into two quarters and test to find the bad quarter, then the bad eighth, etc.

If the chart shows you have an open circuit or poor conduction, the testing is easily done with the voltage indicator. Leave the loco on the track. Connect one end of the lamp to one power terminal, Fig. 12-4. Touch the other clip to the other terminal just to be sure the power is on, then move it out to the loco site. If the lamp burns again, the break is in the wires, feeders or rails connecting between the two clips. Now connect the clip only half way out to the loco; if the light still burns, come in half the distance again toward the other clip. But if the light stops burning, then you know the trouble is between the last two places you tested. In this way, you can narrow the region where voltage is lost to find the exact location. Divide and divide and conquer. All the while, you can leave one clip at the power terminal if that's convenient, just moving the other.

A short circuit is a little more trouble to track down. If you are checking in the locomotive, slip a piece of paper between a motor brush and the commutator or disconnect the motor wire temporarily. If the trouble is in the track, remove all lighted cars and locos from the offending circuit. This is so the ammeter or continuity tester indicates only short-circuit current (not current through the normal load). Turn the power down so the ammeter reads only about ¼ a. or just enough so you can still see the motion on the needle.

Now the trick is this: The circuit is supposed to be open because the train is off the track or motor disconnected. But current does get through. Somewhere along the two feeder wires and rails a metal object is touching from one feeder to the other. If you disconnect a wire from its terminal, or remove a rail joiner, the current will stop if the break you make is part of the path to the short-circuit spot. But a disconnection in wires beyond the trouble spot makes no difference.

A good place to start is to disconnect the block feeder at the main terminal strip, Fig. 18-4. If current stops flowing, you know the trouble is beyond. Put the wire back right away and make another disconnection in the trouble half of the circuit. Again you divide and divide again to narrow down to the exact spot. You may even have to saw through a rail joiner to make a test.

Elusive troubles

If tests seem to be contradictory, proving the trouble isn't here and it isn't there either, you may have the trouble between the two areas checked. Dirt on track or wheels can fool you this way, the loco and the track both testing OK but not working when combined. So can poorly soldered joints and rail joiners that look good.

The other common cause of contradictory test evidence is having two different troubles at the same time. In this case, get the wiring right at the power pack, then as far as the control panel, then to the track, etc. After you find the first trouble, the usual methods will find the second. You may have to disconnect one whole branch of a circuit that has a short circuit in order to find a short in another branch.

Erratic troubles are another nuisance. They are troubles that don't stay put so you can test them. A bad rail joiner may be bad only when you push on the table in a certain place. A truck may short under the frame only while a loco is pulling cars but not when stopped, etc. If you can use pulse power and run a train very slowly, that will help you analyze erratic troubles, but sometimes the best you can do is just keep observing when they happen, if they happen with every car or just certain ones. These things will be the clues. You can also look for evidence of burned rail or marks where short circuits occur, pitted wheels, etc. Erratic troubles may be caused by the weight of passing equipment or your hand, by vibration, temperature changes, humidity expanding the wood supports, flanges spreading rails, loose wires, connections, or loose metal objects, and of course by curves and undulations of the track affecting equipment. Almost always they are at places that are able to slip or touch when moved.

Sneak circuits are like short circuits, but between control wires so that power operates something at the wrong time. You can find them by breaking connections here and there in the same way you find short circuits. Such faults are also called "crossed circuits." Fig. 18-5 shows another kind of sneak circuit that can occur with selective-control type turnouts.

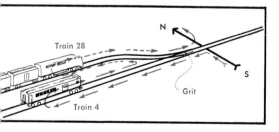

N — Train 28 — Grit — S — Train 4

18 - 5 When I pulled the throttle to start train 4, train 28 on the side track also moved toward the turnout. The turnout was of the selective control type and dirt prevented it from making normal contact between points and stock rail. The result was that both trains were in series; power for 4 followed a sneak circuit through 28 because of their common connection to the frog of the turnout.

INDEX

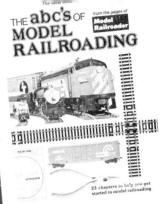

THE abc's OF MODEL RAILROADING

from the pages of
Model Railroader

23 chapters to help you get started in model railroading

POPULAR MODEL RAILROADS you can build

Step-by-step instructions / Bills of material

Ma & Pa/Kinnickinnic Railway & Dock Co.
New York & Quebec/Portage Hill & Communipaw

MODEL RAILROADING with JOHN ALLEN

BY LINN H. WESTCOTT

The story of the fabulous HO scale Gorre & Daphetid Railroad

SCENERY FOR MODEL RAILROADS

BY BILL McCLANAHAN

REVISED EDITION INCLUDING HARD-SHELL SCENERY AND ZIP TEXTURING

HOW THE EXPERTS DO IT
MADE EASY FOR BEGINNERS

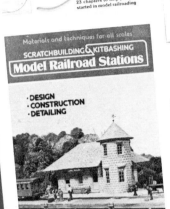

Materials and techniques for all scales

SCRATCHBUILDING & KITBASHING Model Railroad Stations

- DESIGN
- CONSTRUCTION
- DETAILING

REALISTIC OPERATION FOR ALL SCALES

How to OPERATE your model railroad

BY BRUCE A. CHUBB

- Waybills
- Fast time
- Switching
- Timetables
- Dispatching
- And more!

TRACK PLANNING IDEAS

from Model Railroader
58 track plans from past issues

SELECTED BY BOB HAYDEN

how to WIRE your model railroad

Including Wiring for Sectional Track

BY LINN H. WESTCOTT

WIRING made simple and clear for everyone

ALL NEW   FUN FOR THE ENTIRE FAMILY

small railroads YOU can build

EDITED BY BOB HAYDEN

Proven Methods Plus NEW Ideas for Scenery, Wiring, Operation

From Complete Lists of Materials...to Finished Layouts

Edited by Bob Warren and the MODEL RAILROADER staff

764 HELPFUL HINTS for model railroaders

Culled from the Kinks columns of *Model Railroader* magazine

BRIDGES & BUILDINGS for model railroads

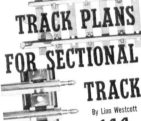

TRACK PLANS FOR SECTIONAL TRACK

By Linn Westcott

144 TRACK PLANS

including lists of pieces needed for rug, table and custom layouts

HO, O-27, S and O gauges

Class 1 railroads • Branch lines • Short lines • Special operations

more RAILROADS you can model

EDITED BY BOB SCHAFER

The wit, whim, and (best of all) wisdom of

John Armstrong on Creative Layout Design

Over 120 pages of ideas, prototype and model photos, diagrams, tabular data, track plans

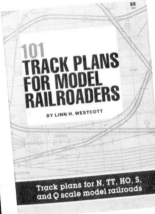

101 TRACK PLANS FOR MODEL RAILROADERS

BY LINN H. WESTCOTT

Track plans for N, TT, HO, S, and O scale model railroads

HO RAILROAD that grows

By Linn H. Westcott

8 easy steps

Start on a sheet of plywood

Including Bridges, Scenery, and Wiring

NEW

Electronic Projects for Model Railroaders

Tested, practical throttles, sound and lighting devices, and signaling systems you can build, and information about command control computers

Complete schematics
Full-size patterns
Assembly instructions
Parts lists
Photos

BY PETER J. THORNE

HO PRIMER

model railroading for all

GETTING STARTED IN HO GAUGE

HOW TO SELECT SETS, CARS, LOCOS, TRACK

HOW TO GET GOOD PERFORMANCE

BUILDING FROM KITS...TOOLS TO USE

BASIC WIRING SIMPLIFIED